Stay Tuned!

Stay Tuned!

Raising Media-Savvy Kids in the Age of the Channel-Surfing Couch Potato

Jane Murphy and Karen Tucker

MAIN STREET BOOKS

Doubleday

New York   London   Toronto   Sydney   Auckland

A MAIN STREET BOOK
PUBLISHED BY DOUBLEDAY
a division of Bantam Doubleday Dell Publishing Group, Inc.
1540 Broadway, New York, New York 10036

MAIN STREET BOOKS, DOUBLEDAY, and the portrayal of a building with a tree
are trademarks of Doubleday, a division of Bantam Doubleday Dell
Publishing Group, Inc.

Book Design by CS Design
Illustrations by Wesley Bedrosian

Library of Congress Cataloging-in-Publication Data
Murphy, Jane, 1945–
Stay tuned: raising media-savvy kids in the age of the channel-
surfing couch potato / Jane Murphy and Karen Tucker. — 1st ed.
        p.   cm.
"A Main Street book"—Verso t.p.
Includes bibliographical references (p.   ) and index.
1. Television and children—United States.   2. Television and
family—United States.   3. Video recording—United States.
4. Parenting—United States.   I. Tucker, Karen, 1949–   .
HQ784.T4M87   1996
649′.1—dc20   95-51465
                            CIP
ISBN 0-385-47690-6
Copyright © 1996 by Jane Murphy and Karen Tucker
All Rights Reserved
Printed in the United States of America
September 1996

1   3   5   7   9   10   8   6   4   2

First Edition

We dedicate this book to our own

"personal peanut gallery"

—our joy—our families.

Credits and Applause

A source of joy for us in producing our videos is the collaborative aspect of the effort—working with writers, composers, technical crews, graphic artists, and editors to create a program. Likewise, this book reflects two seasoned and enduring collaborations we value greatly: our partnership of over twenty years, and the rare and treasured relationships we share with our respective spouses, Jerry Murphy and Jerry Avorn ("the Jerrys"). They are our most enthusiastic cheerleaders and the most rigorous critics of our work.

Beyond these cherished partnerships, we want to acknowledge a cast of contributors to this book and to the ongoing effort to make the highest-quality programming available for kids: Peggy Charren, Diana Huss Green, Kathryn Montgomery, Irene Wood, Martha Dewing, Catherine Cella, Loretta MacAlpine, those all-star champions of children's video and media who write, speak, and advocate for the good stuff. Red ribbons to Annette Rivlin and Cait Murphy for digging up the facts, sources, validations, and background research we required. Honors to Lori Lipsky, our editor at Doubleday, together with Frances Jones, who supported us through this first book publishing experience. Kudos to Chuck Sirois, who designed these pages. Commemorations to Stan Freberg of *Beany and Cecil,* Fran Allison of *Kukla, Fran and Ollie* fame, to Captain Kangaroo, Clarabell, Shari Lewis, *The Mickey Mouse Club* Mouseketeers, and the rest of the children's TV hall of fame characters who impressed us, entertained us, and informed us as we grew up with TV. Much appreciation to all the families and individuals who've shared their views and concerns with us.

And finally, we acknowledge our kids—Cait, Noah, Nate, and Andrew—who remind us every day of the challenges of growing up, who keep us abreast of new trends, from moshpits to websites, and who appreciate the set when it's on and the many other wonderful experiences waiting for them when it's off.

Tune In the Topics

Who Are We and Why Did We Write This Book?

Kids love TV. It gives them enormous pleasure, comfort, and lots of intriguing information. Parents, however, often have mixed feelings about it. They consider TV both a miracle medium *and* a manipulative monster when it comes to their children. Since the average parent has enough to do even before considering the television set, we offer this family video guidebook to support your efforts to get the most out of TV and keep your kids' viewing from getting out of control.

This book is designed to assist you and your children, ages 2–14, in making the best viewing choices for your family. Our goal is to help parents help their children balance the many activ-

Sound-Bites

Mom 1: If I read from now until doomsday, I still couldn't tackle half the parenting books out there.

Mom 2: Besides, you'd have no time for your kids if you did.

ities in their lives and take advantage of TV as the wonderful resource it can be. In getting there, we'll also discuss some universal issues of parenting as they apply to TV and show you how to use your VCR strategically and creatively. The videocassette recorder can help you maximize the best that TV has to offer and help solve the many problems that arise around viewing. With the VCR, you can take back some control over *what, when, and how much* TV your children watch.

In our culture, the terms "TV" and "video" are often used interchangeably, and they truly overlap. In this book, we refer to "video" as your use of the VCR—viewing previously recorded programming at a time you select. The original source may have been broadcast TV or cable, a theatrical feature film, or a made-for-video production. But the crucial difference is that you control the selection and time of viewing.

Finally, this guidebook is not necessarily meant to be read cover to cover, although you can certainly do that. Nor is it meant to be a bible, prescribing what's right and wrong. Think of it as a reference designed to add perspective to your parenting around the screen and to offer some suggestions to unlock the potential of your VCR in enriching your children's TV experience.

We're parents, too. Jane is mother to Cait, 22, and Noah, 19, and Karen's two sons are Nate, 15, and Andrew, 10. As mothers, we've gotten firsthand experience with kids and TV. We're also educators with degrees in child development, as well as publishers and distributors of children's videos. We started our company, KIDVIDZ, eight years ago to produce videos that teach as they entertain. We design our tapes to enrich children's lives by encouraging their special interests and helping support them through some of life's trying transitions. Our live-action videos feature kid hosts as the on-camera experts and principal informants. Humor, original music, and dynamic computer graphics are key elements of our videos, inviting kids to watch again and again. We want our audience to come away with know-how, healthy self-esteem, and the inspiration to exercise their own creativity. The topics of our tapes are diverse, ranging from pet ownership to drawing to surviving a family move, and more. Underlying the variety of topics are the same messages of empowerment: understand your feelings, look to your friends and family for help, trust yourself as you grow, and have a good time.

Our experience as parents, educators, and video publishers has given us a special perspective on video and an insight on what is age- and content-appropriate for young viewers. We understand only too well how invasive the TV can be, how inappropriate certain programs are for kids, and how quickly the new media are challenging parents with new hardware and software choices, fighting for the family's time and discretionary dollars.

In all our years as children's programmers and educators, the questions we're asked most about TV are actually questions about parenting. *"My kids want to watch whenever there's free time. What should I do?" "She does her homework in front of the set. Is that okay?" "How can I get my son to stop watching all the junk he chooses?"* In spite of all the issues and concern about TV, we remain enthusiastic advocates of video as a valuable resource for kids' entertainment and learning. You care about your kids and want to better manage their TV and video viewing. This book will help you teach them to be critical viewers, limit their TV time, and *use your VCR* to become actively involved in what, when, and how much your kids watch.

We are advocates for parents as well as for quality viewing. We believe that if you keep things in balance and assert your parental rights and responsibilities to communicate your family's values, set and enforce limits, and educate yourself about the programs available out there, you and your kids can enjoy the best video and TV have to offer. You can help your kids become discriminating viewers and broaden their view of the world, enabling them to be active participants in it. The goal is to make viewing a choice rather than a habit.

Even with the advantages of video, we all know that TV can be a source of tension and conflict during already stressful times for busy parents. The kids battle over who gets to watch what, and you're drawn in to referee. You search the listings for something valuable that will satisfy both kids, but all you can find is junk, junk, and more junk. Or your brood scatters to different rooms and different sets to browse programs you never dreamed of at their ages—stuff you wouldn't even watch now. Then your son's show is over and so is his TV time, but he's still watching. You have to go to a meeting. He lobbies as you welcome the sitter. You suggest ten alternative things to do. He's a good negotiator and wears you down. You feel guilty as you rush off. The discourse and discord seem never to end.

You don't have to feel that you've totally lost control. This book can help you take back the reins. TV shouldn't be a battleground or an all-or-nothing pastime. It's a unique entertainment and information resource which doesn't always have to serve as a medium for learning, but shouldn't always be the pastime of first choice. Even if you choose to turn off the set for national "TV Turnoff Week," we hope you'll turn it back on with a renewed commitment to get the best it has to offer for you and your kids. We've written this guide to support you in your quest.

This book grew out of our dialogue with parents as they've shared their concerns with us about their children's use of the media. We'd like to keep the dialogue going, so we welcome your comments. Please write to us at:

KIDVIDZ
618 Centre Street/ Newton, MA 02158
http://www.kidvidz.com

Stay Tuned!

....

1 It's More Than Eye Candy

Plug into Your Kid's Viewing and Discover Video's Value

Television can deliver a wealth of entertainment and information into our living rooms, or it can represent a threat to our kids. Used the right way, TV (including videos and new media, such as CD-ROM and online entertainment) can actually be good for your kids.

This chapter begins with a historical perspective on the medium, and it should conjure up some nostalgic memories that will have you acknowledging the impact TV has had on you. We move on to discuss video's many advantages, but no matter how much we may come to defend its benefits, there are many concerns which need to be acknowledged and confronted. This leads to a discussion of how we as parents can get involved. It's critical that you begin by stepping back and evaluating how your children use TV, or rather how you let them. *What* are they watching? *When* are they watching? *How much* are they watching? And how does the time they spend in front of the tube balance with the rest of their lives—their schoolwork, sports, time with friends, music lessons, household chores, time to daydream? This assessment is critical, and this is where video can play a role. Used properly, video can spark family interactions and lively dialogue, take kids to far-away places, illustrate hard-to-see phenomena, introduce fascinating people, and inspire a host of interests and activities.

Tune In the Topics

- The Video Advantage

- From Howdy Doody to Mighty Morphins: A Perspective on TV History

- Concerns About TV

- Getting Involved

- Family Activity: TV in the Year 20__

1

The Video Advantage

Video is an "anytime" medium which offers a range of choices to be viewed at your convenience. You can pretape broadcast and cable shows for later viewing. And they can be commercial-free if you fast-forward through coming attractions and zap through the commercials on tapes you've prerecorded. More important, your VCR is also a playback device for a wealth of rental and for-sale video programming, a huge selection not found on broadcast or cable. In addition to the many old and new movies and TV classics available, there are hundreds of new made-for-home-video titles covering a wide range of topics reflecting children's special interests, concerns, and delights. The accumulated history of movies, TV, and video—combined with the VCR—offers families an unprecedented resource for accessing entertainment and information. Families can use this tool to kick the habit of tuning in to "whatever's on." The VCR can liberate you from scheduled programming!

Although videotaping shows requires some planning on your part, the VCR affords you the opportunity to capture the *best* of broadcast and cable, which otherwise are "real-time" choices, holding the viewer hostage to scheduled time slots. You can watch prerecorded shows as often as you like, and programs produced specifically for video are often designed for repeat viewing. The VCR enables young viewers especially to watch programs again and

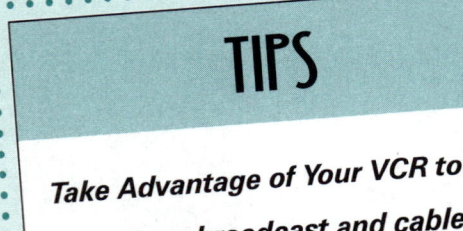

TIPS

Take Advantage of Your VCR to:

- **pretape broadcast and cable programs for later viewing and to maximize the learning and enjoyment of a program: stop, rewind, and watch again.**

- **build a collection of film and TV classics.**

- **expand viewing options with a range of programs made especially for video.**

- **fast-forward through commercials and promos for other shows.**

again. As a matter of fact, children watch favorite videos an average of thirteen times. Just as kids often request the same book over and over, they watch videos again to become more familiar with favorite characters, learn the songs, and perhaps, over time, come to appreciate various points of view. Even before the advent of the VCR, we were enjoying the benefits of television.

From Howdy Doody to Mighty Morphins: A Perspective on TV History

Almost all of today's parents, beginning with the baby boomers, have grown up with TV, and we cherish memories of the times we watched favorite shows with our families and the characters we came to know. Today there are homes with TVs in many rooms, and families don't always watch together. Niche programming to target audiences defined by their ages and interests, together with the vast array of choices available, have given us individual TV menus and schedules. Back in the 1950s and 1960s, TV was more often a shared experience, offering an opportunity for pleasurable family time. We believe we can recapture some of this experience for our families and our kids.

• • • • • Sound-Bites • • • • •

Grandma: When your dad was your age, he used to beg to stay up late so he could watch *The Twilight Zone.*

Larry: Why didn't you just tape it so he could see it the next day?

Grandma: Honey, those were the days of hi-fis, black-and-white TVs, and Hula Hoops. We didn't even dream of computers or phone machines, let alone VCRs!

3

Most every parent reading this book can attest to the fact that TV had some impact on their growth and development. We often mark time by events we have seen on the screen—like the Beatles' debut, the first moon landing, or Nelson Mandela's release from prison. Or we dip into shared TV nostalgia, calling up memories of *Bonanza,* family nights watching *Laugh-In* or *The Wonderful World of Disney,* singing old Campbell Soup jingles, reminiscing about *The Brady Bunch.* TV has played a major role in defining our culture, and it's amazing to consider how much it has developed over the course of the past half century. But the most profound changes may be taking place right now, with advances in computer technology and the new media options available on the screen.

Since their introduction in 1976, VCRs have reached over 77 percent penetration in U.S. households. Personal pizza-sized satellite dishes are appearing on rooftops. CD-sized video discs will soon be commonplace. Each month, it seems, new forms of home electronics gizmos appear in the stores, including portable CD-ROM drives and virtual reality peripherals. And just wait. The French National Center for Scientific Research is testing paper-thin plastic sheets with embedded microchips—video screens that virtually roll up like window shades. So, it's plausible to forecast our future sets being portable (even flexible!) lightweight computing and communication devices. And this is just the hardware, the "set" itself.

But what about the programs? In the early days of TV, there were only two primary sources, the NBC and CBS networks. Now there are four networks (ABC, CBS, NBC, FOX) with two more on the way (UPN, WB), and some sixty cable channels, slated to mushroom to five hundred over the course of the next five to ten years. Pay-per-view and satellite dishes further expand the options, and the proliferation of these channels has created a vast new market for programming, both old and new.

And then there is video: prerecorded programming. We rent, we purchase, we borrow cassettes. We make our own home videos and hire professionals to record our weddings, birthdays, and other important family events. Some of us take advantage of public-access cable facilities, or enroll our kids in school and summer film and video courses.

The VCR was the home entertainment success story of the 1980s. Now that most people have VCRs, rent movies, and tape TV programs, they're demanding more of this electronic appliance. In addition to feature films, people are becoming more interested in information and how-to programs as well as nonfiction entertainment. This pattern reflects the self-education and leisure trends of the 1990s. And these trends influence kids' programming as well. Why not? Look at the growth of children's nonfiction books over the past five years and the variety of kids' magazines available as well. At least fifteen children's special-

As a Matter of Fact...

- In 1947, 14,000 families had TV sets. By 1950, 5 million families owned them.
- Today, 98 percent of American households have TVs and 98 percent of those are color.
- Half the children ages 6–17 have TVs in their rooms.
- There is an average of 2.3 TVs per American household, tuned in to some fifty-four hours of viewing per week.

> 66 Video, the **right** video, can expand a child's universe. It can offer a flesh-and-blood view of history (PBS's The Civil War); it makes science comprehensible and fun (Bill Nye, the Science Guy); it makes learning geography a game (Carmen Sandiego); and it shows us that we can come together (Erase the Hate). All of this is possible when video is used wisely. Not only parents but government must participate in 99 educating our youngsters.
>
> **Diana Huss Green**
> *President, Parents' Choice Foundation*
> *Parent, grandmother of kids ages 3 and up*

interest magazines have appeared since 1992. Video is simply another form of publishing, and at its best it can stimulate our kids intellectually, inspire them creatively, and motivate them to undertake new and exciting experiences. So TV has changed us and our kids, and it will continue to do so, even as it evolves into new forms. The opportunities for personal enrichment, education, and entertainment are truly exciting.

Concerns About TV

Yes, TV can make a terrific contribution to your family's education and entertainment. It allows us all to witness events and encounter worlds we would not otherwise have the opportunity to see. In a single evening, from the comfort of our own homes, we can experience a space shot, a trip to Africa, a concert, a humorous cartoon, or a classic mystery. Milton Chen, director of the Center for Education and Lifelong Learning at KQED-TV in San Francisco, says in his book *The Smart Parents' Guide to Kids' TV:* "The notion that TV is singlehandedly turning kids into couch potatoes and frying their brains is a myth." Nevertheless,

Sound-Bites

Dad: We'll be back by eleven-thirty. There's salad in the fridge to go with the spaghetti.

Mom: Could you remind Alex to clean up his room? And make sure he brushes his teeth before bed

Dad: Oh, and just an hour of TV.

(They exit.)

Sitter: What do you suppose you can watch?

Alex: How about sex, lies, and videotape? I saw it on Mom's desk—it sounds cool.

Family Roundtable

Concerns About TV

My biggest problem, actually, whether you're watching TV or working at a computer screen, is that you don't move except for your fingers. It's not very healthy and I worry about that more than the content.

Father of 14-year-old

I'm mostly concerned about the violence. It's gotten to where it's not a question of whether a program has any violence in it but rather what kind and how much.

Father of 8- and 11-year-olds

I can't stand it that I'm always the bad guy telling them to turn off the set.

Mother of 12- and 14-year-olds

Parents worry too much. Kids mostly want to watch funny, entertaining stuff. I think this whole violence thing is being blown way out.

11-year-old

7

It's More Than Eye Candy

parents express a lot of heartfelt concern about the effect of viewing on their children, and rightly so.

Violence, Sex, and Language

Many parents are concerned about TV's presentation of violence, sex, and language. Young kids are exposed to numerous depictions of violence, which is often portrayed as the solution to a problem. This can lead kids to believe that violence is how you solve conflict, and it desensitizes them to its horror. More important, it can blind them to alternative methods of problem resolution.

Sex is another perennial source of concern, because it's often presented gratuitously, titillating kids who are too young to know what to do with this information. Inappropriate language is another hot button for many families. The use of foul or suggestive language or ethnic or sexist slurs raises flags for many parents in selecting appropriate programs for their children. Words can incite hostile feelings, and the overuse of abusive language can desensitize kids to its impact, as well as give them a distorted sense of what kind of language is acceptable in everyday life. We'll provide some detail in Chapter 3 on how to address these prevalent issues without taking a sledgehammer to the picture tube.

Advertising

Commercials are ingeniously designed to show kids how the advertisers think children should look, act, and play, but these are not always the messages we parents want our kids to receive. How many toys or snack foods have your kids requested that have been pitched heavily to them as members of a valuable target market? We need to protect our kids from being treated as just another consumer seg-

As a Matter of Fact...

- It is likely that the average American child will have watched 100,000 acts of violence on television by the end of sixth grade.

- 77 percent of a survey group of 10–16-year-olds said TV too often portrays sex outside of marriage.

ment. To do this, it helps to show kids that advertisers see them as a target market, and that they create their pitches to be as persuasive as possible. Gerald Lesser, in his book *Children and Television: Lessons from Sesame Street,* acknowledges the impact of advertising: "No child can be bombarded by images of energizing cereals, bumbling fathers in family comedies, exciting toys, and excited mothers winning prizes in game shows without acquiring some stereotypes about people and products."

As a Matter of Fact...

The average American child sees 20,000 commercials each year.

TV can also distort the truth through technique (camerawork, editing, lighting) and has the potential to influence young viewers who aren't yet capable of separating fact from fiction, bias from objectivity. But kids can be helped to become more critical viewers as they develop. We'll discuss this further in Chapter 6.

Viewing Time

American children on average watch twenty-eight to thirty hours of TV per week. The sheer number of hours spent in front of the set is one major cause of parents' concern, regardless of the quality of what's being seen. TV can cut into kids' time to play, explore hobbies, and exercise. Critics charge that television is addictive, fuels aggressive behavior, inhibits reading ability, impairs creativity, shortens attention spans, and even contributes to obesity. This can all be true when kids spend unlimited hours of unmonitored time viewing television. But limiting their viewing to two hours a day or less is one policy that makes a great deal of sense. If your children are heavy viewers, this can be accomplished over time.

Limiting viewing hours can also help to slay one of the biggest dragons: *television as a default activity.* Time limits on

TV can lead to many benefits, but the biggest is that kids will begin to seek other things to do (with a lot of your help) and will not simply turn on the set whenever they're bored or lonely, or for any other reason. As Mary Leonhardt writes in *Parents Who Love Reading, Kids Who Don't:* "I think many children choose television over books simply because it is there." A key first step is to change the "simply there" condition.

Each family is unique and what's right or possible for one family may not be for another. Some families have changing schedules and fragmented days while others follow a regular routine. Parents also have different values and criteria for selecting appropriate programs. So as you read on about programming options, TV schedules, and time allotments, and how to balance all this with everything else in your lives, take what fits for you and know that there are always choices.

Other Concerns

Studies by pediatricians have shown that TV influences eating habits and contributes to increased obesity among our kids. It also influences the amount and quality of reading our children do, and often perpetuates biases by presenting stereotypes and disregarding diversity in its programming.

Unlike children of non-TV generations, today's kids are more likely to watch TV instead of developing hobbies, skills, and special interests. Sometimes the programmers and their sponsors present gratuitous violence, model stereotypical behaviors, and insult our kids' intelligence. Sometimes the government fails to assure and support quality children's programming. Sometimes we parents let TV take over. What can we do about all of this? Plenty.

Family Roundtable

The Right Stuff To Watch

My parents won't let me see a movie unless they've seen it before because they think a lot of stuff isn't right for me to watch.
12-year-old

I wish every product were color-coded for violence, language, and sex.
Dad of 8-and 11-year-olds

Ratings are difficult to go by. You're not always sure who sets them and where they're coming from. Besides, nothing is black and white. We all have our own standards.
Mom of 8-and 11-year-olds

Getting Involved

As parents, you can have a very positive influence on your children's TV viewing. You can simply select appropriate programs and watch some of them together or actively push for legislation that affects programming for children, or anything in between. Whether you choose to get involved in your home or in the community, or both, the issues around children and television are not going to go away. Rather, they will continue to demand all our involvement as the caretakers of our kids.

Recognize the Value of Video

Every day video fulfills its potential to entertain and educate in programs that take us to faraway places, bring cultural masterpieces into our homes, and present complex scientific wonders. So why do many parents think of watching a video as a low-value

 TV: You program it or it programs you. We watch movies that offer a window to an era that seems no longer to exist among today's numbingly violent special-effects extravaganzas and audience-response studies. In our house, comedies or musical comedies rule. Danny Kaye. The Marx Brothers. Billy Wilder. Cary Grant. Carole Lombard. Howard Hawks. Top Hat. These are optimistic, silly, and incredible movies that make us and our children believe in the importance of humanity, creativity, idiosyncrasy, and wit. Add Chinese food on Friday night. Bliss.

__Maira Kalman__
Children's book author/illustrator
Mother of two, ages 10 and 13

activity, suggesting video's redeeming benefit may be in the minutes it occupies a child as a baby-sitter or the role it plays as an incentive to accomplish more important things?

If there's a play or concert that appeals to you and the kids want to go, or they request that you buy a book, aren't you delighted you're raising such cultured beings? Kids don't have to do a lot of arm twisting to attend a performance, get a book, or go to a museum. But many parents treat a video more like candy. It's considered a gift that comes with a certain amount of leverage for you. But Bill Moyers reminds us in his talk, "The Wondrous Power of Television, Video, and the Public Library":

> *There are bad books and good books. There is bad television and good television. Good books and good television ought to be good neighbors, each concerned not only with the art of pleasure but with the art of truth. The enemy of both is mediocrity.*

Entertainment ought to be enriching. But video doesn't always have to be educational or intellectual in nature to deserve our kids' attention. We all need to shift gears and be entertained once in a while. Parents need to appreciate the benefit of down time for children, especially in this age of "the hurried child." Either as education or as pure entertainment, video can have value for kids just as it can for adults.

A major reason to value video is the control it offers parents right now. We can't wait for television to clean up its act. After all, it was over thirty years ago that Newton N. Minow, then chairman of the Federal Communications Commission, called television "a vast wasteland." After nearly four decades of continued debate about TV, Minow's new book, *Abandoned in the Wasteland: Children, Television and the First Amendment,* makes the point that television has been "turned into an instrument of child exploitation and abuse." Broadcasters and advertis-

13

ers who make billions from the public airwaves have taken little responsibility for the public interest. At least parents can turn to video for their kids' entertainment and education while trying to bring public opinion to bear for positive change.

 If we don't guarantee federal support for public telecommunications, we are doing our children and ourselves an incredible disservice. The opportunity to require the communications industry to give something back to the public is right now. After all, they're making out like crazy on spectrum giveaways and monopolistic megadeals.

Peggy Charren
Founder of Action for Children's Television
Mother of two and grandmother
of children ages 9, 5, and 2

Exercise Your Right to Censor as You Teach Your Kids to Judge for Themselves

Would you pay your kids not to watch TV, or put a lock on the set? Some parents do. Others advocate the development of technology to control viewing, such as an electronic lock to prevent kids from viewing until the set is unlocked by a parent. You *should* use your instincts and parental prerogatives to set limits on what you think is unacceptable viewing. But because we feel that locking the TV is saying "I don't trust you" to your child, we offer ways throughout this book to help you both set limits and encourage your kids to become critical viewers who can learn to make appropriate viewing decisions for themselves. In these ways you maintain trust and make locking unnecessary. Of course, it's even more of a challenge to monitor viewing when

14

you're not around. But there are things you can do, and there are suggestions offered throughout the book.

Go Cold Turkey and Reassess

Every April, TV-Free America sponsors a national "TV Turnoff Week," which is endorsed by a coalition of civic groups, schools, and libraries. They prescribe that families leave the TV off for a week and plan other activities as well as talk about the effect "no TV" is having on everyone. After using this book, we hope that you will not need to go "cold turkey" every year because you will have decided how best to use the medium for your family. But turning off the set for a week at any time can be a revelation because it will make you immediately aware of what, when, and how much your family watches. Consider a TV-free week a new beginning. Do some planning and talking, and find alternative activities for when you turn the set back on. But remember, you will need to be especially available during this time and for a few weeks thereafter, so don't try it when you or your kids are facing another big obligation, deadline, or stress. (See Resources section for suggestions on alternatives to watching TV.)

The average American spends fully one-third of his free time in front of a TV set; watching TV is by far our most popular leisure activity. In fact, it's the third-leading human activity worldwide, after work and sleep. All the more reason to attend to what, when, and how much our kids are viewing. In the past fifty years, the TV screen has grown up from a little window of muddy black-and-white images to a multifaceted, full-color interactive display, and two generations of American children have grown up with it as a friend. From MTV to PBS, today's kids are exposed to fast-paced images, sophisticated effects, slick editing and soundbites, instantaneous delivery of the world to their living rooms, and engaging programs that run the gamut from enter-

As a Matter of Fact...

• William Weld, governor of Massachusetts, was one of four governors promoting a TV-free week. However, according to his press secretary, his family didn't have a TV until his wife was away and his five kids "wore him down."

• Televisions outnumber toilets in American households.

15

taining and thought-provoking to mediocre and mind-numbing. But don't throw out the set!

Since you're reading this book, you may feel that you have already lost some control of your family's use of TV. But you can win it back. With the help of video and the VCR, you will be able to make sensible, sensitive rules for your kids (and yourself). The important thing is that parents—all of us—stay involved. We can start by tuning in to the topics. Enjoy!

Personal Notes

. . . .

When Karen was in first grade, she became extremely alarmed by a commercial asking the public to help stamp out TB. How could she live without TV? She worried for days and finally shared the problem with her mom, who explained the commercial was asking for money to find a cure for tuberculosis, a bad disease. She celebrated by watching I Married Joan, followed by I Love Lucy.

Family Activity

TV in the Year 20__

Did you ever read predictions of the future and get a chuckle measuring them up to how things really turned out? Jane's mother saw a demonstration at the 1939–1940 New York World's Fair of the first contact lenses. She wrote in her diary they were huge and would never catch on and really be used by people.

If you think it would be fun to record your ideas now, this activity's for you!

You'll need:

a tape recorder and a blank tape

-or-

**a pad and pen
your imagination**

Keep in mind how much TV has changed in the past ten years. Ask your own parents. In 1985, cable was just starting, there were hardly any VCRs, and Barney wasn't even born yet.

Pull the tape recorder out at dinner or some other time when the family happens to be in the same place at the same time. Take turns predicting TV's future ten years down the road. Will TV be mainly for entertainment or for learning? Will it be important in the family? How? Will it look different?

Record the date on the tape and label. Put it somewhere where you'll find it, and mark on your calendar to listen back at the same time each year, like Thanksgiving. See who was on or off the mark.

	in one year	in five years	in ten years
TV Technology			
Home Video			
TV Show Themes			
Computer-TV Combos			

2 Who's Got the Remote?

Video and Parenting

Video offers yet another challenge and opportunity in raising kids. And, as with most other areas of parenting, it takes skill and sensitivity to be effective. First and foremost, remember you are your kids' biggest role model, ultimately more impressive than the Power Rangers. So begin by reflecting on your own TV behavior, and realize that your use of TV will set an example for your kids.

This chapter focuses on the challenges we all confront as parents and relates them to issues and concerns around TV. We begin with some attention to how children think and learn. This understanding of how kids process information is key in raising them, whether the agenda is video or cleaning up their rooms; and appreciating the differences in kids' ages and individual development is critical.

The issues that surface around video viewing engage you in many of the significant roles you fill as a parent: role model, mentor, limit definer, and rule enforcer. Over the next several pages, we discuss some opportunities afforded you in these capacities. In your roles as limit setter and enforcer of limits, negotiation is integral, involving you in a dialogue with your kids. Listen to them. In this way, you let them know that their point of view matters.

Tune In the Topics

- How Kids Think and Learn

- Age 5, No Way/Age 10, Passé: Age Appropriateness

- Many Hats: The Roles Parents Fill

- The Art of Negotiating and Maintaining Limits

- Testing, Testing, 1, 2, 3: Solutions to Familiar Issues That Surface Around Video

- Family Activity: Make It Legal

The process you follow in making family decisions will influence the outcome. If you include your kids in decision making and empower them with some reasonable responsibility, they'll be more likely to live by the rules. And they should better appreciate the need for limits and the process of making intelligent choices. Of course, there will always be occasions when your kids push against the boundaries. Anticipate this. In the last section of this chapter, we offer some familiar circumstances that arise to test the limits that get set. Find common ground when negotiating, and always try to maintain your sense of humor. It adds perspective and wins favor with them.

You justifiably have questions about your kids' viewing. That's one of the main reasons you're using this book. You wonder if you should limit their viewing or whether watching a lot is okay if it's educational. Then there are times when the kids are safely settled in front of the set, not making a mess, and you can go ahead and cook dinner. But your 4-year-old wants to watch Madonna on MTV and your 7-year-old is asking to see *Hard Copy*. Hold on. Before you reestablish what, when, and how much TV your kids should be watching, get your arms around some basic parenting issues.

How Kids Think and Learn

In your role as a parent, you have values, ideas, rules to pass along. This all necessitates a healthy dialogue with your kids. Start by understanding how they learn, so your messages will be understood by them.

Kids learn best by:

- *doing*
- *repeating*
- *being motivated to do well*
- *being praised*
- *keeping busy*
- *observing and imitating others*
- *responding to simple age-appropriate direction*
- *having their curiosity cultivated*

Kids learn by doing. Kids are hands-on creatures, so they need to be active and involved. Programs that inspire them to read, create, explore, or research after viewing will maximize the viewing experience by taking advantage of the fact that kids learn best through firsthand experience.

Kids repeat activities for enjoyment and to gain mastery. This is one of the reasons younger children in particular watch favorite videos over and over, just as they ask you to read their favorite books to them again and again. They like the familiarity of favorite characters and situations, and they delight in anticipating outcomes. More important, they internalize the

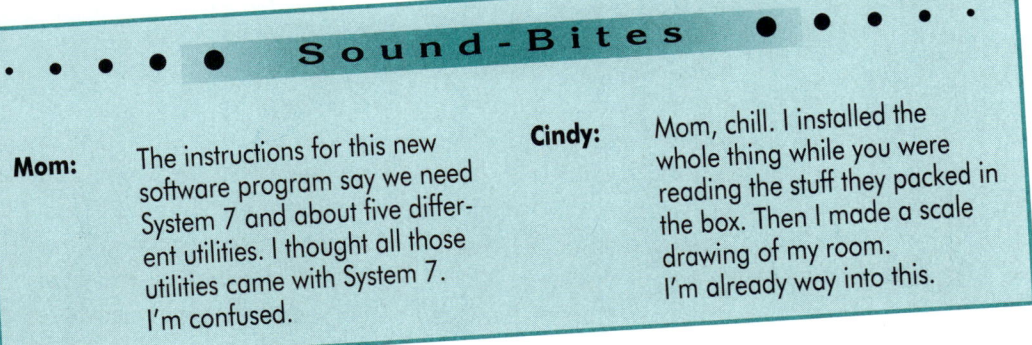

Sound-Bites

Mom: The instructions for this new software program say we need System 7 and about five different utilities. I thought all those utilities came with System 7. I'm confused.

Cindy: Mom, chill. I installed the whole thing while you were reading the stuff they packed in the box. Then I made a scale drawing of my room. I'm already way into this.

message, the process, the "how-to" of what they're watching while they enjoy the repeated experience.

Building self-esteem is a key to encourage learning. As you modify what when and how much your family is viewing, praising your kids' efforts in adjusting to the new standards will go a long way. You can also encourage your kids to choose alternatives to TV by doing them together and by planning fun activities for your kids when you aren't there. They'll stay busy and involved and won't seek TV to fill in the spaces, and being engaged in productive activities will keep your kids excited and primed for learning.

Kids learn by example from parents and others they admire. If you love watching old comedies, they might just join you. If you select only a few favorites to watch weekly, you're setting a good example. Remember, kids are like chimps when it comes to copying you. If they see you channel surf, expect them to follow your lead. If you leave the TV on as background for other activities, they probably will, too.

Kids need clearly presented information in order to "get it." Long-winded explanations and sophisticated rules will turn kids off and invite their appeals to make exceptions. Be brief and to the point about why your family is evaluating how to use TV and video, and include the kids as you develop a plan of action.

Kids want to master new skills and information. Acknowledge their intelligence. Share reviews about videos you think they'll enjoy. They'll discover the value of criticism in making viewing choices, and they'll learn how to weigh and measure what the critics have to say. Involve your kids in recording shows and setting up the family's video library.

In all the ways you authorize your kids to be active participants in their own learning, you will be investing them in the process as well as the outcome. This goes a long way toward reconciling lots of parent-child issues, including TV. But whatever's on your agenda at the moment, keep in mind your child's age and development, and communicate the message in language your child can understand.

Age 5, No Way/Age 10, Passé: Age Appropriateness

Your kids' development is a central factor in setting limits, establishing ground rules, and evaluating appropriate content for them to view. For example, a program that might be scary for your 5-year-old could seem hokey to your 10-year-old. Children of different ages display a wide range in their ability to grasp certain ideas intellectually, appreciate new experiences emotionally, and manage their lives socially. Beyond the general characteristics for each age, kids grow at different rates socially, emotionally, and intellectually just as they grow at different rates physically. In other words, your daughter could be intellectually advanced but less emotionally mature than other kids her age.

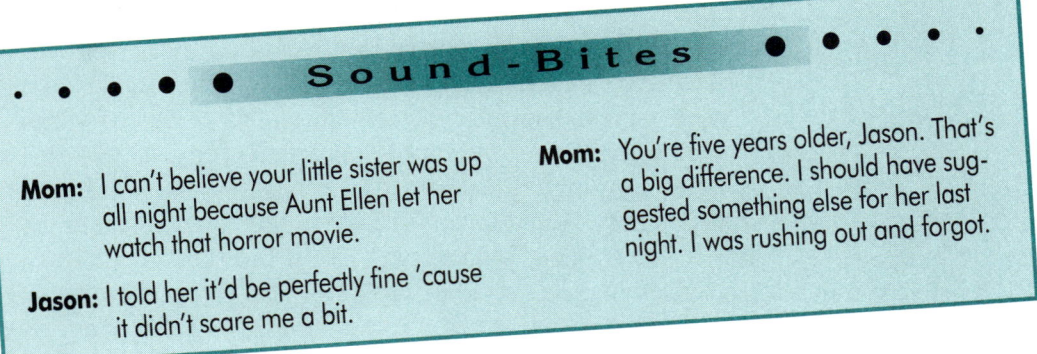

Sound-Bites

Mom: I can't believe your little sister was up all night because Aunt Ellen let her watch that horror movie.

Jason: I told her it'd be perfectly fine 'cause it didn't scare me a bit.

Mom: You're five years older, Jason. That's a big difference. I should have suggested something else for her last night. I was rushing out and forgot.

In addition, sometimes a child is especially sensitive about a particular issue which may not be of concern to her age-mates. For example, your 5-year-old, who worries about being away from her parents, won't sleep over at a friend's house, while another 5-year-old might plead for sleepovers all the time.

Development is also key to how you explain your reasoning in setting certain limits and how you articulate your values. For example, reminding your 8-year-old of your hour-a-day viewing limit will satisfy him, since he's fairly responsive to rules at his age. But be prepared for your 13-year-old to repeatedly challenge you on the reasons behind your hour limit. It's up to you to figure out where your kids are on the developmental scale and match experiences, including viewing, to their readiness and interest levels. To give you a start, we're offering (in very broad strokes) some portraits of different stages of development.

You're better equipped to use video effectively with your kids when you're aware of some of these basic developmental indicators. For example, for your 5-year-old who's focused on himself but loves having friends around, simply choosing a video everyone will like can be an exercise in accommodating his own interests with those of his friends who come to visit. For your 8-year-old who's growing independent from you and is interested in projects, a special-interest video that gives her ideas to make something for someone else could complement her developmental agendas. She could watch a gardening video and plant something as a gift for her grandma. For your 13-year-old who's working on his own identity at the same time he's showing an interest in music, a how-to guitar video could be just the ticket. The fact that you chose the tape for him acknowledges his interest and also gives him an opportunity to work at something that will help define him to himself and to his friends.

Stages of Development

Age	Social	Emotional	Intellectual
2–3	• enjoys imitating • plays alongside others • interested in other kids	• specific fears develop • likes to do things own way • separation issues	• interested in animals, babies, vehicles
3–6	• pretends • cooperates • socializes	• wants to copy parents • asserts own ideas • imagines worries: dark, animals, death • self-centered • discovering separateness from parents	• intense curiosity • active imagination • difficulty distinguishing real from imaginary • understands words and concepts in a very concrete way • absorbing ideas of right and wrong • learning social roles
6–11	• looks for role models • joins groups • peers are important • likes rules • argumentative/bossy	• developing a conscience: beginning to feel guilt and internalizing right vs. wrong • gaining independence from parents	• idealistic • interested in projects
11–15	• close relationships with friends • at 13-15, interested in opposite sex	• groping for identity • rebellious	• identifies intense interests like music, sports

When you consider how your child's own development influences his behavior and perceptions, a number of facts become clearer:

Videos work on different levels for different kids. We've all sat watching tapes with our kids while one zeros in on why a character acts a certain way and the other kid gets totally caught up in the plot. *The Little Mermaid* could affect two kids for two entirely different reasons. One could be enthralled by the theme of disobeying a parent and its consequences, while the other simply delights in the music and animation.

You can't always anticipate how your kid will respond to a particular tape.

We sold our *Hey, What About Me?* video to a toy store whose owner showed her 7-year-old son the tape a year after his sister was born. The kids on the tape talk candidly about the joy, anger, and loneliness they felt when their baby brothers and sisters made the scene. This child, who seemed quite accepting of the baby and didn't talk much about her arrival during her first year, began sharing a lot about his feelings after he saw the tape. His mother was amazed. She never knew he was carrying the emotional load he divulged.

Your kids' individual levels of development are strong indicators of the kind of programs they're likely to enjoy.

Really young viewers enjoy tapes that are close to their own experiences, while 7–11-year-olds will likely appreciate informational videos that introduce them to new experiences or expand their own interests.

Don't feel you need to call attention to the theme or character's motivation in a program even if you know the content is an issue for your child at this time.

It's enough for your kid to just watch and privately benefit from whatever the tape has to offer. The plot of *The Mystery of the Million-Dollar Hockey Puck* features a lead character who comes to appreciate his sister. This could prove an entertaining and apt choice for your 9-year-old who's having friction with his sister.

There are times a program can stir something up you didn't anticipate given where you think your child is developmentally.

If a character or situation portrayed in a video unexpectedly disturbs your child, he may very well turn off the set and walk away. If it's too heavy for her to deal with, she may say it's stupid or a bad movie. If you're watching with her and pick up on her discomfort, you may be able to talk about whatever it is. Otherwise, suggest another program while you make a mental note that the theme may be an issue for her.

Shari Lewis is a children's media guru who's been entertaining kids for three generations, now appealing to the grandchildren of the kids she entertained in the early 1950s. Shari captured the essence of child development in "What Makes Kids Tick," a speech to the media industry:

> *I have met 3-year-olds who can read, and 3-year-olds who can't relate to anything but their blankie. The 3-to-5s are preschoolers, eager to gain skills and knowledge and roll their tongues around big words. The 5- to 8-year-olds are in school, and so, are less willing to sit for teaching or preaching. . . . These little kids want to be big kids and anything that allows them to overcome their lack of size and status is a hit. The 8- to 11-year-old, currently referred to as "the middle-aged child," often has a well-developed sense of humor and gravitates to anything that helps him to hold center stage. Being the center of attention—knowing the punch line that makes others laugh—that's big stuff.*

Personal Notes
• • • • • • • • • • • • • • •

When Jane's son Noah was little, the family took him to see Pinocchio. *It certainly seemed like an appropriate film, and he appeared to enjoy it. That night, however, he had a nightmare and woke up crying out that "Pinocchio wasn't a bad boy." Remember the scene where Pinocchio lies and his ears grow big like the donkey? Obviously, that upset Noah. So even when you know the story, know the kid, know about child development—you can still blow it!*

Many Hats: The Roles Parents Fill

Add media monitor to the roles you fill, along with coach, chauffeur, cook, mentor, teacher. Parents wear many hats—in the course of one hour, let alone in the course of a whole day. Here we profile some of these roles and discuss how they come into play where video's concerned. We begin with Role Model and Mentor. Finally, we focus some serious attention on parents as Limit Setters and Enforcers of Limits. These last two roles require basic

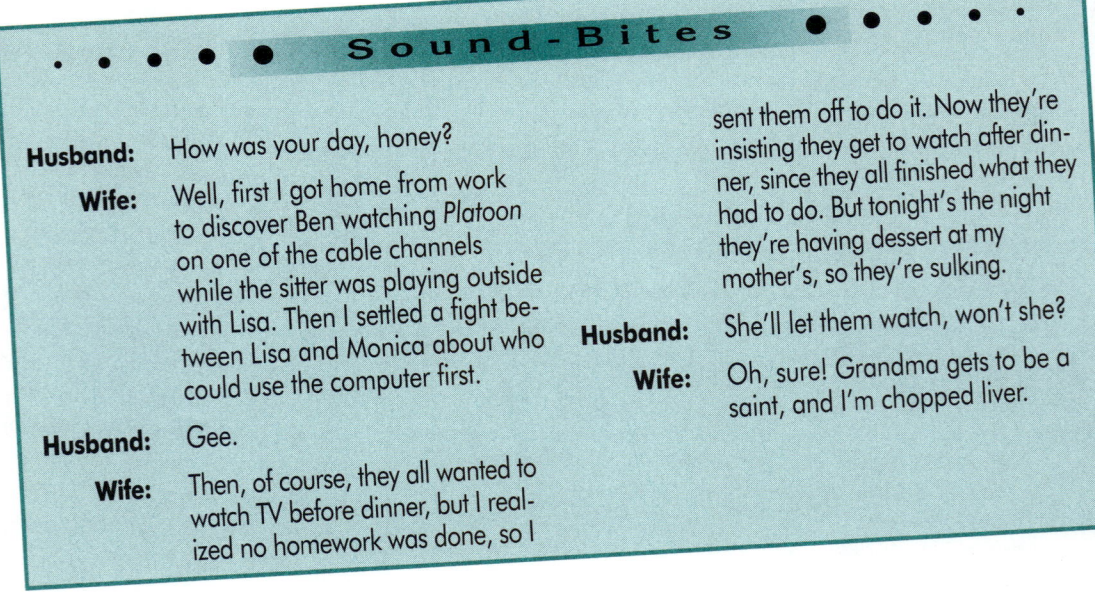

● ● ● ● ● **S o u n d - B i t e s** ● ● ● ● ●

Husband: How was your day, honey?

Wife: Well, first I got home from work to discover Ben watching *Platoon* on one of the cable channels while the sitter was playing outside with Lisa. Then I settled a fight between Lisa and Monica about who could use the computer first.

Husband: Gee.

Wife: Then, of course, they all wanted to watch TV before dinner, but I realized no homework was done, so I sent them off to do it. Now they're insisting they get to watch after dinner, since they all finished what they had to do. But tonight's the night they're having dessert at my mother's, so they're sulking.

Husband: She'll let them watch, won't she?

Wife: Oh, sure! Grandma gets to be a saint, and I'm chopped liver.

training in negotiation, so we've set this off as another section. The hats are familiar; hopefully the following will help them fit more comfortably when you wear them around the TV screen.

Role Model

What parents *do* will always have far more impact than what they *say*. Your own TV behavior sends a strong message to your kids. Let's face it, it's easy and reasonable to turn on the TV to keep you company when you're tired, or to occupy you while you take care of a boring task. However, if you actively turn off the set for yourself once in a while, you're giving the kids a message that there are other ways to entertain yourself.

So take a look at your own behavior. Consider *what* you choose to watch, *when* you watch, and *how much* you watch. In these situations choosing a video to relax can preempt the inclination to default to regular TV, and because video entails a certain amount of decision making and planning—a purchase, rental, or time shift—before viewing, you are sending an additional message about the importance of using TV as a tool. If you don't rent or buy a lot of videos, you might want to survey more of what's available. You may be surprised at how much quality programming there is to choose from. You might become a champion of video as a rich resource for entertainment and education.

If on the other hand you think you watch too much, you should consider the fact that what you do sets an example for your kids.

TIP

Share your passion for certain films or genres with your kids to broaden their taste in programming.

Sound-Bites

Tod: It's not fair. I can't watch my new video because I have a test tomorrow, but you get to see the movie you rented. Don't you have bills to pay or something else you have to do?

Dad: The bills aren't due tomorrow. Come to think of it, I could help your brother fix his tire so he can ride his bike tomorrow. I can watch the movie later.

What are you communicating every day through your own attitudes and behavior around the TV? If you want them to be selective in their viewing and to balance viewing with other valuable activities, then you need to demonstrate the same. If you're a fan of Hitchcock thrillers or screwball comedies, no doubt the kids will also take an interest if you share the experience. And if you search the listings for something you want to watch rather than watching what's on, that's setting an example, too.

Mentor

Try to position yourself as a mentor, not a rule enforcer. One of the most rewarding roles in parenting is counseling and educating your kids—mentoring. Offer advice and counsel when it's appropriate and when you think your kids will be responsive. It's great when you can steer a conversation in such a

Sound-Bites

Alyssa: I really want to go to Meg's basketball game, but I have that paper to write. And we only have one more day for the movie you rented, and I want to see it. Plus, I want to finish the mystery I'm reading so I can find out who did it. It's not fair, I don't know what to do first.

Dad: Obviously, you have to finish your paper. Besides that, think about what you could do another time. What do you think?

Alyssa: Meg has another game on Saturday. I could go to that one. I need about an hour to finish the paper. How about we watch the movie together? Then I'll read in bed.

Dad: Wow, you solved that one. I'll make us some sandwiches with the leftovers from last night. We can eat while we watch the movie.

way that your child discovers solutions and answers on his/her own. As we'll discuss throughout the book, TV offers many opportunities to mentor your kids, like discussing values through programs you watch together. The very process of balancing what, when, and how much your family is watching creates many opportunities to offer your insight and experience.

The Art of Negotiating and Maintaining Limits

Kids are skillful negotiators, especially when it comes to TV. Help them understand that negotiation is give-and-take, and that hearing what the other side has to say is as important as being heard. Encourage them in the process. In this way, you're supporting their willingness to argue their point of view, to deal with other points of view, and to defend their positions. Creative negotiation can

TIP

Try not to solve your child's problem for him; instead be a resource by asking questions to help clarify choices and reach a solution.

. . . . • ● ● ● ● ● ●
S o u n d - B i t e s ● ● ● ● ●

Mom: An hour a day of screen time during the week is enough, considering everything else you have to do.

Rick: You mean computer and TV? That's no fair. What about computer programs that are educational, like the typing one you got me? That shouldn't count as screen time.

Mom: That's true. Okay, an hour and a half, including any other stuff you do—which is mostly computer games. Write it down, and we'll have an agreement we can both live by.

Rick: Tell you what. I'll type it!

help you reach consensus. Keep things nonemotional when you negotiate, and be understanding.

It's also important to structure the negotiation so it's within acceptable bounds. Then it will most likely result in a win-win for all concerned. For example, if your kids are arguing to see a really violent film, find out what's so appealing about that particular title. If you're able to isolate some dramatic context or content that can be found in more acceptable alternatives, come up with a few other titles and give them a choice between those. Leave their initial choice out of the equation. Just identify what it is that attracted them to their first choice and try and translate that to other agreeable options.

How to Talk So Kids Will Listen and Listen So Kids Will Talk, a superb parenting resource by Adele Faber and Elaine Mazlish, can be a valuable reference when negotiating with your family. Based on their book, here's a checklist on problem solving, which should prove extremely useful when planning the standards you set for viewing:

1. *Talk about the child's feelings.*

2. *Talk about your feelings.*

3. *Brainstorm with your child to find a mutually acceptable solution.*

4. *Decide which ideas you all like, which you don't, and which you want to put into action.*

5. *Follow through.*

Making rules and following through on them is one of the most agonizing tasks in

Personal Notes
. . . .

Karen's 10-year-old son Andrew negotiated a night of a Schwarzenegger movie, accompanied by a candy bar, joking that "next time" he'd be willing to watch a "classic" his parents favored, accompanied by carrot sticks.

parenting. But if you keep perspective on the process, practice what you preach, maintain your sense of humor, and include the kids in the dialogue, you should find the job far less daunting. You'll also learn more about yourself and your kids along the way. And when you're not home, be sure that Grandma, Uncle, baby-sitter—whoever is in charge—knows the ground rules and is also upholding them.

Limit Setter

As you begin negotiating, also remember, kids want limits, although they'd never admit as much. Reasonable limits instill a basic feeling of security in children and demonstrate your concern for their well-being.

The way in which we set limits can help determine how successful they'll be. Of course, kids are going to push the boundaries and test the limits, and there will inevitably be exceptions and violations that require ongoing negotiation. But you can do *your* job by defining these boundaries and attending to some basics involved in setting limits.

Limit Setting Involves These Steps in Negotiation

- *State the problem.*
- *Get the kids' input on the problem.*
- *Propose rules and explain the reasons for them.*
- *Get your kids' suggestions for rules and their reasons.*
- *Get your kids responses to your suggestions and respond to theirs.*
- *Formulate guidelines together that are fair.*

State the Problem
I want to talk to you about the amount of TV we all watch because I'm concerned about the amount of time it takes up in our day.

Many parents are afraid of the arguments and disobedience that can result from exerting their authority, or they have difficulty enforcing rules consistently. But using authority doesn't mean being authoritarian. In fact, it's a parent's responsibility to see what limits need to be set and to recognize that limit setting is really a reflection of values. Children appreciate limits that are fair and consistent once they understand the reasons for them.

Get the Kids' Input on the Problem

What's there to do besides watch the tube?

Don't establish limits in a vacuum. Invite your kids' opinions and involve them in your assessment of how your family uses TV and how it can serve you better. Your children will also feel part of the process and will respect you even more if you come together to discuss issues. Kids often raise points that their parents haven't considered and feel more invested in the decision when they're included in the discussion.

I can't believe you won't let me watch that cartoon because you think it's violent. I think it's funny! And it's not real; it's a cartoon. If a real truck ran over Crusader Rabbit, it wouldn't make him look like he was ironed to the street.

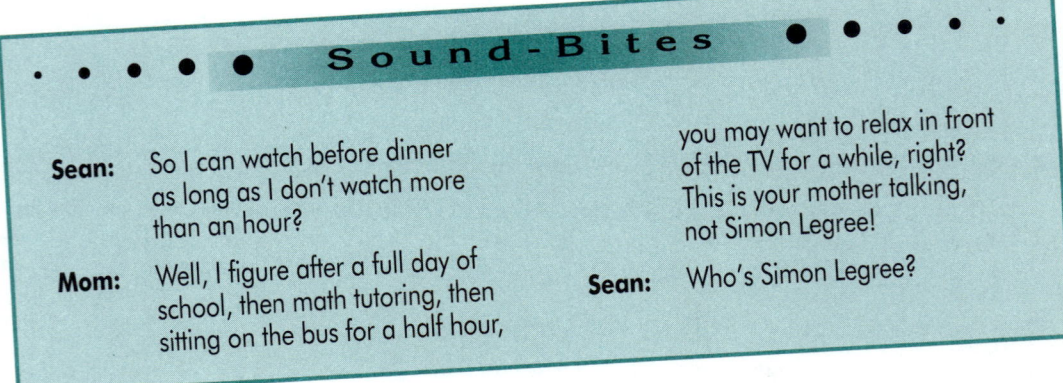

Sound-Bites

Sean: So I can watch before dinner as long as I don't watch more than an hour?

Mom: Well, I figure after a full day of school, then math tutoring, then sitting on the bus for a half hour, you may want to relax in front of the TV for a while, right? This is your mother talking, not Simon Legree!

Sean: Who's Simon Legree?

They may test your assumptions or the basis on which you established certain rules, but that's only fair. Remain open to their rebuttals. The kids' arguments will help fine tune the rules while confirming their participation. They will also learn to listen to you and better appreciate your point of view.

Propose Rules and Explain the Reasons for Them

It's really better when you plan ahead what you're going to watch. TV should be a choice, not a default.

TIP

Setting limits lets kids know you care.

Instead of simply declaring the rules, try to explain how the rules reflect your values. For example, if you feel that "swear words" are offensive, insensitive or rude, and never justified, let them know. If, on the other hand, you are comfortable with certain language when taken in context and seen as a reflection of the character, say so. This, of course, depends on the language you're comfortable using at home.

Of course, we all bring certain biases to various situations, so you need to make an honest judgment as to whether certain content is objectionable, harmless, or just not your taste. For example, you may not be a fan of the language in a video on grunge music, but a show that features a grunge band's struggle to succeed in the music business might be a worthwhile program for your preteen who aspires to be a rock star. In fact, such a program could encourage individuality and independence, values you probably espouse.

Get Your Kids' Suggestions for Rules and Their Reasons

Why do you feel three hours of screen time a day is what you should have?

Remember to listen to your kids' ideas and try to understand what the core issue really is. You never know when they'll come up with a winning position. They often consider details and circumstances you haven't entertained, such as having the option to switch their TV time when a friend is visiting and there's a special video they want to watch together. Your kids represent another point of view, which will force you to consider whether the limits you want to set are really fair and reasonable. Most important, though, is the fact that by truly negotiating with your kids, you're demonstrating a respect for their ideas and a willingness to involve them in setting standards that directly affect them.

Get Your Kids Responses to Your Suggestions and Respond to Theirs

Two hours should really be enough. Just think about it. If you spent three hours watching each day, how would you find enough time for all your after-school sports and the Y and visiting friends, to say nothing about homework and other stuff around here? Of course, you could give up dinner and sleeping . . .

It's important to have a back and forth and let everyone have an opportunity to react to the ideas and suggestions that are being discussed. Remember humor as a key to keeping things from being too heavy-handed.

Formulate Guidelines Together That Are Fair

How do you feel about choosing ahead so the TV doesn't get flipped on the minute you can't figure out what to do? I know there are times you're tired and just want to flop down and watch for a while. Let's deal with those as they come up.

It's important that the rules respect reality and individual situations. If your kids' time is taken up with a lot of studying and chores, a rule that TV time be at the end of the day may leave no opportunity for a justifiable break. If your child tends to procrastinate, scheduling TV as a break or incentive can work well. On the other hand, if you have a diligent student and homework is not an issue, then holding back screen time until after homework may be immaterial.

Maintainer of Limits

Listen to your kids' arguments when you need to enforce rules that had been agreed to by everyone but come into question again. Sometimes what kids are asking for has nothing to do with TV. For example, if they're arguing for more time to watch, maybe they're bored and need some alternatives. If they are pleading to watch a particular show, and you're uncertain about the content, find out what has them so interested. Maybe there are other choices to satisfy them. Or maybe their case

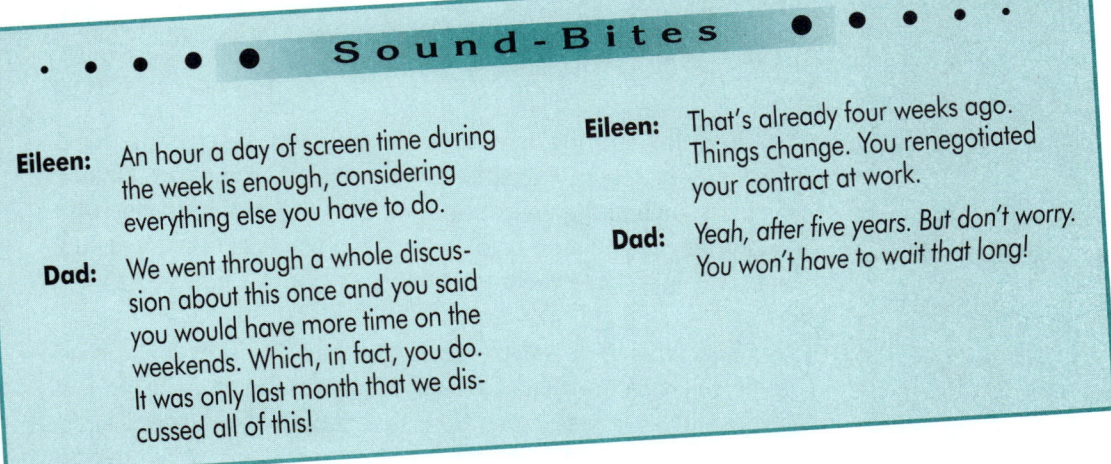

Sound-Bites

Eileen: An hour a day of screen time during the week is enough, considering everything else you have to do.

Dad: We went through a whole discussion about this once and you said you would have more time on the weekends. Which, in fact, you do. It was only last month that we discussed all of this!

Eileen: That's already four weeks ago. Things change. You renegotiated your contract at work.

Dad: Yeah, after five years. But don't worry. You won't have to wait that long!

will convince you to watch with them so you can discuss any questionable segments. Perhaps you can tape and preview the show if it's on broadcast or cable. If you take the time, there's usually a solution that will satisfy everyone. Even if you wind up holding the line, working on a problem together will make your kids feel they were given a fair shake.

Enforcing Rules Involves These Steps in Negotiation:

- *Recognize valid exceptions to the rules.*
- *Restate the rules clearly and in positive terms.*
- *Be consistent and follow through on the rules that were set.*

37

Recognize Valid Exceptions to the Rules

I know you said I can only watch an hour a day, but today's history assignment is to watch either a documentary on civil rights or to watch the news and look for a story that relates to civil rights or civil disobedience. Can't I add that to my hour?

When someone doesn't feel well or it's a rainy day without plans, then it might be fair to bend the viewing rules a little. There will always be times when you're not sure how you feel or how you should respond—those gray areas that crop up to test your assumptions and the limits you've set. Be prepared for these situations, and deal with them in a way that doesn't confuse the established limits.

You can maintain your authority without being rigid. There'll always be exceptions, and it's important to recognize them as such and go with the flow. The main thing is not to let exceptions *become* the rule. Treat them as exceptions, and your kids will appreciate them for what they are.

Kids have to deal with exceptions, too. The schedule can become so clogged with an after-school sport, a party, a doctor's appointment, or a visiting relative that time for homework slides later and later, and that hour of viewing at the end of the day becomes more and more elusive. Sometimes kids just have to let it go. Acknowledge these difficulties, and work with them to make up the loss. Add time to the weekend viewing schedule, time shift a favorite program, or offer a surprise bonus half hour to stay up.

Restate the Rules Clearly and in Positive Terms

So we've agreed, you get two hours of screen time a day. That should work with your busy schedule and still give you enough time to enjoy viewing, when you fit it in.

Remember, the way you state the rules can make all the difference. *"You can have up to two hours of screen time a day for the TV and computer"* sounds much more positive than *"No more than two hours of screen time a day."*

Be clear about the boundaries and your reasons for setting these limits. If your rule is that homework comes before video, then explain why homework takes priority. If you state the rules clearly in the first place and spell out the consequences, then there should be no confusion or resentment when the ax falls because someone has crossed the line.

Cara came over to shoot a few hoops and to work on math, not to watch the show you taped yesterday.

Be Consistent and Follow Through on the Rules That Were Set

I'm disappointed that you watched your show before you finished your paper. We agreed on the rules, so you won't have any more video or TV for the rest of the week.

Don't change the rules or make an exception for every new circumstance that arises. When you make the rule, acknowledge some exceptions that might crop up. Then when those exceptions arise, it will be clear what *can* happen.

It's not enough to make the rules. Obviously, they must have force behind them in order to work. This requires monitoring, since no matter how cooperative kids may be, they're bound to challenge even clear, fair, and consistent limits.

You should also ensure that the ground rules are in force at home even when you're not around. When someone else is in charge of the kids, be sure they know the rules and are comfortable maintaining them in your stead. If the kids are home alone, be sure they have activities that will occupy them. Besides homework and chores that need to be done, suggest fun activities that will keep them entertained. Of course, there are those occasions when the kids are at someone else's house,

39

where you have no authority. But behavior is portable. As your kids internalize the rules and find alternatives to using TV as a time killer, they may influence their friends to do the same. If your kids watch more TV at their friends' houses or watch something they know you would consider inappropriate, invite them to share this with you so you can discuss their experience in a nonjudgmental way. Use it as a learning opportunity.

If more than one adult in the household is setting limits, it's crucial that they agree. Of course, adults don't always agree on anything. Some may have a level of comfort about the presentation of sex and may feel that nudity, if warranted in terms of the story line or program, isn't an issue at all. For others, anything more than pillow talk and a peck on the lips may be unacceptable. This often means that whoever is home at the time sets the agenda, unless you've ironed out differences in advance. Without clear agreement between adults, kids will see one as the "good guy" and the other one as the "meanie."

S o u n d - B i t e s

Bobby: Dad said I could watch the movie Billy loaned me. You were out at a meeting when he told me. He promised.

Mom: Are you sure he knew it was Misery? Now Dad's at a meeting. We'll have to wait until he gets home and have a chat about this, since I don't agree.

Bobby: I wish you guys would get your act together.

Family Roundtable

Living By The Rules

I have rules. It's a struggle because the rules are good, but they're not always enforced because I'm not always there.

Mother of 12- and 14-year-olds

I know what you mean. The baby-sitters we get are nice, but real pushovers. That's why we try and pick something ourselves for our daughter to watch when we go out.

Father of 4-year-old

Yeah, but what about when they come home from school and you're at work?

Mother of 8- and 11-year-olds

We see some of the best stuff when we have a baby-sitter. But we also do all this other stuff like draw and read and call Grandma, so they think we didn't watch at all.

10-year-old

Grown-ups may have to compromise. You may have to strike a bargain that brings you a bit over the line of your "comfort zone." Usually, those who take the time to discuss these values before presenting them to the kids can find a solution that will be motivated by a shared concern for the kids' well-being. No matter what, keep in mind that limits that were negotiated together will still get tested down the road.

TV and video are only part of the territory of parenting. But if you model the behavior you'd like for your kids, set reasonable limits, follow through, and listen to your kids in the process, there will be less conflict and confusion regarding TV and more consensus about its use by the family.

Testing, Testing, 1, 2, 3: Solutions to Familiar Issues That Surface Around Video

Constant testing is a sign of any normal kid's search to find boundaries and to grow beyond them. And TV has its own classic confrontations: kids who want to watch a lot, younger children who demand to see the same programs as their older siblings, kids visiting friends' homes where viewing may not be appropriately monitored by other adults.

TIPS

• *Post a list of activities your kids like to do that they can refer to when looking for an alternative to TV.*

• *Post the screen rules for all to see.*

You may feel like your kids are expert negotiators and that you must become a specialist in conflict resolution. You often wonder if *everything* isn't up for negotiation. How do you maintain the peace without tearing your hair out, engaging in shouting matches, or going for the Kleenex to deal with the tears that flow when kids don't get what they want? It takes patience and forbearance to listen to kids' arguments, to deal fairly with siblings vying over the VCR and their respective schedules and viewing rights, and to peacefully settle differences so everyone comes out satisfied.

Dad: Who said you could turn on the set now?

Lizzie: No one said I couldn't.

Dad: Later you can watch the tape you wanted to watch yesterday when your TV time was over.

Lizzie: How about I watch it now, since Lauren's coming over later to finish up our science project?

Dad: Okay, good enough.

Lizzie: See, now you said I could!

Setting limits often invites resentment, so acknowledge your kids' feelings and assure them that their feelings are normal. Help your kids to understand that you're not trying to deprive them but to enrich their lives by improving what they watch and helping them to find alternatives. When you must remind your kids of established ground rules, take advantage of the occasion to steer them to other engaging activities so they won't feel as if something is being taken away. If it's almost time for dinner, and they go to turn on the set, ask them to concoct a dessert with whatever ingredients they can hunt up, or offer to play a round of cards while dinner finishes cooking.

It will take time for the family to adjust to new viewing patterns. You will experience regression—expect it and address it, since behavior change is never easy. Here are some fictional scenarios that illustrate common conflicts around viewing rights and privileges. The parents' responses here are certainly not the only way to deal, just approaches that might work for you when you feel like you want to throw out the set and retire to

As a Matter of Fact...

It is estimated that 7 million children nationwide are home alone. This makes television a companion, which is difficult to limit. Children alone who must stay indoors in unsafe neighborhoods watch TV as an alternative to outdoor play and visiting.

43

some isolated beach with no TV in sight. Also, notice the versatility of video and the VCR in these resolutions.

Dealing with Special Circumstances

When the need to watch doesn't fit neatly into allotted times.

Maria: *I had a stressful day and need to chill in front of the set for a while.*

Dad: *What do you mean stressful?*

Maria: *I've heard you say that when you sit down to watch.*

Dad: *True. Sorry to hear you were stressed. What happened today?*

Maria: *An argument with Jake, a pop quiz in math, and I sucked at basketball during gym.*

Dad: *Sounds like you need to relax. Go for it. Why don't you watch the* Mystery Science Theater 3000 *I taped for you last week? It's only a half hour. Then we can go over your math.*

Don't be so rigid that you can't recognize when a little TV provides valuable relaxation, especially when it works that way for you.

Peer Pressure Situation 1: Confronting Different Expectations at Someone Else's House

Considering your child's development and age when judging whether they should watch a (scary for a particular kid) program that's being shown at someone else's house.

Jeff: *It's not fair. I'll be the only one not going to Rick's party because my mom won't let me see* Friday the 13th. *That's going to go over real big with my friends. Everyone will think I'm a weenie.*

Mom: *I certainly don't want to put you in an awkward position with your friends. But you have some choices here. First off, let me remind you, you don't particularly like scary films. You can go to the party and say you have another obligation with me and can't stay for the movie. Or you can skip the party. Or you can stay and watch the movie and possibly wind up a bit freaked out like you were when Uncle Sean baby-sat and rented* Alien. *Remember? Maybe Rick would consider another film if you suggested a few you could bring.*

Jeff: *Maybe we could rent* Stand by Me. *I know it's one of his favorites.*

This one was particularly successful because the kid winds up making the decision. It's always better when you can offer them some choices.

Peer Pressure Situation 2: Choosing a Video at the Video Store with a Friend

Christi: Dirty Dancing's *great. I've seen it, and there's nothing really bad in it. I can't believe your mom won't let you watch it. Anyway, what can she do after you've seen it if you watch at my house? Come on, let's get it.*

Anne: *No, let's see* Grease *instead. It's really cool with lots of great dancing, too. It's one of my favorites. I can't believe you haven't already seen it.*

Anne might have rehearsed this one with her parents, she was so quick and self-assured in her handling of the situation. It's terrific if kids have some comebacks in their back pocket for just these kinds of situations.

Setting Limits on Violence

The benefit of a preview when in doubt.

Ken: *Why do you say it's too gory? How much is "too gory" anyway? Is a cup of blood too much but a quarter cup okay?*

Mom: *I searched through it last night after you pushed me into renting it, and I thought the violence was excessive and totally gratuitous.*

Ken: *What does that mean?*

Mom: *Unnecessary. I think the story would have actually been more dramatic without all the close-ups of blood and guts. Sorry, it registered over an eight on my violence scale. When I returned it, I rented a few other tapes I thought you'd enjoy instead. Choose one for now. You can make some popcorn to go with it.*

It's hard for Ken to dismiss the fact that his mom took the time to preview the tape. Kids do appreciate your caring. You need to make it clear, however, that it's not a matter of your trust in them, but that it's hard to know where to draw the line if you haven't seen the program in question. The ratings systems leave a lot to be desired and are really arbitrary guidelines that don't speak to everyone's value system.

Here are some ways you can make judgments on tapes you haven't seen. (It would be impossible to preview all tapes your kids want to see.)

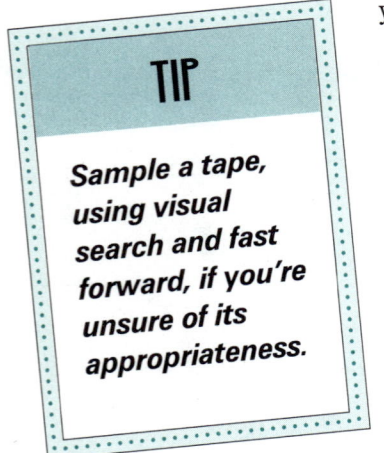

TIP

Sample a tape, using visual search and fast forward, if you're unsure of its appropriateness.

- *Look at the sleeve. The video cover is the main tool of the studio's marketing department. Even if sex and violence play a small part in the program, they will probably be featured on the cover. The ratings, genre, and the blurb can help, too.*

- *Do a visual search/fast-forward. Once you get it home, it doesn't take long to sample a tape by fast-forwarding or searching through a few times.*

- *Search online. The major online services have film reviews.*

- *Check out CD-ROMs. A few of these, such as* Cinemania *(Microsoft Home), include reviews and cross reference titles by directors, bios of stars, and subject matter.*

Accommodating Different-Age Kids

Siblings with different choices and a time conflict—who goes first?

Rachel: *Anna and I both finished our homework. Now we want to watch our shows. I go first 'cause I'm the oldest.*

Mom: *Is that a fair reason for you to go first? I thought you had to go to Nina's to drop off her book, and there were a few calls you wanted to make this afternoon. Why not let Anna go first? This way you'll get all your gottas over with and only have your wannas for the rest of the evening. After Anna goes to bed, you can watch the show you taped last week. I'll watch with you if you like.*

Rachel: *I'm heading out to Nina's. Be back in half an hour.*

Making the Rules Clear and Fair

Kids try to internalize the rules but sometimes get it wrong and need clarification.

Lydia: *I'm not supposed to tell you, but Willie saw a movie over at Jake's house that had naked people in it.*

Mom: *How do you know?*

Lydia: *I heard Willie tell Kevin on the phone.*

Mom: *Seems like we have three issues here. One is that Willie saw a program with naked people. Well, I know he did. It was about Australia, where some of the Aborigine people who live there don't wear much clothes. Jake's mom told me they bought it for the family because they enjoyed it so much when they saw it on cable. But there are two other issues here. How is it you were listening in on a phone conversation between Willie and Kevin? And do you think you should be telling me about what Willie did behind his back?*

Lydia: *Strike three. I'm out.*

Are you exhausted yet? Take a deep breath and remind yourself you are doing your job as the parent, but also remember they're doing their job as the kids.

Holding the Line

Kids try to bend the rules and are often persistent in trying to win your sympathy.

Trying to Bend the Rules

Tim: *Wednesday is my hardest day in school. I really need a break before I start my homework and I already rode my bike around for a half hour. I need to relax and have a TV break. It's time for* The Simpsons *reruns.*

Mom: *I'll tape them. You have your room to clean up and homework to finish before TV. If you really need a break, lie down on your bed and read your* World Magazine *that came in the mail today, or put on the radio and draw for a while.*

Okay, Tim exercised his body, but how about his creativity? Kids need to be reminded there are other choices for taking a break, regardless of how valuable the programming is. Sometimes, it's just a matter of rechanneling their energy instead of the set.

Being Persistent and Trying to Win Your Sympathy

Diana: *Come on, Dad. I finished everything I have to do and Steve loaned me that dog movie we've been trying to rent for weeks. I have to return it to him tomorrow. Can I watch it all today and just not watch tomorrow?*

Dad: *Fine. But are you sure you want to spend tomorrow's viewing time now? That's two hours today. I don't care how you decide to use it. It still adds up to two hours.*

Diana: *Dad, you're so into keeping score!*

Using her time allotment at once may come back to haunt Diana, but she has to make the decision and accept the consequences.

Being Consistent Within the Family

Communicate with each other so you can follow through and maintain consistency on the rules.

Diana: *I'm almost done with my homework. I can't wait to sit down and watch that video Grandma sent.*

Mom: *I thought you already watched today's hour yesterday when you watched Steve's movie.*

Remember to update each other on what the kids have seen. We *told* you it would come back to haunt Diana.

Handling Inappropriate Viewing Requests

What's forbidden can be very appealing, so don't make a big deal of your refusal.

TIP

A film you rule out, like Speed, *may have a behind-the-scenes "making-of" that may satisfy your kids' interest.*

Nicole: *But I want to see* Raiders of the Lost Ark. *I need to see it. It's really important. It even won an award, I think.*

Mom: *It's got some pretty scary parts. You can see it when you're older. Let's rent* Willy Wonka and the Chocolate Factory *today.*

Nicole: *Can we get some M&Ms to go with?*

Acknowledging the Kids' Point of View

The VCR can be a solution.

Clare: *It's the season opener. I've been looking forward to seeing this game all summer. I just won't watch any TV tomorrow.*

Dad: *So it's a two-hour special. You still have piano to practice and thank-you letters to write. Sorry. An hour of TV is all you have time for. It's enough. Watch the first half, and we'll tape the second. You can watch the rest tomorrow.*

Often the VCR offers the flexibility to resolve conflicts. You can select different programs for different kids according to their ages, development, and personalities. Video is a more flexible approach to allocating your family's viewing time because you can easily split programs into separate viewing installments.

When parents exercise their role with confidence and sensitivity, they can avoid many confrontations. Listening to your kids and negotiating fairly will help resolve the issues that do arise. Then you can all move on from the potential video battleground to create a climate in which everyone can share their views and learn from each other. You and your kids will feel more empowered. Your kids will benefit from being involved in these decisions, and you will have the confidence that your kids have internalized the family's values and respect the viewing ground rules.

Family Activity

Make It Legal

We've all heard: "Write it down so you won't forget." It's usually true. When people agree to something, they often write it down to seal the deal. Then they can go back to the written document if anyone tries to stretch things or really does forget. Why not draw up a contract when you're working out limits around the TV? Someone can design it in markers or on the computer. Post it on the fridge or just keep it handy for those "reminding" times.

Get everyone together to negotiate what, when, and how they will watch in a week.

You'll need:

paper
markers

-or-

a word processor or typewriter
and a willingness to compromise

Here are some items to consider including in your contract. They reflect some of the issues you'll want to include in coming up with guidelines everyone can accept.

What

What kinds of programs must I watch with an adult?

What types of video and television are unacceptable for viewing?

When

Can we watch before homework, as a break?

Can we watch every day?

How Much

If I watch during someone else's screen time, does it count for me?

Can I "bank" screen time I don't use now for another time?

3 Is TV Only for Dessert?

Video as Part of Daily Life

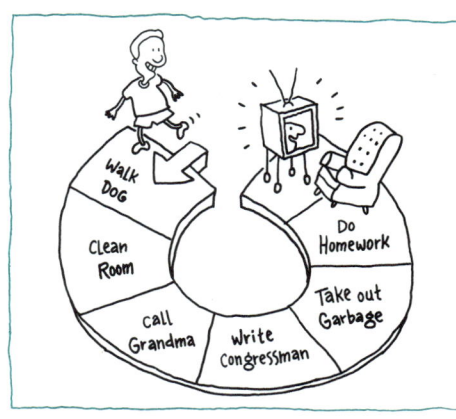

Video can be an entertaining reward and a valuable educational resource when parents get involved in their kids' viewing. In this chapter, we help parents grapple with the *what, when, and how much* of TV viewing.

What to watch is perhaps the most highly charged area, since it involves the hot topics of violence, sex, language, stereotypes, and negative role models; and on top of all that is the concern about scariness. Then there's the matter of balancing the kinds of programs your kids watch so that they're exposed to a variety of formats and genres. Here in Chapter 3 we address these broad-based issues you confront in expressing your own philosophy and orientation regarding viewing decisions as well as ensuring you introduce your kids to a mix of program styles and categories. Chapter 4 follows with a more specific treatment of how to judge individual programs.

When to view forces an examination of daily activities and priorities. For instance, should your kids watch before homework? On school nights? **How much to view** addresses the question of TV's ultimate value in your kids' lives and how it balances with everything else that's fighting for their time and attention.

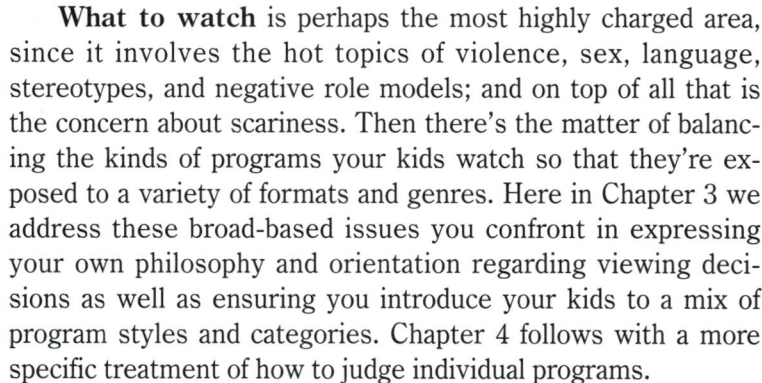

Tune In the Topics

- **Those Colorful Gray Areas: Violence, Sex, Language, Stereotypes, Negative Role Models, and Scariness**

- **A Balanced Viewing Diet (What to Watch)**

- **Fitting It All In (When to View)**

- **A Video Allowance (How Much to View)**

- **Lessons Learned**

- **Family Activity: Design Video Coupons**

Your answers to these questions of quality, balance, and quantity will form the basis for your family's policy about TV in your home, and the process will also enable you to make similar decisions about other screen options like video games and online services, if your kids have access to them.

Again, the VCR can be a lifesaver. Use it to watch programs, not to "watch TV." Select what you want to see, watch it, then turn off the set. And consider locating your TV centrally, so it's obvious when and what the kids are watching. We hope this chapter will make your balancing act easier and offer some ways to manage the tricky issues that every family confronts, even after your policy is in place.

Those Colorful Gray Areas: Violence, Sex, Language, Stereotypes, Negative Role Models, and Scariness

Just because Billy's folks let him see Robo Cop *doesn't mean you can.*

We're confronted by major and complicated decisions when we select programs for our kids. There are many gray areas, especially regarding appropriate programming. *"Where do I draw the line on violence?" "What kind of language is acceptable?" "Should I totally rule out programs that present stereotypes?" "What's left to watch?"*

Violence

Over 1,000 studies have shown connections between violence in the media and violent behavior by children. Dr. William Dietz, a researcher in the field, states simply, "Children do what they see." He goes on to say that children watch approximately 12,000 violent acts per year on TV. Most major profes-

Family Roundtable

Kids Know a Lot About What's Available to View

My kids pick a show a night they want to watch for thirty minutes, but you'd be surprised how familiar they are with all the shows that are on that they're not watching . . . or supposedly not watching.

Mother of 11- and 14-year-olds

We talk a lot about the shows with our friends and I feel like a dork if I don't know the show.

2-year-old

My mom lets me see some extra stuff once in a while so I know what it's about, even though I don't watch it all the time.

10-year-old

55

sional organizations of educators and doctors have recommended that parents limit their children's viewing of violence because of the evidence that viewing violence is strongly linked with aggressive behavior. One-third of kids ages 10–16 polled in Los Angeles in 1992 said they often want to try things they see on television. In 1993, the *Yankelovich Youth Monitor* surveyed kids ages 9–17, and two-thirds of them thought there was too much violence on TV. The American Psychological Association encourages parents to protect kids from feeling that the world is unsafe, from becoming insensitive to the pain and suffering of others, and from imitating negative things they see. Limiting what and how much TV our kids see is one very effective way to work toward these recommendations.

As a Matter of Fact...

The average child grows up watching 20,000 murders before he or she turns 18.

Since violence takes so many forms on the screen, from cartoons through reality-based "docudramas" to the news, it's a constant challenge to determine what's appropriate for your own kids. Your child's maturity and emotional makeup are always factors in making these decisions. If you were given a list of choices that included *Rocky, Butch Cassidy and the Sundance Kid, North by Northwest, The Terminator, Close Encounters of the Third Kind,* and *Woody Woodpecker and Friends,* which would you let your kids watch? If certain titles are okay, why is their violence acceptable? What is it about the violence in the other films

TIP

Explain the real consequences of violence, and how they can be different from what's shown on the screen.

Family Roundtable

Different Kinds of Violence

I tape After School Specials for my kids to watch later on.

Mother of 8- and 11-year olds

Yeah, but those real-life stories scare me to death. I think it's harder to watch shows that are about abuse and things like that because you know it's the reality.

10-year-old

The more realistic it is, the more I get upset. The Schwarzenegger movies aren't scary be-cause they aren't real.

11-year-old

57

Is TV Only for Dessert?

that's inappropriate? You'll probably ask yourself some of these questions in your deliberations:

Things to Consider

- *Should I allow cartoon violence that doesn't show the real consequences of violence and is often funny?*
- *Is "authentic" violence in context okay, even if it's gritty and real, such as in a war film or a documentary?*
- *If the perpetrator's goals aren't served by violence, and aggression is shown to be a poor choice, should I let my kids watch?*

What You Can Do

- *Explain the real consequences of violence, and how they can be different from what's shown on the screen.*
- *Plan ahead of time so you know what they will be watching.*
- *Limit how many hours your kids watch.*
- *Talk to your kids about ways to solve conflict: talking it out, walking away, finding common ground.*

Realistically, it's impossible to screen out every bit of violence that's portrayed on the screen. And it's probably not a good idea to do that anyway, since violence is part of our human condition. The issue and decisions around it involve your particular kid, the context and presentation of violence, and whether your child's watching alone or with you to share the experience and offer commentary. Writer Elizabeth Weld Nolan in a *Boston Globe* article, "The Human V-chip," harnesses the violence beast so well when she writes: "How can software or a dark television screen compete with the power of a parent's outrage at violence, compassion in front of bad news, horror at human cruelty, reinforcement of kindness? How can children learn to handle violence in man and nature if they never see it at all, or if they see it unrefined and uncomforted by adult sensibilities?"

Sex

We've come a long way from *I Love Lucy,* where Ricky and Lucy slept in twin beds and Lucy couldn't even use the word "pregnant," which she clearly was at the time. The American Psychological Association estimates that American teenagers are exposed to 14,000 sexual references and innuendos per year. Sex is on the soaps, in commercials, and in promos for upcoming shows. Kids can easily get the idea from

As a Matter of Fact...

Teenagers are exposed to 14,000 sexual references and innuendos per year on TV. Only 150 of these deal with responsibility, abstinence, or birth control.

> **66** *Tim recently started enjoying some older, more adult-type movies. He loved Harvey and Some Like It Hot. But with A Fish Called Wanda and Saturday Night Fever, I'd completely forgotten about the nudity and the sex scenes. That's why it's important to watch videos with your kids—so you can hit the fast-forward button when those scenes you forgot about come up and surprise you.* **99**
>
> **Maria O'Meara**
> *Independent writer of children's multimedia and video products, Mother of three children, ages 10, 7, and 5*

television and movies that sex is the dominant aspect of relationships and one they should sample soon. They may get the message that it's the only way for boys and girls to relate, and that everybody's doing it.

Every parent has his or her own point of view regarding the presentation of sex. However you feel, you need to clarify your

59

own feelings first, then you will be confident in presenting them to your kids.

Things to Consider

- *Do you feel that if sex is associated with love, and its presentation serves the story, it's okay?*

- *Are you uncomfortable with your children seeing any presentation of sex, no matter what the context and how subtly it's presented?*

- *How do you feel about your child viewing a portrayal of any of the following sexual topics: married sex, childbirth, homosexuality, AIDS, teenage pregnancy, or rape?*

Personal Notes

Many years ago, Karen enthusiastically recommended Ruthless People *to Jane, encouraging her that her son Noah would love it. On the basis of Karen's enthusiastic suggestion, Jane and her husband Jerry took Noah and were surprised by a rather inappropriate (albeit short) rape scene that transpired within the first fifteen minutes of the film. Since there was nothing really questionable for Noah in the rest of the movie and the scene was not really integral to the plot, Karen had entirely forgotten about it.*

What You Can Do

- *Plan ahead of time so you know what they will be watching.*
- *Talk to your kids about other ways for boys and girls to have fun together and get to know each other—talking about common interests, joining clubs, or playing sports.*
- *Watch together.*
- *When a sexual situation is presented while you're watching together, use it as a teachable moment and offer appropriate information on relationships, responsibility, abstinence, birth control, and how love and sex may or may not be related.*
- *Limit how many hours your kids watch.*

Language

Another touchy area, language, may reflect a character's point of view, an historical context or a cultural bias. We should sensitize our kids to its impact. And, we should be aware that if we use a fair amount of "rich" language at home, it will be

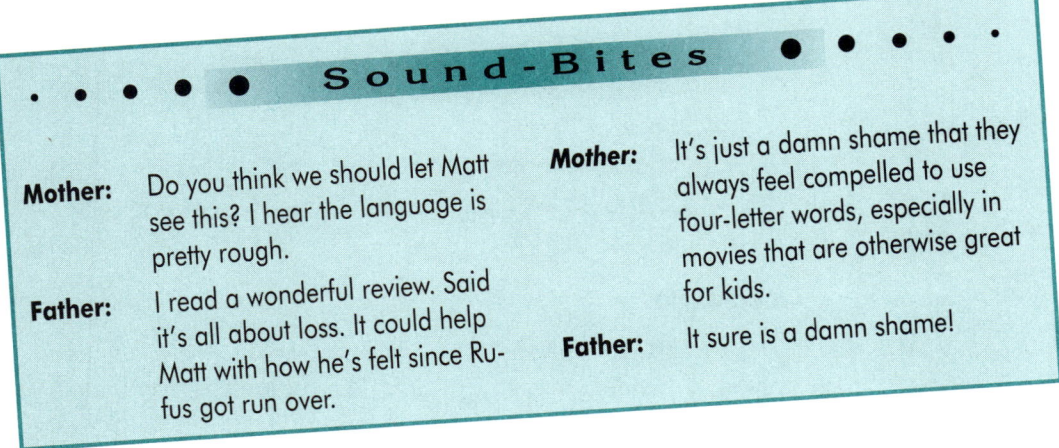

Sound-Bites

Mother: Do you think we should let Matt see this? I hear the language is pretty rough.

Father: I read a wonderful review. Said it's all about loss. It could help Matt with how he's felt since Rufus got run over.

Mother: It's just a damn shame that they always feel compelled to use four-letter words, especially in movies that are otherwise great for kids.

Father: It sure is a damn shame!

tough to rule out some programming on that basis alone. In fact, cursing language once considered aberrant by mental health professionals is no longer used as a diagnostic criterion for certain emotional disorders. Dr. Timothy Jay, in *Cursing in America,* writes that while dialogue in 1940s gangster movies was limited to "You dirty rat," *GoodFellas* in 1990 had 400 curse words.

Things to Consider

- *Is all programming with swear words out of the question, or might some colorful language expressing strong emotions be acceptable?*
- *How do you feel about racial or ethnic slurs that may reflect a character's prejudice or the thinking of a time or place?*
- *Are your kids old enough to understand what "slander" means?*

What You Can Do

- *Discuss with your kids how language is a powerful tool, one that can both cause and resolve conflict.*
- *Sensitize your kids to words that are hurtful, culturally biased, sexist, ageist, racist.*
- *Watch programs together, and point to instances where language may reflect a bias of a character or of the writer.*
- *Help your kids appreciate how some words can cause hurt feelings, and others can build self-confidence.*
- *Limit how many hours your kids watch.*

Stereotypes

TV and video are full of presentations of characters stereotyped by gender, ethnicity, or age. The references may be subtle enough to elude us, or our own biases may filter our awareness. It's important to be alert to stereotypes and to consider whether they are truly inappropriate for our kids or whether they represent an opportunity for discussion.

Things to Consider

- *How do you feel about a racist character if he's a figure in an award-winning film that is historically inaccurate? (For example,* The Birth of a Nation, *one of the first major films ever made.)*

- *If you have a child who's fairly savvy and appreciates satire, would you consider a comedy that includes a parody of feminists?*

- *Do your kids ever play-act people in stereotypical ways? If so, what do you think was the source of these notions?*

What You Can Do

- *Plan ahead of time so that you know what they will be watching.*

- *Watch programs together and point to characters who are presented as stereotypes. Discuss how this impacts the story and the other characters' behavior.*

- *Talk to your kids about stereotypes and how they themselves could be misrepresented by stereotyping of their ethnic background, or height, or other characteristic.*

- *Limit how many hours your kids watch.*

As a Matter of Fact...

- African Americans make up only 5 percent of the casts in children's programming, while, in fact, they make up 12.1 percent of the population.
- Even though 10 percent of the population is Hispanic, a child sees only 1 Hispanic character every other weekend out of the 123 characters on Saturday morning TV.

Of course, there are many outstanding examples of films and TV programs to view that will meet all your criteria, except for some foul language, a short interlude of sex, or some degree of stereotyping. These are the best occasions to watch with your kids. Use these opportunities to discuss your displeasure or discomfort, and learn how they feel.

Negative Role Models

Characters in film and television sometimes act in ways you wouldn't want your kids to imitate. Cheating, drug and alcohol abuse, and disrespect of teachers and parents are frequently portrayed. How the plot gets played out is key when these issues arise. Are there negative consequences for these types of behavior? The mix of what your kids watch is also important, since an occasional example of drug abuse may well be counterbalanced by other viewing. Of course, your kids' ages are significant indicators as well.

Things to Consider

- *Would I feel okay having my children watch if consequences are faced in the end, even though cheating is successfully accomplished for most of the movie?*

- *Is a light comedy that features a parent character who is the butt of jokes a good movie choice?*

- *Is drug use shown in all its gritty reality a good lesson that will warn my kids away or too detailed and tough going for them?*

What You Can Do

- *Plan ahead of time so you know what they'll be watching.*

- *Discuss the real-life consequences of the negative screen portrayals.*

- *Limit how many hours your kids watch.*

Scariness

Next to violence and sex, scariness might seem like small potatoes. Truth is, the scariness of dark closets, monsters, and things that go bump in the night is another big issue to tackle in selecting appropriate viewing for your kids. And it's hardly ever an obvious decision. Certainly, age and development can provide guidelines for what are classic concerns at various stages, but what constitutes "scary" really comes down to the individual child and what they may be worrying about at the time. Often you can judge "not scary," "okay scary," or "too scary" by whether the scene, circumstance, or character in question are cartoonish and exaggerated or too real for comfort. Some kids don't mind shoot-'em-up action-adventures but can get worked up over real-life situations that are too close to home. For instance, for a young child who's anxious about his mom who's away at work or visiting relatives even *Bambi* could be upsetting since Bambi's mother dies in a fire.

In *The Uses of Enchantment,* celebrated child psychologist Bruno Bettelheim's book on the value of fairy tales, we learn that "scary" may have a rightful place in children's lives. Bettelheim maintains fears and aggressions children experience as part of their normal development get confronted and resolved through these classic stories. The predicaments of Hansel and Gretel, Little Red Riding Hood, and a cast of thousands of other familiar characters help kids feel less alone about their own feelings. Of course, this point of view doesn't give us license to let the kids watch everything. Reading or hearing stories are less graphic than seeing the same themes treated on the screen, so care must be taken. Consider the following when you're wondering if *Raiders of the Lost Ark* would be okay for your 5-year-old or *Predator* acceptable for your 12-year-old:

Things to Consider

- *What might frighten* your *child to watch—cliffhanging danger, a monster or brutish character, a sea of snakes, an orphaned child?*

- *If something you never considered scary does frighten your child, is he able to be helped by talking with you?*

- *Can monsters be frightening and explosions okay?*

What You Can Do

- *Plan ahead of time so you know what your kid will be watching.*

- *If you have any doubts about a part of the show but feel overall it would be fine, prepare your child for the part or character.*

- *If you allowed your kid to see something that wound up being scary, explain you made a mistake and you're sorry. You didn't realize that it would be upsetting. Use the instance as a teachable moment and discuss what was scary and why. Talk about how the characters handled the situation. Be assured that in most cases, lasting harm will not be done and this too can be a learning experience.*

Hosting Other Children

These colorful gray areas are factors that must also be considered when you have other children over, so you need to be sensitive to what they're viewing. If you have any doubt about whether the programming is right for them or okay with their parents, check ahead of time to get the green light. In fact, if you're planning a party or another occasion where kids will be watching a tape, poll the kids ahead of time on what they'd like to see and get clearance and ideas from parents. Everyone, including the kids, will appreciate this consideration, and your kids' friends and their parents may reciprocate in the future. As we mention throughout this book, there are hundreds of videos that are excellent and clearly fine for everyone, and this kind of networking will extend the kids' and parents' awareness of worthwhile titles.

The Gray Areas Are Never Black or White

It's impossible to be a purist in making choices in these ubiquitous gray areas. Many wonderful films and programs succeed in carrying a valuable message, presenting an engaging story, or offering great entertainment, except for one scene, one objectionable character, or stereotype. For example, *Old*

Yeller is a classic heartwarming story about a family dog and a boy's growing responsibility. There are, however, some inappropriate references made to Native Americans in this story, which is set in the 1860s American West, and the dog gets rabies and must be killed by the owner, who loves him. What do you do? You need to make these decisions based on your knowledge of your own child. If you feel your kid can handle the dog dying, go ahead and let him watch, and discuss the fact that this 1950s movie presents some outmoded and unfair comments about America's original inhabitants.

Some films can be interpreted one way by one person and perceived another way by someone else. *Home Alone* has come under attack because it features a child who's forgotten by his family as they rush off on vacation. The child is seen in a variety of comic circumstances protecting himself from a couple of bumbling thieves with ingenious, albeit violent shenanigans. Others counter the criticism by explaining that the kid proves himself independent and resourceful, taking initiative (not unlike Hansel and Gretel). He comes from a loving, although flaky family. And, the defenders add, the violence is cartoonish. Here's where only a parent can select for his child. Will the abandonment ignite an issue your child is already sensitive about? Is robbery an issue too close to home?

A technology you can consider for restricting access to selected programs is the "V-chip," which would censor violent programs. Parents could program their sets to not show violent programs (indicated as violent in TV listings). By the time this book is published, the V-chip may be inserted into televisions on the assembly line. This means that only new sets will have the chip, therefore affecting only those families who can afford to replace their sets. We feel the major drawback to the chip is that someone somewhere will predetermine for your family what's considered too violent. The Motion Picture Association of America (MPAA) ratings of theatrical movies are often steeped in controversy, since one person's PG may be another's PG-13. The V-chip will stir up similar disagreements. A rating system that balances context, nuance, and taste is pretty near impossible. Should pictures of war be censored on the news? Some censorship advocates go further and propose a "C-chip"—the choice-chip—enabling parents to eliminate talk shows with sexually explicit language. The complexity of this technology could make it impractical for some families. After all, one third of Americans don't even know how to program the VCR to tape a show when they're not at home. Since most kids have such facility with new technology, they would most likely learn how to deprogram the chip before their parents figured out how to program it. So we feel it's really best to draw up your own criteria and advise advertisers of your support for government and industry guarantees of programming designed specifically for children.

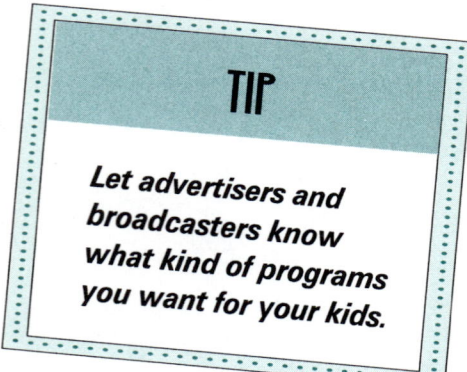

TIP

Let advertisers and broadcasters know what kind of programs you want for your kids.

An interesting spinoff of the chip issue is that proponents hope that advertisers will shy away from programs likely to be blocked, and support more acceptable shows instead. But why wait for a chip to encourage sponsorship of quality programming? An interesting alternative to the V-chip is a "zapping chart." Different organizations can produce charts letting their constituents know their viewpoints for what should be eliminated from a child's viewing. Then the parent selects the chart that matches their own values, just like when you read the critic you like best.

These gray area predicaments may require you preview—if you can—or watch together if you have your doubts. Whatever the issue, begin your deliberations by considering your kids' ages, maturity, concerns, and personalities. These will be the factors that will contribute the most to your making the right decisions for them.

A Balanced Viewing Diet (What to Watch)

Most of us don't want to put our kids on a TV starvation diet, but we're not anxious for them to move headlong into a TV junk food pig-out, either. We want them to watch and appreciate a variety of programs, not only cartoons and licensed character videos.

Videos, like books, aren't just about blockbuster titles, pulp fiction, or sensationalist unauthorized bios. The video choices now available offer a whole library of entertainment and information about other cultures, other times, how-to activities, music, science, literature, and more—selections that reflect a broad diversity of subjects and genres, such as drama, comedy, mystery, action.

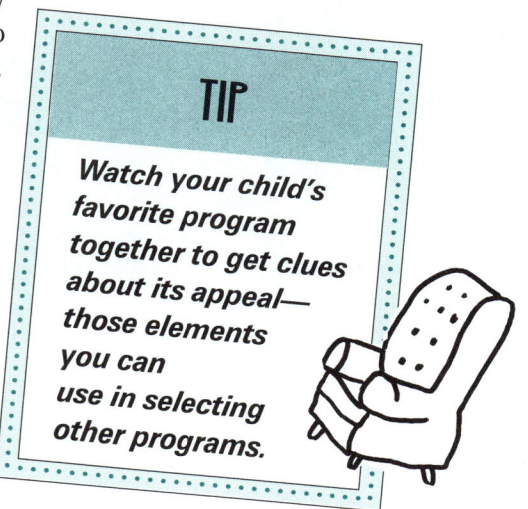

TIP

Watch your child's favorite program together to get clues about its appeal—those elements you can use in selecting other programs.

One way to expose kids to this diversity is to take turns once a week and have a different family member choose a program for a time when everyone can come together and watch. When you discuss choices for watching or taping, let your child know why you think he'll like your choice and why you think

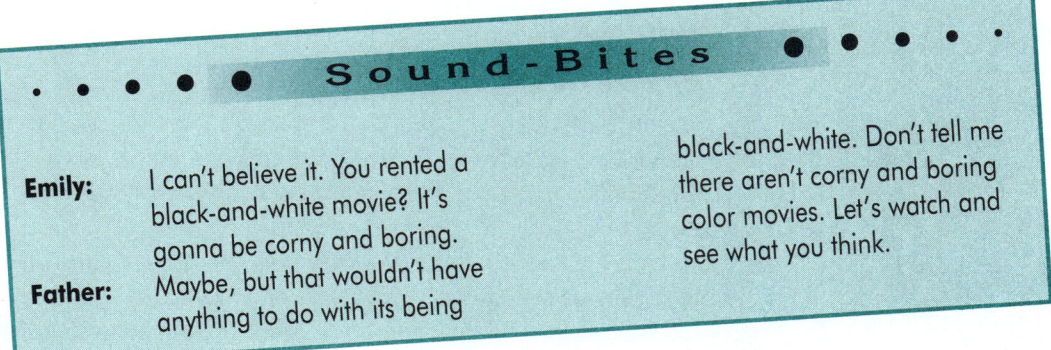

Sound-Bites

Emily: I can't believe it. You rented a black-and-white movie? It's gonna be corny and boring.

Father: Maybe, but that wouldn't have anything to do with its being black-and-white. Don't tell me there aren't corny and boring color movies. Let's watch and see what you think.

it's a good program, and get him to do the same. Some things will surely be a turnoff for some folks, but there will be lots of surprises. This is an opportunity to introduce the kids to the Marx Brothers or Buster Keaton, to watch a documentary on airplanes, a travel video on a place the family is going to vacation, a behind-the-scenes view of an animation feature, even a sports blooper tape. Taking advantage of this shared viewing time will broaden everyone's video experience and open you all up to the wide variety of programming available. It will also afford you the chance to expand the bandwidth of what you will allow your kids to choose from when they make their own choices.

Widening the universe of choice can also present opportunities for siblings to enjoy an activity together. Having more viewing choices also affords kids more latitude in making selections with friends when they're presented with options they know wouldn't be acceptable at home or choices that simply don't appeal to them. Armed with a roster of possibilities, they will be in a position to better help their friends come to consensus on what to watch.

Look at this catalog that I got at the music store—I didn't realize they had all these guitar videos! Can we buy the Eric Johnson one? He's unbelievable. It'll be like having a pro give me a lesson at home.

Not only can video complement a special interest like guitar or soccer, but it can also be an excellent resource at a critically emotional time when your kids may require special supports, such as the arrival of a new baby in the family, or a new pet, or a family move—topics we tackle in our KIDVIDZ line of children's videos. Video can enhance your kid's experience at school, expanding their knowledge of topics covered in the classroom. And it's always fun (although often a disappointment) to see the movie version of a book they just read. In fact, the disappointment in the movie by comparison with the book can be *good*, by showing them the strengths and limits of each medium.

Use Video to Bring the Kids Back to Books

It's been suggested that too much viewing can slow a child's reading development. We place a very high value on reading. It's a crucial skill which requires practice and dedicated time, and can be a source of unending pleasure. Video often serves to support reading, bringing kids back to the books on which the programs were based or to seek out more information on a topic they discovered through video. Kids frequently turn to books after they've been inspired by dramatizations of famous novels and biographies, or by characters who they see involved in reading and writing. Book-based videos for young children also enhance their enjoyment of favorite stories from writers like Maurice Sendak or Doctor Seuss.

Both books and video are forms of publishing which can effectively handle a wide range of genres, from fiction to non-fiction. Both media are now equally embedded in the fabric of our culture and our everyday lives. We and our children need to attain literacy in each of these media—the written word and the screen—in order to maximize their benefits. TV uniquely reflects our culture and defines it, in its legacy to our language (rerun, prime time . . .), its cultural contributions (*Roots, Baseball, Sesame Street* . . .), its immediacy (moon landings, Desert Storm, elec-

TIP

- *After your child finishes watching a book-based video, have the book readily available.*

- *Check out* **Parents' Choice Magazine Guide to Video Cassettes for Children** *(Green, Diana Huss, Consumers Union 1989), which lists companion books for all annotated videos in its compendium.*

71

> ## TIP
>
> **Plan ahead when you use your VCR to time shift:**
>
> - **Check the TV Guide listing and preselect what to tape.**
>
> - **Learn to program your VCR.**
>
> - **Keep tapes labeled and easily accessible.**
>
> - **Consider VCR Plus in your next equipment purchase.**

tions, Olympics), and its parade of personalities (Lucy, Lassie, Johnny . . .) who've joined us in our living rooms. We are all products of and participants in the media culture. So, as parents, educators, family, and friends, we have an obligation to bring into our homes and our children's lives the best that both TV and books have to offer.

Time Shift to Maximize the Best of Broadcast and Cable

Try to set aside time each week to check the listings and select what you may want to view and tape. Cable stations and public television have expanded listings in their own publications. You'll enjoy the advantages of being freed up from the broadcast and cable schedule, having the opportunity to prescreen questionable programs before deciding what's appropriate for the kids, and enjoying the expanded program options available to the family. Learn how to program the VCR or have your kids learn how. They probably already know. VCR Plus is also an excellent feature that is available on many VCRs. You program it by using the numbers printed in the television listing. Try to keep all your tapes labeled, and include running times. And set up your tape library in an easily accessible location.

Include Home Videos in Your Viewing Menu

And don't forget your own home videos. If you own or have access to a video camera, then besides documenting family events, the kids have the chance to make some of their own programming. Also, if you don't have any home videos but have dusty boxes of old Super 8 and 8 mm home movies, have some of them transferred to video. Many video stores now provide this service, and some companies can also add musical tracks that you select or even integrate family photos. Of course, prices vary, depending on the amount of material and sophistication of the production you want.

TIP

Schedule screenings of your own home videos. It's sure to be a hit with the whole family.

TV and video are really like a diet. Many of us like to encourage our kids to try new tastes at the table and recognize the need for balance and quality. The message is that video can offer new feasts for their minds, eyes, and ears without loading them up with junk.

Fitting It All In (When to View)

We're all busy with lists, schedules, appointments, and wall-to-wall commitments, and so, for better or worse, are our kids. Many of us feel we don't get enough exercise. Some of us feel we spend too many hours in front of a computer screen or behind the wheel, driving from work to Little League practice, to school, to the store, and back again. Kids often feel the same way. And they don't have your perspective and experience to ap-

As a Matter of Fact...

Nearly a third of Americans don't know how to record a program when they're not home.

preciate that the time they spend doing fun things like sports and socializing usually far exceeds the time they devote to homework and chores.

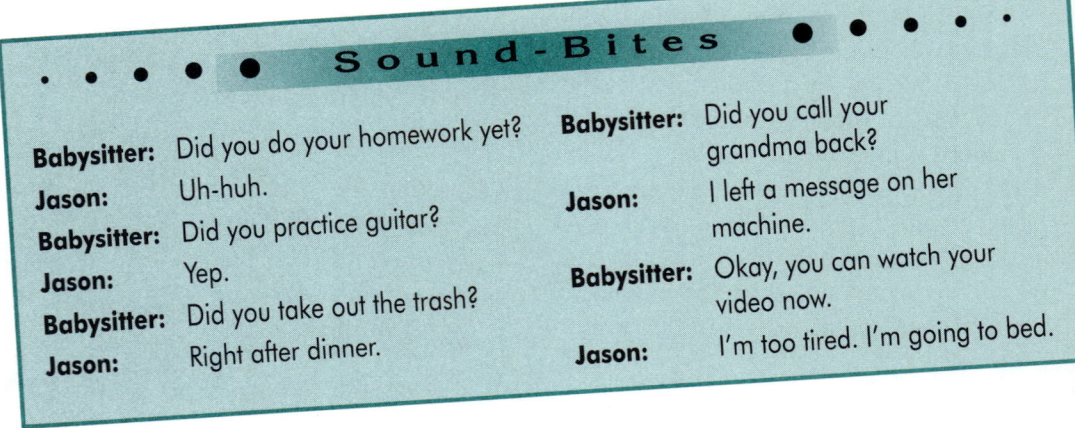

Sound-Bites

Babysitter: Did you do your homework yet?

Jason: Uh-huh.

Babysitter: Did you practice guitar?

Jason: Yep.

Babysitter: Did you take out the trash?

Jason: Right after dinner.

Babysitter: Did you call your grandma back?

Jason: I left a message on her machine.

Babysitter: Okay, you can watch your video now.

Jason: I'm too tired. I'm going to bed.

In the best of all possible worlds, we and our kids would be healthfully occupied in a mix of athletic, intellectual, and social pursuits during all our waking hours. The kids would all do their chores, homework, parties, get-togethers, and obligations on time with few management hassles on your part. Fat chance. Parenting involves management, and in most situations the TV screen looms as an obstacle. But it doesn't have to become the ever-present electronic intruder, and you don't necessarily have to pack it away.

TIP

Keep track, by hours and minutes, of how you or your child spends one day.

When to View

Take a look at how your family spends its time, individually and together. Sometimes if we take the time to notice how we spend time, we discover better

> **" As a family, we don't watch much TV. If parents watch a lot of TV, then the kids learn to watch a lot. We try to use videos most of the time. We don't have set rules about how much they can watch, but we have a sense of when it's been enough. How much and when they watch is usually dictated by what's happening in their day. They watch mostly for a quiet time after playing outside or to relax or to cool out after a spat with each other. The little guy uses it to fall asleep at naptime. It's a real calmer. "**
>
> *John Kusiak*
> Composer and Music Producer,
> Anacrusis Productions, Boston
> Father of three children: two sons,
> ages 3 and 8, and a daughter, age 22

ways to use it. How does video presently fit into your family routine? Does everyone default to TV when they want to unwind? Is it a prize? A sedative? A time for TV is okay, but TV shouldn't be just a filler for anytime. Many of us complain that there's never enough time to get everything done. Yet most of us watch a few hours a day of TV. If we trim our TV time, we'll find a new reservoir of hours to do more things.

With defined times earmarked for video, kids will feel challenged to fill the rest of their time with other activities that help them unwind or serve as a reward, like playing a board game, working on a puzzle with a friend or sibling, or building a model. If kids are really busy, they'll be much less likely to default to TV, their viewing time will be more valued, and they'll become more discriminating in selecting what to watch.

Tommy: Get real, Mom. If I'm going to get to see Josh's animation class video *Mighty Action Hero Gets the Flu*, I can't clean up my room and finish my homework.

Mom: You should have considered that yesterday when I told you your room needed to be clean by tonight. You knew you'd have homework today, too.

Tommy: How about I clean my room, watch the video, and then do my homework. It shouldn't take me that long, and I can do it in bed.

Mom: In your dreams! Homework and room first. You can finish watching the video tomorrow.

Tommy: But tomorrow I have a soccer game, and Friday is Jona's birthday party, Saturday's the yard sale, Sunday . . .

Mom: Sounds like Mighty Action Hero will have recovered by then.

Factoring Age and Development into the Time Equation

As with all the other issues, the question of when to watch will depend on your kids' ages and personalities. Clearly, a younger child who doesn't have homework may have more flexibility regarding when he can watch, but he will probably be going to bed earlier, so he has his own particular limits. On the other hand, for a child who needs short-term goals and rewards after doing chores, homework, or other obligations, it might be wise to divide the daily TV allowance into a few time slots.

Balancing Activities

It's also important to balance active and passive activities. And, when it comes to video, it's essential to balance viewing and doing. Everyone has to find the schedule that works best for them. Here's a checklist of likely activities to consider when trying to balance your family's time:

- *Is everyone getting some exercise every day?*
- *Are your kids getting their homework and extracurricular activities done before the last minute and without constant battles?*
- *Are your kids doing their share to pitch in around the house (garbage out, laundry shifts, dishes)?*
- *Does everyone have a fair shot of time on the VCR and computer (if you have one)?*

TIP

Check out a chapter on time management and kids in Confessions of a Happily Organized Family *by Deniece Schoefield (Writer's Digest Books, 1984).*

Mastery of the time domain is a major issue for most families. Of course each of us develops routines in response to our own unique work and leisure schedules and lifestyles. People behave as differently around time as any other area, and a lot of TV's appeal is that it's always available to fill the gaps, however long or short.

Making a Schedule

So how does all this translate into a workable schedule that accommodates the TV screen so that it doesn't take over and isn't ruled out? Not everyone can live by formal routines and charts. Everything doesn't go smoothly for those with rigid schedules anyway, nor is life always chaos for those folks without a written-down agenda. One way or another, however, you and your kids should agree on some schedule guidelines for selected activities and obligations if you want to balance things and make viewing a planned-for activity. The most important thing is to agree in advance on time allotments that are realistic and fair. Remember to get the kids'

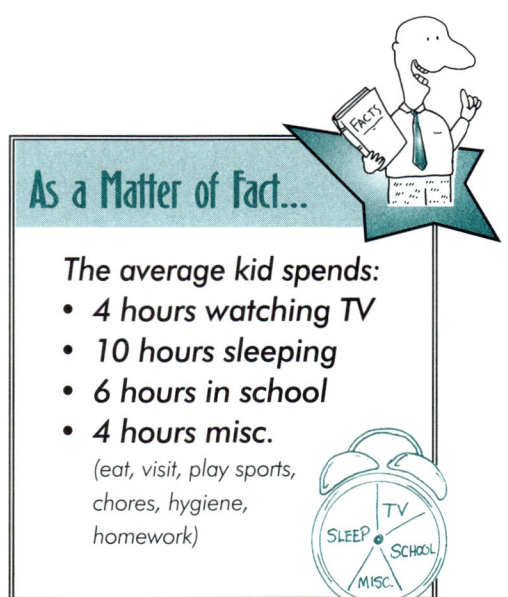

As a Matter of Fact...

The average kid spends:
- *4 hours watching TV*
- *10 hours sleeping*
- *6 hours in school*
- *4 hours misc.*
  (eat, visit, play sports, chores, hygiene, homework)

77

TIP

Post a list of fun activities, so your kids will have an alternative to just turning on the set.

feedback on the schedule and make sure it reflects a balance of activities.

Consider assigning video/TV time and computer time for weekends or apportioning appropriate amounts of time for your kids each day. If certain days are heavy on lessons, chores, and other obligations, it might be a good idea to allow some video time before homework, so kids won't feel that their lives are just a list of "gottas." Having a half hour or so for entertainment or specially selected programming can refresh them for returning to homework. Likewise, they may not feel a need for TV time at all on days filled with sports, clubs, and socializing, so they can spend extra time at home on pleasure reading or hobbies. And be aware of the amount of exercise and outdoor time your kids do each day. If the weather is bad and the school schedule doesn't offer much in the way of exercise, then time in front of the set may not be the best for the body or the mind. Some indoor exercise could be a good alternative.

Okay, okay, so I didn't have basketball today and it's pouring. It's a perfect day to plunk down and watch. How about we rent an exercise tape? But that shouldn't count in my TV time since I'll be exercising!

You decide how to handle that one. He might have a creative solution!

A Video Allowance (How Much to View)

Sitting in front of the TV screen can be mesmerizing and addictive. With broadcast and cable, one show leads into another, and young children sometimes can't tell when one leaves off and the next begins. But with a video, it's

As a Matter of Fact...

Your children may have watched up to 22,000 hours of TV by the time they graduate high school.

Mom: We agreed to one hour of TV each weekday and two on weekend days. If you don't use your time that day, you know you lose it. We're not getting into saving hours and keeping track of what you use and what you don't. That's nine hours of TV a week, more than enough.

That comes to about forty hours a month or four hundred and eighty a year. Wait, that sounds like too much—that's twenty full days!

Scott: Don't do the math, Mom. It always complicates things.

very clear when the show's over, which makes it easier to enforce viewing time limits.

A good way to treat the issue of "how much" with older kids (6–12-year-olds) is to give them a viewing time allowance. Kids this age are ready to take some responsibility for selecting when they watch and learn to apportion their viewing. Just as with a money allowance, each family will have different views on how much and on what terms. Kids can learn to budget their time and make wise choices, just like they do with their dollars and cents.

How Much Screen Time?

Parents often wonder, is a half hour a day too little to allow? Is two hours a day too much? Should younger kids have more time available for TV, since they're not in school or at least they're not getting homework and don't yet have commitments of after-school sports and other activities? What's right? What's healthy?

79

The statistics are chastening on how much kids watch. According to Dorothy and Jerome Singer, codirectors of the Yale University Family Television Research and Consultation Center, elementary-school-aged children on average watch five to six hours of TV a day, or twenty-eight to thirty hours of TV a week.

Restricting viewing to a certain number of hours is something each family struggles with. Experts agree that you should set time limits, but there's no "gold standard" or consistent recommendation, since a child's age and other commitments are also important factors. A guideline we endorse comes from the American Academy of Pediatrics:

- *no more than one hour of TV per day during weekdays*
- *no more than two hours of TV per day during weekends*
- *no more than two hours of total media time per day (including TV, video games, and computer)*

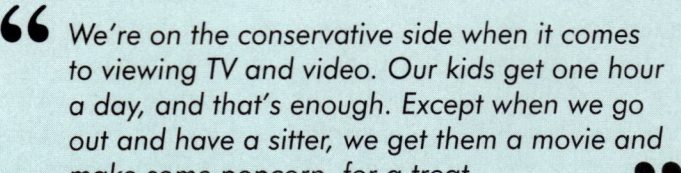

66 *We're on the conservative side when it comes to viewing TV and video. Our kids get one hour a day, and that's enough. Except when we go out and have a sitter, we get them a movie and make some popcorn, for a treat.* **99**

Bill Littlefield
National Public Radio host, It's Only a Game
Father of kids ages 6 and 9

Some considerations in tackling the issue of time and TV:
- *apportioning viewing time equally over weekdays, with more on the weekend*

- *allowing viewing on weekends only*
- *making exceptions to time allotments for sick days, holidays, special movies, or longer-running programming selected in advance*
- *agreeing on whether to accumulate time not used on a given day*

Some recommendations for tackling the issue of time and TV:

- *include computer time with TV time*
- *work out issues regarding sharing the VCR—who gets to see and when?*
- *factor age and other commitments that dictate appropriate amounts of time*
- *exclude school-relevant, educational TV from being included in their time limit*

Balance Activities

Sometimes it's helpful to take a snapshot of how your kids spend their time over the course of an average week, what goes on, what gets done, what doesn't. It ultimately sets you all up for working toward realizable goals in apportioning time and balancing activities. Use the following chart as an exercise to "guesstimate" how your kids presently spend their time (real) and how you'd prefer to see their time spent (ideal). Later, adjust your "real" schedule to reflect how things are changing as you work toward your "ideal" schedule.

TIP

Include computer and video game time in your screen allotment along with TV.

	Real Schedule (Date)		Ideal Schedule	
What	**How Much**	**When**	**How Much**	**When**
Screen Time: *TV* *computer*				
Homework				
Chores: *pets* *room* *other*				
Music Practice				
Sports/Outdoors				
Play				
Other				

• • • • • ● S o u n d - B i t e s ● ● ● ● ● •

Mom: You've already watched for a half hour today, Joey. It's time to turn off the set.

Joe: Uh-uh! This is my first show to-day.

Mom: Oh? What were you doing with Billy this afternoon while you had your snack? Wasn't that your baseball tape I saw playing when I brought you guys some cookies?

Joe: Gee, Mom, you have a memory like an elephant!

82

Helping the Schedule Work Successfully

Obviously, you can't just set time limits and waltz off with an "end of discussion" attitude. Your kids will be testing and bending the rules, even if they were included in setting them. Be prepared to remind them of the regulations and follow through. It will be easier to remind them if you actually drew up a contract in the first place. You'll have something concrete to point to that they helped formulate.

Get together with your kids to develop a list of nonscreen activities they like to do. Then post the list. When they say they "have nothing to do" and want to watch television, you'll have ideas immediately accessible. Get your kids to ask permission each time they want to do some viewing, just like they'd ask permission to go to a friend's house or run an errand. Why? This is a way for them to check in when they want to watch. Find out what program they want to watch. Don't just agree to turn on the set.

Consider using coupons to help your kids self-regulate their viewing and help you in the monitoring department. The kids use the coupons to redeem their weekly viewing allocation. This arrangement might be fun and helpful for one family and a pain for another. It all depends on your family's style and needs.

The main thing is to be watchful of the clock and monitor viewing so that the experience doesn't become a runaway train. The objective is that every-

TIPS

Help your children learn to self-regulate how much TV they watch:

- Be prepared to restate your guidelines and follow through.
- Get your kids to ask permission each time they want to do some viewing.
- Try using coupons for viewing to help the kids self-regulate their viewing and help you monitor.

one in the family becomes aware of how much time each spends on various activities and manages their time most productively and happily.

Lessons Learned

Confronting the big questions of *what, when, and how much* to watch can offer your kids valuable insight into life skills: making choices and sticking with them, budgeting time, balancing activities, sharing, planning ahead. TV is an emotional area

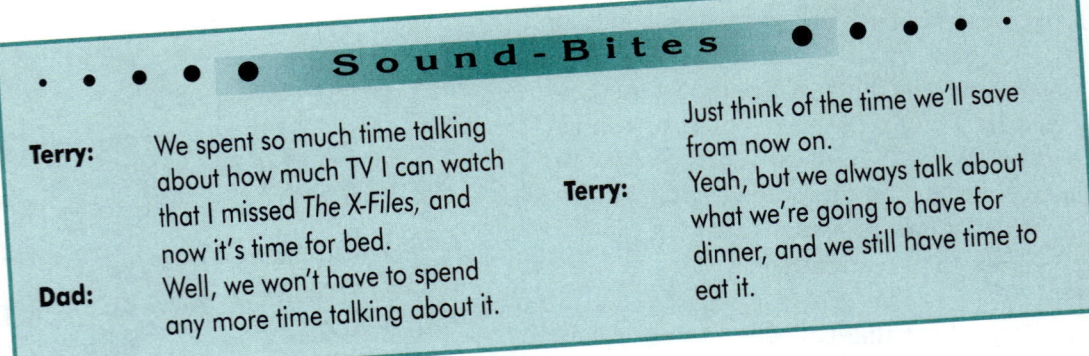

Sound-Bites

Terry: We spent so much time talking about how much TV I can watch that I missed *The X-Files*, and now it's time for bed.

Dad: Well, we won't have to spend any more time talking about it.

Just think of the time we'll save from now on.

Terry: Yeah, but we always talk about what we're going to have for dinner, and we still have time to eat it.

and lessons learned here will apply to many other parts of your kids' lives. In the bargain, they'll also learn about many different genres of programming and realize the impact violence, language, and stereotyping can have on them. They'll come to appreciate the difference between pure entertainment and informational programs. And hopefully, they'll become more selective in their own viewing and gain a better sense of how they spend their time. A little more empowerment and self-awareness; a little more media savvy and critical acumen; a little less dependency on the tube—what could be better?

Family Activity

Design Video Coupons

Sometimes it's hard to keep track of what you've watched and when, even though your family has agreed on viewing times. Coupons can be a fun way to stay on top of your TV viewing, and you can create your own. Kids get a number of coupons each week and turn them in for viewing. When the coupons are gone, no more TV that week.

You'll need:

paper
markers
-or-
a computer art program

Before you start, consider:

Will you put your coupons on sheets of paper or bind them into a book?

Will the coupons be assigned for individual days, a week, a weekend?

Should your coupons show the length of each viewing?

Do you want the coupons to mix up genres so you're guaranteed to see lots of different kinds of programs?

What kind of border or drawing will you put on your coupon?

4 No Guns, No Sex, No Swearing, and They Want to Watch It Again?

How to Select What to Watch

At one time or another you're probably baffled by your kids' viewing choices, defeated by their insistence on watching something that's unacceptable to you, or simply frustrated by not being able to respond to their requests with better alternatives. Don't despair when they ask to watch programs that are totally out of the question. Just take charge. Consider a few basic criteria, discussed in this chapter, that can help you and your kids choose the best productions out there to rent and purchase.

Content, genre, treatment, price, and overall value will factor into the choices you make in your effort to develop yourself and your family into savvy video viewers.

You don't have to spend hours weighing choices and reviewing a mile-long checklist before making the popcorn. Instead, you can use our "Green Light Test" and review the criteria of the four recognized industry authorities we have included to help you develop your own standards for judging what can get onto your tube. The criteria you use to choose will become familiar as you get more involved in your children's viewing.

Tune In the Topics

- **Does It Pass Muster?**
- **Standard-Bearer Ratings, Awards, and Criteria**
- **A Rich Mix Means More Choice (Lots of Genres)**
- **What Do Your Kids Want to See?**
- **Read the Sleeve**
- **Family Activity: Design a Video Cover**

87

In addition to guiding you through the evaluation process involved in choosing appropriate programs for your kids, this chapter emphasizes the benefit of a mixed viewing diet. We propose ways you can accommodate your kids' choices *and* introduce new genres that will entice them to expand what they watch instead of turning them off. We suggest a variety of genres, culled from pretaped broadcast and cable shows and video programming available for rent and purchase. We point to the sleeve as an informative tool and discuss how to read it to learn more about a video you aren't able to preview. In the end of the chapter, you'll find a basic glossary of video jargon to help you when reading about videos and looking at their covers.

The evaluation process is a valuable experience, helping everyone become more discriminating in their viewing choices and priming the whole family to enjoy a rich selection of quality programs without wasting time in heavy negotiations or unwelcome conflicts.

Does It Pass Muster?

A checklist of criteria, like the "Green Light Test" below, is useful when reviewing a video to decide if it's appropriate for your kids. Most of the points on our list assume you're able to see clips, preview the whole tape, or read a review. That's not always possible, and you obviously aren't going to preview everything your kids are likely to watch. But for those titles which you're really dubious about or for when you're watching together with your kids and debating the value of purchasing the tape (if you've rented or borrowed it), this list will help you in your considerations.

When you want to preview a title, remember it may be available for rental at your local video store, or you might be able to preview parts of the tape in a store that sells it. You can

Nancy: Mom, I really want to get this tape. I'll chip in five bucks and that'll make it only $10 for you. I saw it at Chuck's last week. It's got great animations. All award-winners. Cool music. No bad language. Not sexist. Not racist. Totally politically correct. So what do you say?

Mom: No gratuitous violence?

Nancy: Not even a water gun.

also go to the public library, your child's school librarian, or ask to borrow it from a friend who already owns it. If you can't preview a video, you can read the reviews and consider our advice on "Reading the Sleeve." You can refer to the "Green Light" checklist while reading reviews and sleeves. Many of the points should be answered in the review or on the cover. The "Green Light Test" reflects our own standards as well as those most often mentioned in other lists we've reviewed.

Green Light Test

- **Age and Development Appropriate**

  Is the content developmentally appropriate to my kids' age range?

- **Intellectually and Creatively Stimulating**

  Is the content and its presentation intellectually and creatively stimulating, asking kids to learn new information or skills, question assumptions, solve problems, and think critically?

- **Entertainment Value**

  Does it have high entertainment value? Even for programming with a strong educational agenda, it's important that the video be entertaining, or it won't succeed

89

in winning the attention of a young audience.

- **Repeatability**

  Does the content and presentation invite repeat viewing: fun story, engaging talent/characters, winning music, a lot of information packed in so that one viewing won't suffice? If yes, this will argue for purchasing the video.

- **Diversity**

  Is there a socioeconomic mix of talent and a sensitivity to diversity in treatment of content, where appropriate?

- **Positive Values**

  Does the program reinforce positive values like nonviolence?

- **High Production Quality**

  Does the video reflect high-quality production— professional presentation, strong writing, polished camerawork and editing, and capable talent?

- **Awards**

  Has the program won any awards, especially those specifically for children's programming? And, if you're considering a purchase . . .

- **Fair Price**

  Is the price fair (usually in the $12.95–$19.95 range)?

Standard-Bearer Ratings, Awards, and Criteria

Parents' Choice, the Motion Picture Association of America, the Coalition for Quality Children's Media, and the Film Advisory Board are leading organizations which have established guidelines for judging the appropriateness of programs for children. These guides can be very helpful when you are unable to prescreen. Addresses of several of these organizations are provided in the "Resources" section for this chapter. You can contact them for lists of titles that received their awards and endorsements.

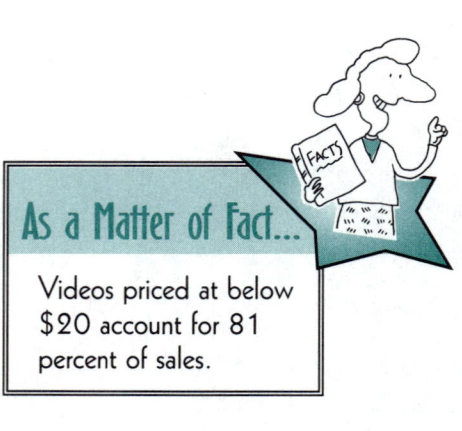

As a Matter of Fact...

Videos priced at below $20 account for 81 percent of sales.

Parents' Choice

This is the oldest nonprofit newspaper resource for children's toys, books, videos, audios, and software in the country. Parents' Choice Foundation Awards are selected annually in over two hundred sites by approximately 3,700 parents, children, teachers, psychologists, pediatricians, and other experts. Awards include the Parents' Choice Gold, Parents' Choice Honor, and Honorable Mentions. Publisher Diana Huss Green reviews the winners on *Good Morning America*. Criteria considered in bestowing these awards require that the material should:

TIP

Preview tapes by renting from the video store, watching on retailer's in-store monitors, borrowing from the library or from friends.

- *stimulate imagination*
- *help the child grow emotionally, mentally, socially, or physically*
- *be in good taste*
- *appeal in an attractive package and presentation*
- *be true to its intent without racial, religious, or gender bias*
- *adhere to basic safety considerations where applicable*

Motion Picture Association of America

A rating board made up of eight to eleven parents discusses each film and votes on the rating, making an educated guess as to which rating most American parents would consider the most appropriate.

Theme, language, violence, nudity, sex, and drug abuse are among those content areas considered in the decision-making process: mostly the same criteria you as a parent use in deciding what's suitable for your child. The rating board also considers the context of each of the content areas without placing special emphasis on any. The board considers and examines all these elements before giving a rating.

According to the Motion Picture Association of America, the latest polls indicate that 74 percent of parents with children under 18 found MPAA ratings to be "very useful" to "fairly useful" in helping make decisions for their kids' movie watching. Still, the MPAA urges parents to learn as much about a film as possible before they permit their children to see it. Keep in mind that some profanity or a little bit of sex can skew a film to a stricter rating, whereas a fair amount of awful violence can get by a PG-13. For instance, if you select videos simply by ratings, you might choose Woody Allen's *Annie Hall*, rated PG, for your 9–13-year-old. The fact is you'd likely wind up considering it inappropriate, since much of the dialogue centers on sex.

MPAA Ratings and Definitions

G   *General Audiences. Content for viewing by children that wouldn't offend parents.*

PG   *Parental Guidance Suggested. Parents urged to give guidance. May contain material some parents might not like for their young children.*

PG-13   *Parents Strongly Cautioned. Urges parents to be cautious. Some material may be inappropriate for preteenagers.*

R   *Restricted. Contains some adult material. Urges parents to learn more about the film before taking young children with them.*

NC-17   *No Children Under 17 Admitted. Indicates patently adult material. Children are not admitted.*

MPAA Update: Reasons for ratings are now provided to the press, so reviews are more likely to include information on questionable language, violence, and sex. For example, a PG-13 would clarify if the rating reflects nudity, language, violence, and so on.

Films do *not* have to be rated by law, so use extra caution when you don't see a rating. "No rating" may also apply to foreign films, old films, documentaries, or educational tapes.

Coalition for Quality Children's Media

This national nonprofit membership organization seeks to inform the public about quality programming for children by endorsing excellent children's media and facilitating its availability to families. All CQCM endorsed titles receive stickers and are put into their *Kids First!* collection, which they bring to the attention of retailers. Members receive an annual directory of endorsed titles complete with a CD-ROM, a newsletter, access to an online service and to their Kids First! Kids' Club.

CQCM evaluates tapes all through the year by assembling both a child jury and an adult jury, drawn from national pools of adult professionals and children from varied economic, geographic, social, and ethnic backgrounds. A title is judged on the basis of its appeal to children, content, technical proficiency, and overall benefits. According to CQCM, a quality children's program should be engaging for both children and adults; appropriate for the age and the developmental level of the children for whom it's targeted; stimulate curiosity in learning; provide appropriate challenges; be esthetically pleasing and technically proficient; be able to sustain repeated watchings; respect diversity and individuality; if informational, provide information that is accurate; and model positive behavior.

A Kids First! endorsement means:

- *no gratuitous violence or sexuality*
- *no verbal or physical abuse*
- *no bias in terms of race, gender, culture, or religion*
- *no condescension toward children.*

Film Advisory Board

A nonprofit international organization dedicated to recognizing and supporting quality children's and family entertainment with its Award of Excellence. Awards are voted on by FAB's Reviewing Committee, composed of professionals in television, video, film, audio and CD-ROM software, books, and entertainment. For products targeted specifically for children, a child panel is used as well.

Products must meet the following requirements:

- *stimulate one's imagination*
- *raise one's awareness*
- *be created in good taste, justly representing its subject matter*
- *be safe where applicable*
- *encourage positiveness and ambition*
- *be attractive and entertaining*

Products must not contain the following:

- *gratuitous, profane language*
- *gratuitous violence*
- *strong sexual content and gratuitous nudity related to sex and titillation*

As we've indicated, Parents' Choice and the Film Advisory Board grant awards. Other esteemed groups offer annual

Family Roundtable

Rating the Ratings

I usually watch PG or PG-13 because I understand what's happening. Some kids might not understand, so that's why their parents say they shouldn't watch it.

11-year-old

PG-13 doesn't mean a thing. Sometimes we've rented a PG-13 and the language wasn't appropriate for a 13-year-old.

Mother of 10-year-old

It's hard to find out why it's an R rating or even why it's PG. I think that's very frustrating.

Mother of 14-year-old

I think the ratings are a guide, but you've got to be familiar with what the content is and if your kids can handle it.

Father of 8- and 11-year-olds

No Guns, No Sex, No Swearing

awards for top children's programming, including the National Educational Film and Video Festival, the Houston Film and Video Festival, the National Association of Parenting Publications, and the International Film and Video Festival of New York.

A Rich Mix Means More Choice (Lots of Genres)

Squeeze some old movies, how-tos, and documentaries between the *Ninjas* and *Jurassic Parks* on your video shelf. The

Sound-Bites

Dad: Cartoons, cartoons, cartoons—all you ever watch is cartoons!

Danny: Documentaries, documentaries, documentaries—all you ever watch is documentaries!

growing library of original children's videos now at hand encompasses a mix of genres, the quality and age appropriateness of which vary a lot. As suggested earlier, start by considering your own kids' interests and concerns as well as their maturity.

> **TIP**
>
> **Ensure that your kids watch a variety of genres of programming.**

Plan a viewing diet that includes your kids' suggestions, and clip reviews and titles you've heard about to add to your own recommendations. Keep in mind options in the video store beyond the children's section, like comedy, music, and drama. Build a list to review before going to rent or buy, and keep it handy so everyone can add to it. Whenever possible, expose your kids to the widest selection of stories, portrayals, and presentations of the human experience.

A Survey of Genres

Movie Classics offer a treasure chest of entertainment and a sense of history and the larger world. Sample Hitchcock mysteries, classic books on film like *Great Expectations* or *Moby-Dick,* classic comedy from Buster Keaton to the Marx Brothers and the timeless Charlie Chaplin, or a family tearjerker like *Old Yeller.* These choices transcend the generations. Some classics offer the fun of comparing the original version with a recent release, like the classic 1933 *Little Women* with the 1994 release, or 1957's *An Affair to Remember* with 1993's *Sleepless in Seattle.* Other classic and contemporary pairs include *West Side Story* and Franco Zeffirelli's *Romeo and Juliet, The Tempest* and *Forbidden Planet,* the *King Kongs* (Fay Wray and Jessica Lange versions), and the old and newer *Supermans.* These pairings will attest to Shakespeare's timelessness, the enduring pleasure of selected stories, and the impact more sophisticated film technology can have in retelling classic tales.

In some classics, your kids may encounter Hollywood stereotypes of ethnic groups—especially Native and African Americans—as examples of how members of our society were once viewed. This can provide a valuable opportunity for discussion. For example, in John Ford's *Stagecoach,* a classic epic Western which influenced most Westerns made afterward, note examples of inappropriate and outmoded representations. Watching movie classics with grandparents is an added bonus, since they may have stories about when they first saw a movie in the theater or remember the stars and periods presented.

Contemporary films like *Big* and *Aladdin* are usually the biggest attraction. Try to include some foreign choices, such as *Europa Europa* or *Cinema Paradiso* (for the right ages), and smaller American films that might not have been giant theatrical hits, like *Fried Green Tomatoes* or *Dead Poets Society.* While

97

contemporary selections may feature child-friendly themes, they are more likely to contain graphic language and treat violence or sexual situations quite explicitly. Also, your child could get upset by the sadness or grittiness of a theme's context. Such an example is *Alan & Naomi,* a coming of age story of a young Jewish boy set in Brooklyn toward the end of World War II. The story centers on Alan's friendship with a neighbor who is a catatonic French refugee girl suffering from her experiences in the war. The themes of responsibility and friendship in this PG-rated film are portrayed beautifully and offer much to discuss. However, Naomi's illness and her flashbacks to her father's murder are very sad. This is a film you will want to watch with your children. When you don't have the opportunity to view together or to spot preview, keep in mind the movie's reviews, ratings, and other criteria, which will help guide you in your choices.

Classic TV series have been repackaged for home video. Although cable offers some classic reruns, there are quite a few series available only in video specialty stores. Bear in mind that old TV can be a hit-or-miss proposition with 1990s kids. Parents may be nostalgic about shows they grew up watching, yet these same shows may bomb with their kids—or even today with parents themselves, who may have romanticized how great they really were. However, there are some excellent classics, and it's fun for the kids to get a view of what you enjoyed at their age. Try *The Twilight Zone, Laurel and Hardy, The Little Rascals, The Honeymooners, I Love Lucy, The Fugitive, The Addams Family.* Watching old TV shows offers kids a chance to see how our society has changed, too. Did fridges and cars really look like that? Did women really stay at home in aprons? These videos will let you talk with your kids about the way we were when "we were their age." *I Love Lucy* will be a winner with most families because of its humor and slapstick elements. It's also interesting to talk to the kids about how much of the humor came from Lucy trying to scheme around the authority

of her husband, a type of relationship that is not as common in the 1990s.

Music videos include a range from contemporary rock and live-performance videos to singalongs for younger kids, opera, ballet, and classical-performance videos. Video can be a great way to introduce the kids to different kinds of music. If you read a summary libretto of a fun opera like *The Magic Flute* and then watch the video, you might cultivate a taste in your kids. (Hope springs eternal if you're an opera fan.) Many readers will want to introduce their kids to early rock and roll, and a great film to do this is *A Hard Day's Night*, considered the Beatles' best film. It's also their first (made in 1964). The film is inventive and borrows from the works of other directors from Busby Berkeley to Fellini. The story takes place over the course of thirty-six hours of touring. Lots of laughs and fabulous music make this a good choice, although you might have to do some selling to get the kids to watch in black and white. This film was made before the ratings system was instituted and it's an example of a good family film you would miss if you chose by ratings alone. Some other titles to look for include *The Glenn Miller Story; Peter, Paul and Mary in Concert; Jazzball—Louis Armstrong, Duke Ellington, Peggy Lee;* and *Les Miserables.*

Exercise videos as a genre are popular with kids and grown-ups. Kids have been exposed to plenty of commercials and direct response ads on the tube for everything from Jane Fonda workouts to Richard Simmons, and now there's an expanding selection of exercise tapes for kids themselves. American kids are fatter and less fit, in part because of the hours they sit watching TV. Here TV can be part of the cure. Look for *Sammy, Kids in Motion,* or *Hip-Hop Animal Rock,* an especially creative tape where kids exercise to a theme of endangered species.

How-to videos extend from playing classical guitar to constructing a birdhouse, cooking, crafts, team sports, and camping. This category, also dubbed "special interest" in the video stores, is growing by leaps and bounds because it offers a wide selection of topics for all ages, abilities, and interests. In other words, if your kid is "1960s retro" and into tie-dying T-shirts, there's probably a video for him. However, you'll find most special-interest product in catalogs and specialty retail stores rather than in the traditional video store or mass merchants. So, if your child is a budding musician or an avid fan of a particular performer, try the music store or music catalogs. If art is her interest, try your art store. A sample of how-tos includes *Yo-Yo Man, JuggleTime, Frisbee Disc Video, Balloonacy,* and *Look What I Made.*

Documentaries can provide wonderful windows on past events, tickets to faraway places, previews to places you plan to visit, invitations to other cultures and encounters with natural phenomena, environmental subjects and animals in their natural habitats. In short, they open your kids' minds to new information and events. Documentaries often feature interesting on-camera hosts and subjects such as writers, artists, educators, anthropologists, and men and women on the street who speak directly about their experiences, offering oral history on tape. They afford the opportunity to "bring home" and make real a subject your kid is studying in school. Documentaries can explain complex scientific subjects and present them in engaging ways that take advantage of the versatility of video technology. One such video is *The Miracle of Life,* an excellent presentation of human conception and birth. For an ecological focus, seek out *50 Simple Things Kids Can Do to Save the Earth,* which includes ideas for recycling, picking up garbage, and planting. The PBS series *Baseball* and *The Civil War* are also available on video, bringing to life important periods of history and our national heritage. And the recent documentary on basketball and the American dream, *Hoop Dreams,* will even appeal to nonbasketball fans in its presentation of the aspirations of kids and their families.

Sports tapes run the gamut from instruction in team sports to bloopers to snorkeling. Unfortunately, many instructional and how-to tapes can be teachy or just plain boring, but this may not deter sports enthusiasts. For baseball, check out *Play Ball with Reggie Jackson,* enjoyable because of Reggie's obvious enthusiasm for the game and for helping kids improve through simple activities easily done at home. For basketball, try *Teaching Kids Basketball* with John Wooden; and for snorkeling, *Snorkeling for Kids of All Ages.* Sports bloopers, such as *ESPN's Amazing Biff, Bam, Boom, Anything Goes Sports Bloopers,* are usually big winners for the whole family.

Animation is a perennial hit with young kids. Cartoons are full of wacky humor and wonderful characters. Full scale animated features are all too often the first thing parents think of under the heading of "children's video." This has largely been due to the dominance of Disney, which has an almost inexhaustible catalog of titles for video release and new blockbusters coming out all the time. There are excellent choices in this category, too, including *An American Tail: Fievel Goes West* and *Cinderella.* In addition to Mickey, Donald, and Goofy, look for Disney's *Fantasia* and *Silly Symphonies.* Try some classic cartoons, such as Betty Boop, Felix the Cat, Bugs Bunny, and others from studios like Warner Bros. Although even these contain some pretty violent episodes. Smarty Pants Video distributes some less-well-known animations from Canada, including *Tender Talk of Cinderella Penguin,* a recent Academy Award nominee. You can also find sophisticated computer animation tapes and animation festival programs featuring many award-winners. New animations are hot now, although not all are kid-appropriate, so choose carefully. Look for a fabulous new show, *Wrong Trousers,* a funny clay animation on the theme of friendship and loyalty between a man and his humanlike dog.

101

Literature-based videos are very popular for the preschool and early primary set. Video versions of some wonderful books make the characters pop off the pages into animated life or move the camera across the illustrated page, highlighting images that complement the narrative, often read by famous actors. Dramatic presentations of popular stories also afford your kids the opportunity to compare print and video or to compare a performance by an actor with the character they may have originally imagined from their print experience. Excellent series for the younger set include: Madeline, Winnie the Pooh, and the Maurice Sendak Library. Some wonderful video adaptations of popular books also include *Anne of Avonlea, Abel's Island, Runaway Ralph,* and *The Lion, the Witch and the Wardrobe.*

Miscellany incorporates a range of content and includes a hodgepodge of original "made-for" videos never distributed in theaters, specially edited selections like holiday and travel tapes, strictly instructional tapes like *Table Manners for Everyday Use,* and ABCs *(Animal Alphabet)* and SATs, which can come in handy for even the brainiest kids around.

Many recent quality videos deal with family matters such as divorce, moving, having a pet, or adjusting to a new baby in the family. Drug issues are treated in *Cartoon All-Stars to the Rescue. When Mom and Dad Break Up* deals with the normal feelings kids have when their parents divorce. *Let's Get a Move On!: A Kid's Video Guide to a Family Move* and *Hey, What About Me?: A Video Guide for Brothers and Sisters of New Babies* treat these major live transition issues. These may not be the titles you select for pure entertainment over *Power Rangers.* However, the best of them can really help kids going through a life transition, empowering them to take control of their feelings and their behavior during stressful or trying times. These are the tapes you really want to preview before showing the

TIP

Remember professionals, such as guidance counselors, psychologists, social workers, and health care professionals can also be sources for suggestions.

kids. Many have received awards and endorsements, offering you the confidence that they have handled their subjects sensitively and successfully for their target age.

With all the new and rereleased product coming onto the market, it's getting to the point where you'll have to put in a database for your home video library. Of course, much of what's out there isn't even worth the rental fee, but you're now armed with discriminating criteria to help you make the best choices.

As a Matter of Fact...

Parents with kids under 18 rent videos more frequently than any other market segment.

What Do Your Kids Want to See?

As we advised, it's a good idea to include your children in evaluating and selecting videos. Let them contribute to your own "Green Light Test." Read the sleeve together (coming up), and point out the elements on the sleeve that are clues to the value of the tape inside. Introduce the kids to the categories the video store and catalogs use to merchandise titles. Discuss what genres of programming are your favorites and why. Ask

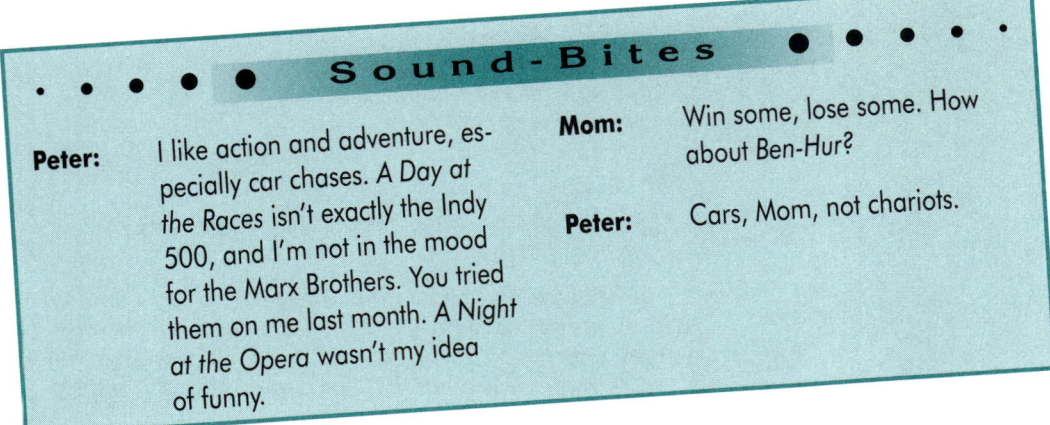

Sound-Bites

Peter: I like action and adventure, especially car chases. A Day at the Races isn't exactly the Indy 500, and I'm not in the mood for the Marx Brothers. You tried them on me last month. A Night at the Opera wasn't my idea of funny.

Mom: Win some, lose some. How about Ben-Hur?

Peter: Cars, Mom, not chariots.

them why they gravitate to certain kinds of programs. When you suggest programs for them, offer a wide enough range of titles. Either use the listings in your *TV Guide* or suggest videos you've noted in your reading or shopping so the kids have room to assert themselves in making selections. And apply your checklist criteria to titles they request.

When you want your kids to watch the programs you've selected for them, keep in mind that the way you present your choices can make all the difference in their attitude and willingness to watch. It's all in the presentation.

- *Select a video you think the family will enjoy, preview it first if there's any doubt, and then whet the kids' appetites by describing elements you know they'll enjoy, like the funny antics in* Duck Soup, *or the main characters who are children in* To Kill a Mockingbird, *or stirring themes like facing down bullies in* High Noon. *These introductions should catch your kids' attention.*

- *Don't recommend the program too strongly or make it feel like a serious "This is good for you" experience. Have fun.*

- *Share your enthusiasm.*

- *See if you and the kids can watch a bit at the store if they are reluctant to rent. This usually persuades them one way or the other.*

- *Watch without them, if they don't seem interested, or tell them you rented the movie for yourself. They'll no doubt stop by to watch what you're watching, and they'll end up joining you.*

- *Watch in segments if the kids are enjoying the video but are getting antsy.*

- *Include black-and-white films in your selection, although children aren't always eager to view them. Counter any arguments by explaining that color wasn't in widespread use until the 1950s and that black and white can convey a feeling or a sense of time and place, such as in* Schindler's List.

> **"** *A good way to encourage children to sample a variety of genres is to tie what they watch into their schoolwork. I think a teacher would be delighted to share a rundown of her curriculum with a parent who wants to select companion videos for home viewing. Example, if a first-grader is studying the author Ezra Jack Keats, then the parent could get one of the book-based animated videos for home viewing. In science if the class is studying the jungle, a live-action animal video might fit in. Any parent can do this across all disciplines—math, weather, geography, etc. I would also encourage parents to get cable and PBS guides so they can tape from TV. A class can chip in 25–50 cents per student for the guides or they might even get them free. The parent could share the results of his or her research with other moms and dads (a terrific thing to do).* **"**
>
> **Diana Huss Green**
> *President, Parents' Choice Foundation*
> *Parent and grandmother of kids ages 3 and up*

Combine kid and parent interests and selections to expand each others' exposure to the variety of programs out there. Key in on the topics and characters that knock their socks off so you can highlight these things in your "sell" to get them to watch some of your recommendations. Schedule a regular time for family viewings, like an "old movie" night once a month, preceded by favorite animations, so you all can see Goofy *and* W. C. Fields.

105

You might want to consider keeping a log of videos you've viewed together. Include your own system for categorizing and rating them. You can also come up with your own rating system—thumbs-up or thumbs-down, zero to five stars, or zero to five bowls of popcorn. You decide! This will give everyone an opportunity to revisit the list when you want to return to favorites, make suggestions to friends, or base new choices on old favorites. Ideally your log will also indicate how fair and balanced your selections have been in accommodating everyone's choices.

Be sensitive to the types of programming and content that are popular with different ages and sexes. Below are some guidelines to help you gain some perspective on what your kids will be drawn to at different stages in their development. Aside from individual interests and concerns, you can pretty much count on the unique and focused interests of particular ages. The following descriptions aren't the only agendas of the different age groups, but they're a start:

Two- to four-year-olds are very interested in other children and in becoming more independent. Good choices for these ages are programs that show other children and families, such as *BabySongs* and *Kidsongs,* and that show children achieving mastery such as *Preschool Power.* This age is also prime for stories, rhymes, and songs they will want to hear and view over and over again. Videos such as *Corduroy* and *Other Bear Stories,* the Wee Sing series, or *Peter, Paul and Mommy* are good choices.

Five- to seven-year-olds are more focused on their own developing skills, so there's a high interest in superheros with super powers such as *Power Rangers* (mostly boys). Girls and boys will enjoy gymnastics, so a good choice would be *Fun with Bela Karoly* to help them begin some skill-building. Their imaginations are growing now, too, so tapes that tap into creativity are good choices. *Sea Dream and Two Other Titles* celebrates the imagination, and *101 Things to Do* is a good tape for kids to learn how to make crafts, tell riddles, and play games.

Seven- to nine-year-olds are keenly interested in peers and are beginning to get involved in projects. The Babysitters Club videos are perfect for this age (especially girls). Programs with friendship themes, such as *Charlotte's Web* or *Bill and Pete,* are good choices. Project-related programs based on your child's interests will be sure hits. For example, *Squiggles, Dots, & Lines* can get kids drawing and *Making and Playing Homemade Instruments* does what it says.

Nine- to twelve-year-olds are keenly interested in fitting in socially and will be interested in stories like *Molly's Pilgrim,* about an immigrant girl who's teased for being different. *Chariots of Fire* will also work well with this age because of the issue of social acceptance and the kids' overriding interest in competition.

Young teens are interested in a much wider range of topics. *Stand by Me* depicts twelve-year-old boys on the cusp of young adulthood and the mixed feelings of isolation and belonging so familiar to this preteen territory. *The Elephant Man,* involving a man with a disfiguring disease who becomes a respected member of society, will resonate for kids who are concerned about appearances.

Read the Sleeve

How can I tell if it's good without watching it myself?

If you read reviews and talk videos with friends and family, you've probably got the makings of a list of likely selections. But when you go looking to rent or purchase them, you'll come

Nick: It's not so violent, Dad. Jamie said he's watched it twice already.

Dad: Did Jamie think it was good?

Nick: He didn't really say.

Dad: Why do you want to see it then?

Nick: The cover looks exciting with all the people exploding and the tank and the guy with the gun and the fire in the back.

Dad: Remember the cover on the movie we rented last week? You weren't interested in seeing that because the cover was "boring" and you thought the movie would be bad because it was in black and white. You'd never seen Alfred Hitchcock before. Then I told you it was the kind of "whodunit" mystery you like, and you loved it. How about another Hitchcock?

Nick: Which one?

across other titles you hadn't heard of or read about. What can you do? Actually, you can tell a lot about a video from its cover, so it's important to know how to read the sleeve.

Most video sleeves offer a fair amount of information that can help you in deciding whether the tape is worth renting or purchasing—something your child will enjoy and come back to for repeat viewings. Ask yourself:

- *Is there a description on the cover that gives a clear synopsis of the content and elements in the video?*

- *Is a suggested target age indicated?*

- *Has the tape won significant awards or notices from the press and media?*

- *If it's a special-interest tape, are there endorsements from key experts on the topic?*

108

- *Are there endorsements from experts in education, children's media, or other professions related to children's health and development?*

- *Does the cover art invite curiosity and reflect quality?*

- *Are there print inserts, such as activity guides, that may offer added value?*

- *Is the publisher or label one that you recognize and trust? If you're satisfied with the quality of other titles produced under the same label, you can be fairly confident in their product.*

Keep in mind that a sleeve can also be misleading. It is, after all, a marketing tool. For example, a picture of a child actor on the cover doesn't always guarantee it's a kid's movie. *Good Son,* with Macaulay Culkin, is not at all appropriate for his younger fans who are likely to be attracted to it because he's on the cover. Culkin plays a preteen psychopath who cruelly terrorizes his young cousin while fooling the rest of the family into thinking he's a good kid. And beware, sometimes the suggested ages are off the mark or at least not accurate for your child and his own level of development. On the other hand, a cover may play up a romantic story for marketing mileage, but this angle may misrepresent a video that actually devotes only a small part of its screen time to romance and contains a story kids will enjoy.

TIP

Shop the video by using the sleeve as your guide and look for:
- descriptive blurb.
- target age.
- awards and notices.
- value-added inserts.
- endorsements.
- recognized supplier, personality, writer, and so on.

109

The sleeve should provide you with some answers. If it doesn't, you might want to think twice before committing to a rental or purchase. If you're in doubt, go home and look for a review in one of your resources, call the library, or ask your friends if they've heard about it.

Sure, there's a lot of time involved in selecting the best for your kids to view. But the process itself can be a fulfilling experience for you and your family, and it makes you all more discriminating consumers and viewers. You'll not only cut down on dissent over what to watch, but you'll discover a bounty of programming options that should please all of you—most of the time.

A Video Vocabulary

It can be helpful to know a small glossary of terms often used in advertising, packaging, and selling videos, terms that can also crop up in reviews and articles. So here are a few of the most common:

Bouncebacks and inserts. Flyers, catalogs, coupons, activity guides, and other print materials, including promotional and ordering materials packaged together with a videocassette.

Closed captioned. Text captioning is encoded on videotape for hearing-impaired viewers (not on all programming) and you need a decoder box or, in new TVs, you can get a decoder chip.

Copying (dubbing, duplicating). The process of making one or more video copies from a "master" tape. Some people attempt to make copies of VHS tapes they borrow or rent. This is against FBI regulations. Although this activity is obviously difficult to police when done at home, it's important to understand the implications of illegal copying. Just as a practical consideration, you will generally get poor-quality copies with VHS as a master. In addition, the producer/publisher is in business to sell tapes, not to give them away, so the law protects the industry from loss of revenue through illegal duplication. In the end, illegal duplication impacts the ability of smaller, more independent producers to generate the funding for future titles. Many videos now in release are "copy-protected," or encoded electronically to render garbled and unwatchable copies.

Dropout. The momentary loss of visual information, resulting in reduced quality or resolution on the video, as a consequence of excessive wear or poor dubbing from a source tape.

Effects. The digitally or editorially designed visuals used to highlight a segment of a program or to transition from one scene to another. Examples include wipes, iris opens and closes, dissolves, and other techniques that replace one image with the next or overlap one image with another.

EP. Stands for "extended play," which means that the copy of the video was made in speeded-up time, not in real time, and so the quality may be somewhat compromised with grainy or streaked sections or an overall playback that is less crisp or less clear. This is cheaper to produce, since more dubs can be made in shorter time. Be aware that videos which are steeply discounted or sold for under $10 are often duplicated in EP.

Format. Refers to the design and organization of a show. For example, is it magazine-style, documentary-style, with or without a host, and so on?

Genre. A type or category of programming sometimes indicated by a label on the tape or merchandised in a dedicated section of a store or section of a catalog: action-adventure, comedy, musical, animation, family, and so on.

111

Live action. The format features real people or actors in real-life contexts as opposed to animation.

Real time. This is usually used in reference to how a video is duplicated (SP mode or "standard play"). The resolution or quality of the tape is usually markedly better when duplication is performed in actual or real time rather than in an EP mode, which is a speeded-up time or "extended play" (although the technology is much improved for this today).

Running time. The length of the program.

Sleeve. The paper cover or jacket for the video.

Target age. The recommended age range that is suggested as an appropriate audience for the specific program. When this age range is based on content and child development standards, it can be helpful. Unfortunately, ages indicated are often arbitrarily assigned without any developmental expertise involved.

Time shift. The ability to tape from television and record a show when it airs but save it on tape for future viewing, thereby having control over when you watch.

VHS. Half-inch format tape cassette and video playback equipment predominately in use in the United States.

Family Activity

Design a Video Cover

Some say it's all in the packaging.

Haven't you ever bought something because of the cover—a book, a game, a video, even a bag of cookies? If you're wondering whether what's inside is worth the price, then the information on the cover can help you make a good decision or it can fool you!

Consider the impact a cover can have and design one for a film or video you've seen or one you make up.

You'll need:

paper
markers

-or-

word processing and
drawing programs

Check this list to be sure you include all the necessary elements:

- title
- descriptive blurb
- target age
- awards and notices
- activity guide inserts
- endorsements
- familiar studio label, star, director, and so on.

113

5 | Homework for Parents

Research Can Lead to Buried Treasure

We always seem to know what we don't want our kids to watch, but having good choices for them is where we often draw a blank. To find the best programming for kids, we're challenged to be tenacious researchers, savvy consumers, and lobbyists. This chapter points you in the right direction. You might need to find the right retailer or get to the library. You can also read the reviews and comb through some worthwhile catalogs and useful compendiums.

In addition to suggesting where to look for quality products, there's the question of whether to rent or buy them once you find them. We discuss the advantages of both and how to decide, and we point out what you can do to have better access to the good stuff in the first place. Read over the next few pages and equip yourself with new resources to turn to in your search for viewing for your kids. A little bit of homework will make your parental halo shine, and you'll be rewarded.

The Video Store and Beyond

Your local video store is a great place to go to find movies and cartoons. It most likely features recent Hollywood releases

We've rented that 15 times already, Abby, don't you want to see something else?

Tune In the Topics

- The Video Store and Beyond

- The Big Dig: Mining Press and Media Reviews, Book Compendiums, Selections, and Community Networks

- The Library, Catalogs, and Specialty Retailers

- Rent or Buy?

- Take the Initiative: Flex Your Muscle as a Consumer

- Family Activity: Prepare a Video Calendar

and the highly publicized titles of the giants of the industry. Many stores have also devoted significant space to their children's sections, separating their offerings into subcategories, like Disney, cartoons, musicals, and so on. Some video stores also specialize in documentary or special-interest titles.

TIP

Ask your video store if they can restrict PG-13 or R ratings when your kids rent by themselves.

We recommend you go to the video store now and then without your kids to look for titles they might not select but might prove enjoyable and worthwhile. At least you won't have the pressure to choose something they want to see *now*. There are some outstanding video stores that have gone the extra mile, adding a family viewing section or a section with staff recommendations, but this is not the norm. Look in all of the sections, not just the children's area. Some stores emphasize selling tapes, while others focus on rentals. Either way, you can ask your store to order the titles you want.

But don't stop there. If the video store is the only place you go to rent or buy videos for your kids, your choices will be somewhat limited, since most video stores give the impression that the only titles in existence are hit movies, cartoons, repackaged TV shows, and the licensed character programs (*Barney, Pocahontas, Tommy the Tank Engine*) you've seen advertised in magazines or on TV. Luckily, this is not the case. There's a universe of alternative titles available, everything from karate for kids to videos all about bugs. There are even tapes on being an airline pilot and on the circus. This probably has you wondering, *"If there's so much out there to choose from, why don't I know about it? And why isn't it available at my neighborhood video store?"*

The Business of Home Video

Over one-third of all videos sold are kids' videos, and about 90 percent of that is Disney! Rather astounding when you come to think of it. The economics of the video publishing industry limit the availability of a wide range of quality product. The major studios have a broad list of titles and deep pockets for advertising and merchandising. Therefore, they can dictate what's offered in the traditional retail outlets because they dominate the shelf space in the video stores and the major mass merchants, from the Kmarts to Toys "R" Us. If one title isn't moving, they can switch it with any number of other titles they own. They can spend significant dollars introducing a new title through co-op advertisements (they give the stores money to run ads featuring the studio's own titles), special introductory discounts and premium offers, and incentives to retailers to get them to strategically position their studio displays in heavily trafficked areas of the stores. So buyers' decisions are affected by a multitude of incentives—not what's the best tape but often what's the best deal. Smaller suppliers and independent producers can only fantasize about having such resources, since they usually have limited product lines and minimal capital to spend on advertising and these other incentives to retailers.

Cartoons, movies, and old TV shows are great entertainment. I'm happy to have my kids watch them. But the world's bigger than Gilligan's Island, and it's populated by lots of beings besides Mickey, Pluto, and Goofy.

As a Matter of Fact...

- Many stores prohibit R rated films to kids whose parents opt for that restriction when they sign up with the store.
- One video chain reports that it brings in four to six new children's titles for rental per month and ten to twelve for sale.
- Only 5.7 percent of the videos recognized with a Parents' Choice Award in 1994 are available in Blockbuster Video stores.

117

Take heart. There are recent indications in the marketplace that a wider variety of product is squeezing its way in. Special collections of award-winning children's videos are now available through distributors to the retail outlets in displays that are set apart from the more mass-merchandised product available in the stores. For example, Baker & Taylor, one of the video industry's major distributors, is now offering a Parents' Choice collection dubbed *Lotsa Fun for Kids*. This particular assortment of Parents' Choice award-winners includes a range of titles from small independent producers as well as larger studios, and is making its way to video stores and large retailers. Another collection of award-winning product called *Kids First!,* put together by the Coalition for Quality Children's Media, is available through select retailers. You can call the coalition to learn which retailers are carrying the Kids First! titles. And there are many more places to look for original made-for videos and special-interest titles beyond retail—the nooks and crannies you can search out to find a variety of quality product.

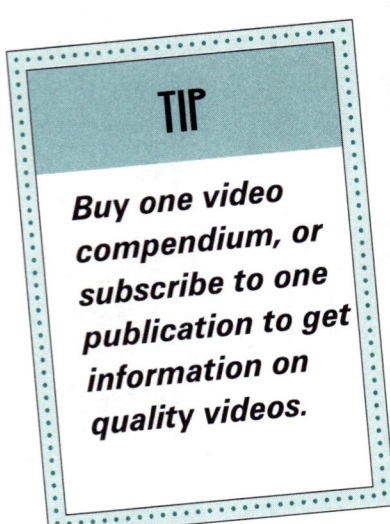

The Big Dig: Mining Press and Media Reviews, Book Compendiums, Selections, and Community Networks

Reviews, resource books, compendiums of quality titles and industry award-winners will point you to what's out there. (See "Resources" section for this chapter.) And don't forget your own networks of other parents who can often provide a wealth of fresh suggestions for your kids. This section will help you out in your search for qualified filters to good programs.

Children's Media Reviews

Magazines and Newspapers

Children's video critics—who themselves hail from backgrounds in education, children's media, and child development—now specialize in reviewing children's programming. They write for magazines, newsletters, and newspapers that cover the video marketplace, responding to the demonstrated concern of parents who seek quality programming for their kids.

These publications offer everything from ongoing reviews of newly released products to features on the TV industry and its impact on American culture. The critics devote a fair amount of attention to the children's segment of the industry, and they have emerged as a reliable panel that identifies the "good stuff" available.

We recommend *Parents' Choice,* a terrific periodical published by the Parents' Choice Foundation in Waban, Massachusetts. As mentioned in Chapter 4, this national quarterly convenes respected experts to confer annual awards in all children's media as well as games and toys. *Child* and *Parenting,* two magazines you can find on newsstands, also have excellent columns on video. Local parenting publications, such as *L.A. Parent* and *New York Family,* do a good job of reviewing videos, often by themes like "sing-alongs" or "truck tapes." Check out Joanne Bracco in *San Francisco Parent* and Steven Rea in the *Philadelphia Inquirer* and *Family Fun.* And each fall *TV Guide* publishes a children's television issue that previews cable and broadcast selections as well as made-for home videos for children. *Parental Discretion* is a newsletter which reviews theatrical releases for parents every three weeks. A synopsis, age recommendations, and warnings on sex, violence, and language are included in their reviews.

As a Matter of Fact...

Children's video represents over a third of the entire video marketplace.

Children's video critics tend to write for a variety of outlets. Some of the ones we find most on target are: Loretta MacAlpine, Catherine Cella, Martha Dewing, Moira McCormick, Terri Payne Butler, and Terry and Catherine Catchpole.

Other sources for reviews are found on newsstands in magazines such as *Entertainment Weekly, Premiere, Billboard,* and in columns in national and regional newspapers and women's magazines. In addition, in-store magazines such as *Pulse* (Tower Records) occasionally review children's product.

Sometimes special-interest magazines on topics as diverse as personal finance and home and garden will review a children's video title if its subject matter is relevant. For instance, KIDVIDZ' *Let's Get a Move On!: A Kid's Video Guide to a Family Move,* has been reviewed in publications from *The New York Times* to *House Beautiful* and *Builder Magazine. Piggy Banks to Money Markets: A Kid's Video Guide to Dollars and Sense,* received coverage in family and parenting magazines as well as in *Nation's Business* and *Money Magazine.*

Another way to learn about quality children's programming is to look at references and resources listed in articles on topics that interest you or your kids. Parenting columns in magazines

> **❝** To some extent, word of mouth influences what we choose for our kids to watch, and we preview things when we can. We'll watch things with them if we have doubts. **❞**
>
> **Bill Littlefield**
> *National Public Radio host,* It's Only a Game
> *Father of kids ages 6 and 9*

and newspapers often mention videos by theme, since their authors frequently write about kids and families and may concentrate on particular subjects or issues. For example, an article on kids and exercise may mention one or two of the more worthwhile movement and exercise tapes for kids.

Broadcast/Cablecast Reviews

Broadcast journalists are also including children's titles in the mix of programs they review. Siskel and Ebert now exercise their thumbs up and down on the subject of kids' programming on their syndicated show. On PBS' *Sneak Previews,* Jeffrey Lyons and Michael Medved regularly cover kids' video releases, and children's programming is featured on a number of daytime news and magazine shows such as on *Good Morning America,* which features Diana Huss Green, publisher of *Parents' Choice.* Your local news programs and cable shows may also include parenting segments or media reviews. And don't forget radio. National Public Radio often reviews general video products and occasionally covers kids' titles.

Book and New Media Compendiums

Video compendiums are proliferating on bookstore shelves, both for children and for general audiences. For families, we highly recommend *The Family Video Guide* by Terry and Catherine Catchpole, which selects the best from the entire world of Hollywood films. The Catchpoles' section on movies by theme is especially useful when you're selecting movies for a particular interest or if there's a topic you want to introduce. You can find a list of fifteen themes, including courtroom and backstage dramas, movies about the press and science gone amok. In addition, the starter section introduces you to old favorites that will appeal to the whole family. Ratings and age suggestions are also included.

Family Roundtable

Finding Out What To Watch

It's hard to find something for the whole family to watch. I wish there were some sort of database you could search for both kids and adults to figure out what's out there that might meet your standards or be about your interests.

Father of 14-year-old

You can read TV Guide or remember reviews from the newspaper.

10-year-old

But videos don't come out for months after the review. I spend a lot of time figuring out what to watch on TV or rent.

Father of 14-year-old

122

We also recommend Catherine Cella's *Great Videos for Kids: A Parent's Guide to Choosing the Best,* which reviews films and videos made specifically for children. The selections are well organized into useful sections, such as book-based, holidays, and instruction. Suppliers and age recommendations are included here to assist you in deciding if titles are appropriate and give you a first step in finding them if they are. Especially helpful is the appendix, "A Baker's Dozen of Best Lists," which includes "Best Videos with Positive Black Roles," "Best Videos Fostering Imagination," and more. *Inside KidVid,* a newer book by Loretta MacAlpine, reviews feature films as well as made-for home video productions, which are divided into user-friendly chapters, including music, fun activity tapes, and more. Interviews with people in the industry are interesting inclusions.

The *Parents' Choice Magazine Guide to Videocassettes for Children* reviews both films and made-for videos and includes books that tie in to each recommendation. An appendix also lists titles by appropriate age groups.

Also take a look at *Video Movie Guide* by Mick Martin and Marsha Porter, a huge compendium of films that is updated annually. The guide describes over nine thousand movies, including MPAA ratings and a star rating recommendation system. The listings are organized much as a video store might be, so you will find sections on children's viewing/family, drama, comedy, and so on. In addition, cast and director listings guide you to more films by an actor or director who intrigues your kids. A family viewing index is also included.

If you own or have access to a CD-ROM, *Cinemania* by Microsoft lists over nineteen thousand titles. Its cross-references by author, director, and title are fun to explore. You can do a search by any number of categories, including title, credits, genre, topic, and cast. Once you select a film, you can see clips or stills, hear famous dialogue, or learn more about the music. Thorough synopses, ratings, awards, and reviews from well-known critics, including Leonard Maltin, Roger Ebert, and Pauline Kael, round out the information. A listmaker allows you to customize your own list to take to the video store or to order from sources suggested on the CD.

If you get hooked on searching out videos that are just right for your child's interest and for family fun, you can ask your librarian for more resources. Look for *Children's Video Report,* edited by Martha Dewing, as well as her book, *Beyond TV: Activities for Using Video with Children; Booklist,* published by the American Library Association; and Eveline Carsman's *Children's Video Review Newsletter.* These resources are aimed primarily at teachers and librarians, but parents will enjoy the enlightening, child-sensitive descriptions.

KIDSNET is a national nonprofit computerized clearinghouse devoted to children's media. Their monthly *Media Guide* lists descriptions of broadcasts, cablecasts, and video releases, along with corresponding notes on grade level and curriculum area. You can subscribe by calling the number in our "Resources" section or through America Online.

Awards, Top Picks, and Selections

If you want to devote a little more time and trouble to your big dig for worthwhile videos, you can also contact the major film and video festivals, as well as publishers and foundations that confer awards. The top awards for childrens' videos are listed in this chapter's "Resources" section, and again, we encourage you to call or write them for lists of their awardees.

Certain magazines do annual or semiannual best-picks lists in addition to the regular reviews they run. *TV Guide* offers

As a Matter of Fact...

One video reviewer we know gets information on 100 new children's releases every week.

their Top 10 Kids' Video List annually, as does *Parents* magazine. Most of the major family, parents', and women's magazines have holiday gift roundups which include ratings and suggestions of kids' videos. Unfortunately, these lists are often dominated by the studio blockbusters which deluge the stores at the holidays, but you can find a few gems.

Your Community Networks

Other parents you know, teachers, store owners, and your neighborhood children's librarian comprise another potential well of information and suggestions. With the rise of two-income families, the playground bench is no longer much of a place for sharing experiences and advice. So pick up the phone, ask at the next PTA meeting or during those chance encounters in the supermarket aisle. And don't hesitate to recommend titles that you and your kids have enjoyed.

Develop Your Own List: Some Suggestions

I can't remember the name of that tennis tape I saw on ESPN. And it was only yesterday. My brain cells are definitely going.

To take advantage of magazine and newspaper reviews or notes you jot down when watching reviews on TV, make a list for that time when you'll be shopping for videos. We've received many orders for our KIDVIDZ title *Paws, Claws, Feathers and Fins: A Kid's Video Guide to Pets* from parents who read reviews as much as two years prior to getting a new pet. They simply saved the review for a future need which they obviously anticipated.

TIP

Keep a list of video titles that interest you for the next time you go renting or shopping for your kids.

You might keep pencil and paper near the phone, why not near the TV, too? When an interesting tape or program is mentioned, you won't have

125

to commit it to memory or dash out of the room in search of a pen while they flash the 800 number and ordering address. Keep a pencil and paper handy so you can capture that information for a time when you'll want it.

The Library, Catalogs, and Specialty Retailers

It can be a frustrating game of hide-and-seek. Once I learn what's available, I often can't find it to rent or buy.

Videos are available through a variety of outlets beyond the exclusive domain of the video store and big mass merchants. Check out the library as well as the unending stream of catalogs, specialty retailers, and on-line computer shopping options to find what you're looking for. These resources will often turn up other appealing titles as you search for what you've preshopped through reviews and resource books.

The Library

Your local library is a good place to begin your search (and research) for the videos on your list. A few years ago, only a small percentage of public libraries purchased video for loan. Now over 80 percent of America's fifteen thousand libraries have some kind of video collection. The American Library Association has encouraged more and more libraries to purchase titles not readily available in video stores or through mass merchants, helping to build collections that offer the best of special-interest, documentary, arts- and literature-based programming. For information, the American Library Association welcomes your call and will send you a list of awards and recommendations.

TIP

Turn to all the outlets available beyond the video store to find what you want:
- *library.*
- *catalogs.*
- *specialty retailers.*
- *online shopping.*

In a recent survey on children's video collections, libraries reported that nearly two-thirds of their children's video collections are in circulation in any given month, indicating the popularity of the subject matter. In fact, children's video is the highest-circulating genre in all library video collections. Video is now outcirculating books in some libraries. This means more money in library budgets will be allocated to purchasing video to keep patrons coming back.

Catalogs

Specialty and children's product catalogs and general video catalogs are another key resource. Troll Communications, Critics' Choice, and Columbia House all feature offerings from many quality children's video labels. Catalogs sometimes present selected titles along with toys and books clustered around a particular interest area like arts and crafts or a particular target age range. This chapter's "Resources" section lists some of the best catalogs we've found offering children's videos.

Specialty Retailers

A new kind of retailer has also entered the marketplace—the educational, learning product retailer. These new chains include the eleven-store chain GBH Learningsmith (from L.A. to Boston), Zany Brainy (mainly on the East Coast), and Imaginarium, with sixteen stores nationwide from San Francisco to New York. In these stores you'll find a fascinating mix of learning products—games and audio books, music anthologies, construction and science kits, educational CD-ROMs and video. Many specialty retailers, including boutique toy and gift stores and independent bookstores, have led the way in offering quality children's videos.

Online Sources

With the wave of new media technologies, new online retail outlets for video surface every day. You might want to sample the

127

S o u n d - B i t e s

Mom: Where's your dad?

Eli: I think he was browsing the on-line mall and fell asleep at the computer.

Mom: This gives new meaning to "Shop till you drop!"

Noodlehead Network or Compuserve's Electronic Mall, both of which include kids' videos.

Rent or Buy?

Buying a video for under $10 and watching it two or three times may be worth the ticket for pure enjoyment, since there are plenty of comparable purchases like the movies, a video arcade, or the candy shop. Certainly, a purchase for $13 to $20 takes a little more weighing and measuring, but again, it's more than worth the money if it represents hours of enjoyment and the added benefit of passing it along to friends and family when you're through.

But you don't need to buy videos. Sometimes it makes sense to rent the video you want or ask around to see if anyone will loan it to you. It may be a program that your kids will view only once. If it's not available to rent and you don't know anyone who owns it, maybe you can get someone else to invest with you. If your child is in a playgroup or other group of friends with kids of similar ages and interests, start a video library or video club for sharing programs.

Of course, if you decide to buy a tape, you can always get back part of your investment by selling it at a yard sale. When

As a Matter of Fact...

- In a survey on video purchases, over 80 percent of parents surveyed said they purchased at least one video in the preceding month, compared to 56 percent of respondents without children.

- Parents of young children are the biggest group of video purchasers.

128

Tony: I don't get it. You'll spend over $40 on a computer program for me or even $15 or $20 on a book. You even agreed to get me those new sneakers I want which you thought were too expensive. So why do you have so much trouble plunking down

$15 for a video? And look, it's won all these awards.

Mom: You're absolutely right. But then you'll have to choose between the shoes and the tape.

Tony: I can't believe I walked right into that.

your videos are just collecting dust, add them to your sale pile, and earmark the funds for new video purchases. Or give a bunch to your local library or school and take a tax deduction.

Linda: Where's the tape with the show about scuba diving? I want to show it to Kevin.

Dad: I think Mom taped one of *The Frugal Gourmet* shows on it. She thought you were done with it.

Linda: She should have her own tape. What a pain!

Dad: Take a look at it—maybe it's about tuna fish and you can both enjoy it.

Linda: That's not funny, Dad.

129

If purchased or taped-off-TV videos are starting to collect around the house, it's helpful to find a space to devote to your video library. Clear a shelf, and include some blank tapes and labels, and maybe some index cards to log shows you want to time shift and save for future viewing.

Renting or borrowing a video is a great way to preview it before plunking down the money on a purchase. Keep in mind that copying videos is a "big no-no" (i.e., FBI and copyright regulations). You wouldn't shoplift in front of your kids or steal a book out of the local library; setting a good example about not stealing video content is just as important.

As a Matter of Fact...

• Americans rented approximately 4 billion videocassettes in 1995.

• Renting a video is a more popular leisure time activity than buying a book, CD, audiotape, or going to a movie.

For the most part, the quality supplementary diet of children's viewing—special-interest how-to, arts, literature-based, documentary, and so on—isn't available for rental. Occasionally, a toy store may carry these titles and have an in-store monitor for you to catch a glimpse, or you may find what you're looking for in the library. But the unfortunate reality is that most products available from smaller suppliers and independent producers are available for sale only, so you usually can't rent or borrow them to preview. This has much to do with the structure of the video distribution business, but in the end it means your family's options as consumers are diminished.

The message here is to rely on the reviews, endorsements, and awards to help you find quality titles. Get to know the reviewers and other experts who prescreen videos for you and your kids, and you'll have a basis for a buying decision. And remember children watch a favorite video an average of thirteen times, so the repeated rental of a good video won't be cost-effective.

Take the Initiative: Flex Your Muscle as a Consumer

You'll read a review of a wonderful program, just the thing for your son who's into camping or your daughter who's obsessed with horses. You search and search, but nowhere is the tape to be found. And the review didn't include any ordering information, address, or phone number. Don't despair. You can find it.

Distributors

If you learned about a particular video in a review, you can call the magazine or newspaper and contact the reviewer directly to ask for the phone or address of the producer, also known as the supplier. Then call the producer and see if you can order directly, or ask where their tapes are sold or who their distributor is. You may have to make another call to the distributor to find where the tape is being sold, or the distributor might sell to you directly. Silo and Rounder Kids are two distributors who carry a lot of good tapes for kids and will sell to you directly.

This may seem like a lot of work, but making a handful of calls and getting to know a quality distributor is certainly worthwhile if you're seeking entertaining and educational video for your kids.

As a Matter of Fact...

- A favorite children's video is watched an average of thirteen times. Renting thirteen times, for $2.50 each time, would cost $32.50. If you buy this video for $14.95, you save $17.55.

- The two largest groups of video renters are society's most stressed-out segments: dual-income married couples (53 percent) and parents of kids under the age of 18 (50 percent).

Local Retailers

Find a video store, bookstore, or toy store whose video selection is varied and reflects attention to quality for kids. Tell the manager about the videos you'd like them to purchase for rental and loan. Retailers are usually responsive to these requests, especially if your friends and other parents you know are making the same recommendations. Be prepared to provide the name of the producer or distributor if you know it. The two largest video distributors are Baker & Taylor in Niles, Illinois, and Ingram Entertainment in LaVergne, Tennessee. Neither distributor sells directly to consumers, but you can ask your store to order from them on your behalf just as you would ask your bookstore or library to order a book.

Ask for the Good Stuff

When you come across videos you and your kids really enjoy, look into other titles by the same producer, since the one you like may be part of a line or a series. Ask your video store or toy store manager to order other titles by the same company, and let them know how much your family appreciates having this type of product available.

There are also opportunities to introduce quality children's videos at school—at school bookfairs, in PTA roundtables, and through sponsorships of speakers who are experts in the field of children and media.

Keep in touch with the children's librarian at your public library, as well as the librarian in your school, and suggest tapes you think would be valuable for the community. Get your PTA to put together video recommendations and publish them in the PTA newsletter. Send them to your community library and to retailers in your area as suggestions for purchase.

Retailers and librarians consider you an important customer, so you should feel comfortable letting them know about the programs you would like them to offer. The key is to find some time to write, call, and lobby those people who can make a difference. It's just as true for TV and video as it is for other issues that affect the welfare and well-being of your family and your community.

As a Matter of Fact...

A family of four pays approximately $23 for movie tickets as opposed to $12.95–$19.95 to buy a video they'll probably watch multiple times.

133

Remember, there are other opportunities for building communal lending video libraries: with a playgroup, preschool, church, or neighborhood group. Organize a local video library or club, either in your neighborhood or through the PTA. This is a cost-effective way to develop a collection of worthwhile videos for many families to enjoy, and it's an opportunity to learn more about what's available.

As a proactive parent, you'll reap the best rewards for your kids. Read, watch, call, research, and request, and you'll find a bounty of viewing that will enhance the value of your VCR and provide "quality screen time" for your family.

TIPS

- **Ask retailers and libraries to purchase quality programs you read or hear about.**

- **Speak up for what you want:**
    - **Ask your retailer to order what you want.**
    - **Help organize school book fairs that include video.**
    - **Offer suggestions to your school librarian and children's librarian at your local library.**
    - **Organize a neighborhood video library.**

Family Activity

Prepare a Video Calendar

Spontaneity is great, but sometimes a little planning delivers a bonus of fun. Anticipate your family's video needs and get together to make some choices for future reference. This way, you won't have to worry about eleventh-hour party plans or forgetting about selections you've already made. And you'll have the satisfaction of having lots of prearranged viewing to enjoy.

Plan ahead for holidays and family events. Target titles that fill the bill for everything from a rainy day to a dinner for the soccer team. Use our calendar below as a guide.

You'll need:
paper/marker /ruler

-or-

word processing with a table format

Event	Topic	Title	Distributor
Leah's slumber party	teen comedy or thriller	*The Babysitters Club: Claudia and the Missing Jewels*	Good Times Video
Little League dinner	sports drama	*Rookie of the Year*	Fox
Vacation rainy day	action-adventure	*Star Wars*	CBS/Fox
Jake's birthday party	art	*Be a Cartoonist*	Mid-Com
preparing for camp	camp comedy	*KidSongs: A Day at Camp*	Viewmaster Video

6 Rewind and Play Again

A Fresh Look at What Kids Do While the TV's On and How What's On Influences Them

You can make viewing more valuable for your kids when you supervise what your kids do in front of the set and help them get the most out of what they watch. Two generations of kids have grown up with television, and there's a fair amount of research that's taught us about its influence on kids—its effect on their behavior and how TV's technology, craft, and commercial imperatives shape the messages kids receive. We've learned the set often gets turned on just for the company it provides. Other times an entire social event, like a birthday party, may be built around viewing. The kids are tuned in during many daily activities, like dressing, eating, and doing their homework. In this chapter, we survey some of what goes on while the TV's on and point out how you can monitor eating and homework in front of the tube and set limits you feel are appropriate.

Beyond TV's impact on our kids' behavior, how they "read" TV is another focus here. How do kids understand what they watch? After all, the "cool medium" can color perceptions of reality while it also successfully suspends disbelief through wonderful dramas created just for its small screen. Recent attention to visual intelligence, together with awareness that many of us

Tune In the Topics

- TV Behavior: Eating, Homework, and More . . .

- Watching Together

- Helping Kids Become Critical Viewers

- Extend the Viewing Experience

- Family Activity: News at Six

learn better through visual images rather than reading, has fostered the development of media literacy programs in schools. These classes teach how the visual media—from billboards and movies to TV—communicate their messages. As in any communications medium, TV programs selectively present information in order to reflect different points of view. Media literacy teaches how its commercials and bottom-line orientation dictate much of what's available, which in turn can sway our perceptions and behaviors. There's no question that TV impacts our tastes and how we spend our money.

In the following pages, we discuss how media literacy programs help us be responsive to TV's influence on our kids. You can teach your kids to be critical viewers, enabling them to understand how programs are built to elicit responses and convey feelings and ideas. You can guide them to become savvy consumers who question what they see on TV rather than passively accept it as gospel. It's also important to help them appreciate the craft involved in making programs that touch their hearts, challenge their thinking, and maybe even inspire their own creativity.

TV Behavior: Eating, Homework, and More...

A lot happens while the TV's on, including homework, chores, and a full sweep of conversations from talking on the phone to talking back to the set. At one time or another, you probably wonder:

What can I do about my son who flops in front of the set to veg?

We all need to veg, and TV's often the place we choose to do it. Just keep the vegging to allotted TV times and realize it comes with the territory. But encourage your child to opt for preselected programs most of the time.

Should I let my kids snack while watching?

We delve into this in a few pages coming up, but basically the message is if it's healthy stuff or a finite "treat" (not the whole bag of cookies), sure go right ahead.

Are homework and TV totally incompatible?

Even if your kid gets straight A's, the answer is yes. After all, if there's a set amount of time to watch and the shows are preselected, just watch. Why muddy the waters—either way?

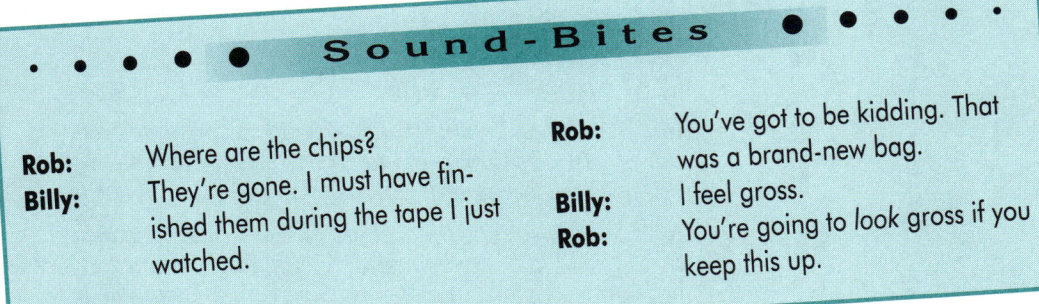

S o u n d - B i t e s

Rob: Where are the chips?
Billy: They're gone. I must have finished them during the tape I just watched.

Rob: You've got to be kidding. That was a brand-new bag.
Billy: I feel gross.
Rob: You're going to look gross if you keep this up.

Location of the TV and VCR

Perhaps the best way to begin a discussion of how TV impacts your kids' behavior is to consider where the TV(s) and VCR(s) are located in your home. Once the set is in place, many ancillary and unplanned activities will take place around it. If kids have their own sets, viewing is less easily monitored or supervised. Yet, even with two to three TVs in most American homes, most families still congregate in the living room to watch together at prime time. Gathering before the set may be the same for us as coming together around the fire at night was for our ancestors.

As a Matter of Fact...

- A marketing survey by Lifescapes revealed 70 percent of viewers tune in to "tune out," while just 20 percent claim to watch "to be in the know."
- 50 percent of children ages 6–17 have a television in their room.

Eating and TV

Research has established a clear correlation between excessive television viewing and obesity in children. A study by Dr. William Dietz, published in *The Journal of Pediatrics,* examined over six thousand children and found that each additional hour of television viewing increased the likelihood of obesity in children when all other factors remained constant. For adolescents, the level of obesity went up 2 percent for every hour in front of the TV. Three separate factors come into play when children spend a lot of time viewing, and these result in obesity:

- *Viewing promotes inactivity.*

- *Kids like to snack while watching and so consume extra calories. In addition, they may lose track of how much they're eating because they're watching at the same time.*

- *Commercials for sugary and fatty foods influence snack choices, and kids are bombarded with ads for unhealthy foods on television. In fact, only 5 percent of a sample of commercials on Saturday mornings during kids' programs was for food products without sugar!*

> **TIP**
>
> *Tune in to your kids' eating habits around TV. How much snacking are they really doing?*

How can you help your kids enjoy their shows and their snacks and avoid unhealthy eating? If your family has a few basic ground rules regarding snacking, stick to them when it comes to viewing. If you put a priority on healthful snacks and limiting snacking to fairly specified times, like right after school, then TV shouldn't be an excuse to change eating behavior.

Set aside a serving rather than let the kids bring a whole box or bag to the TV, so you and your kids can control how much they eat. It's easy to lose track of how many crackers go down if their hands are absently going from the box to their

Family Roundtable

Eating and TV

We don't let our kids watch much TV during the week, but usually they're eating dinner and they're watching it. It's sort of their wind-down time, is how they use it. I don't feel my kids take advantage. They're not like television couch potatoes at all.

Mother of 8- and 11-year-olds

We don't let them watch while they eat dinner, but I think it's a good idea, especially if the kids aren't eating with us or if they had a very busy day.

Mother of 10-year-old

They're so busy! So, usually they're watching the show while they're eating dinner, which I know some people don't allow, but we do.

Mother of 8- and 11-year-olds

We aren't allowed to watch at mealtime. *10-year-old*

We can watch at dinner, after I've got everything done, or if someone's in a bad mood. *12-year-old*

141

mouths while they're concentrating on the screen. If you offer a two-cookie snack, then enjoying them in front of TV is just fine. You can also have yogurt or carrot sticks on hand.

Some people, however, feel it's simply better to never eat in front of the set.

And how do you feel about eating a full meal while watching TV? Some families feel that when kids are eating, it's a time for them to let down and view a show. Others feel that mealtimes represent a time for the family to share and catch up on the events of the day. One family we know sets aside one night a week to have pizza and watch a video. Whatever you decide, be sure the whole family also lives by the rules because your behavior is a model for your kids.

Homework and TV

Families run the gamut on policies about doing homework in front of the TV/VCR. Some are absolute in their refusal to permit any schoolwork to be done in front of the set, while others allow certain activities, like an art project or clipping current events articles from the paper. Some parents don't think this is an issue at all as long as their kids are doing fine in school, even though the average amount of time American kids spend doing homework is twenty-six minutes. Compare this to the three to four hours they watch television, and it's clear that homework shouldn't be accompanied by viewing. If you're really concentrating, it's hard to do two things well at the same time. If you've set limits on how much time you allot to viewing, you may as well decide that your kids enjoy their viewing time for the experience itself and keep homework out of the equation. Also, a footnote regarding the supplicant comment: "But my show is on now, so I'll review the spelling list during the commercials!" Once again the VCR comes to the rescue. Tape the show and do the spelling list without interference.

Family Roundtable

What We Do While We Watch

I think we eat popcorn and stuff while we watch a movie because our hands aren't occupied.

14-year-old

I fold the laundry. That shows how little input you need to put into watching a video. You can watch an entire movie and do five or six loads of laundry at the same time, read the paper, and still get the movie.

Father of 4-year-old

143

Personal Notes

Karen's son Andrew, age 10, whose screen time is limited, observed that sometimes he watches a show he doesn't really like because the remote is so accessible from the sofa where he rests. He suggested, "If my art supplies or reading book were on the coffee table, too, I might use them and turn off the show."

Channel Surfing

With the advent of the remote control, a new behavior has evolved—channel surfing. Switching from channel to channel can increase the likelihood of kids seeing something inappropriate or just junky. With all the cable selections available and the growing programming options accessible through pay-per-view and other channels, the remote becomes a key to a lot of doors you may not want your kids to open.

Channel surfing means you want to see what's on instead of deciding to watch a particular program. Want to avoid channel surfing as an addicting activity and defeat TV's seductive power to get your kids to watch whatever's on? Then agree in advance about what, when, and how much to watch. When you make program selections in advance and you tape, rent, or purchase, you're not held hostage to what's on whenever you sit down to watch. You can also fast-forward past unsuitable ads, even those around a good show. Preselecting your programming prevents the habit of turning the TV on as a matter of course and using it as background noise to fill in the spaces.

Conversation and the Tube

Lots of talk goes on in front of the TV. We talk on the phone, we talk back at the set—often to outrageous commercials or ridiculous characters or plots. Conversation while watching together can be terrific. Programs can become more interactive, generating lively discussions. Kids can ask questions and express their ideas, concerns, or confusion about what's on. The VCR can invite these dialogues because you control the pace, including stopping, starting, and replays. And obviously the VCR's a tremendous convenience when the phone rings or some other interruption occurs. You can stop the tape and return later, or record the broadcast or cable show that's on and watch it another time.

Chores and TV

Some routine tasks seem to be made for TV. Kids can actually maximize their time by doing certain chores while watching. Cleaning out a box or drawer of old stuff, folding laundry, braiding a sister's hair, or helping a parent with a job like stamping a business mailing are all great candidates for TV accompaniment. And rather than sucking your kids into "just watching," this short task-plus-TV interlude might satisfy their need for a little dose of the tube.

> **TIP**
>
> *Pick a few chores you feel won't be compromised while watching TV.*

Watching Together

Do you view tapes with your kids? Do they watch alone or with friends or siblings? TV viewing shouldn't always be separate for the kids and apart from what you watch. Watching alone can be isolating for children and rob you of opportunities to see what they're up to and what interests them. Peggy Charren, founder of Action for Children's Television, writes: "What parents have to remember is that television is like a stranger in the house talking to your children." Steve Bennett, author of *Kick the TV Habit,* says: "There is a loss of perspective if kids are watching shows alone with no parental input or discussion."

Watching programs together can be an important sharing experience. You can learn more about your kids' tastes and interests and see if you're comfortable with the messages "the stranger" is telling them. Your kids' responses to different characters and personalities can give you a window on what scares or concerns them and how they feel about certain issues. Sometimes a topic will strike a chord with your child and offer her a chance to air her feelings about something she otherwise might never have broached, like the loss she feels about a friend who moved away or how she cherishes the memory of a particular family outing that took place years before, something you never knew meant that much to her.

Often, watching a show with your kids or with your child and their friends can be like driving the car and listening to them in the backseat. You can be privy to conversations you wouldn't otherwise hear. It can be both delightful and enlightening to listen to the exchanges between your kids and their friends as they respond to what they're viewing and how they interpret certain concepts and characters.

Watching together can also become a teaching opportunity, and talking afterward about what you saw together can help your child better understand the program . . . and you. The main thing is to "be there" as often as possible. Experts agree that for television's positive messages to really sink in, it helps for them to

> 66 *Videos offer us the opportunity to share an at-home experience together as a family. We do it about once a month and it's always gratifying.* 99
>
> **Paul Binder**
> *Founder and Artistic Director, Big Apple Circus*
> *Father of two children, ages 8 and 10*

be reinforced by the adults in kids' lives. That means parents should actually watch at least some of the shows and then talk about them with their kids—advice that will come as a blow to those who have used toddlers' TV time as a chance to get dinner started, or just for a break. Michael Loman, executive producer of *Sesame Street*, notes: "We've found that children learn more when they talk about the show with adults." So make it a priority to do some of your viewing together, and plan some social viewing occasions that may relate to another experience, like *Hoop Dreams* after a basketball game or *Beethoven Lives Upstairs* before or after a concert or music lesson.

Helping Kids Become Critical Viewers

To help your kids get the most out of TV and video, you need to get them to become more "media literate"—to understand how programs are constructed and that television and video are businesses.

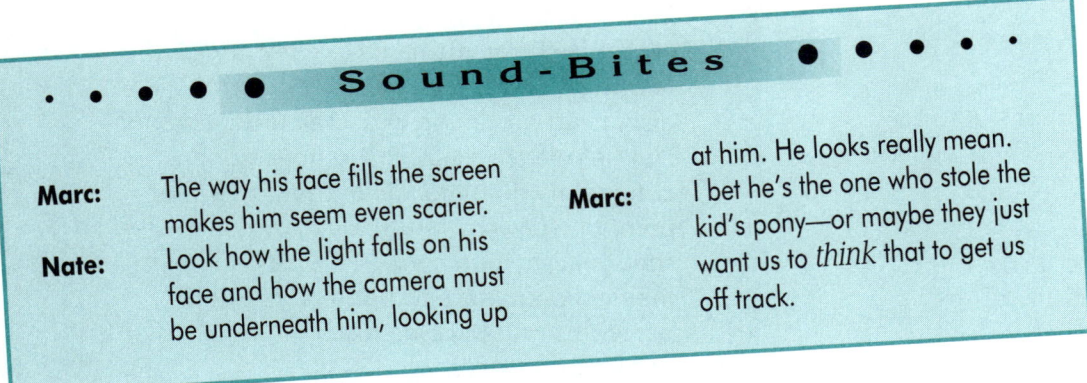

S o u n d - B i t e s

Marc: The way his face fills the screen makes him seem even scarier.

Nate: Look how the light falls on his face and how the camera must be underneath him, looking up

Marc: at him. He looks really mean. I bet he's the one who stole the kid's pony—or maybe they just want us to *think* that to get us off track.

When we help our kids learn how and why programs are produced, we enable them to be consciously involved in what they watch and invite their responses. Their understanding of

147

Father: Here's the tape I rented for you. You can watch while I make dinner.

Millie: Could you sit with me for a while? I feel like company. Just because I have a tape doesn't mean you can't be here, too.

the medium will enable them to question what's presented and may inspire them to produce their own media messages and programs. It may even summon their political instincts to get involved in today's dialogue about the role of government and industry in what's produced and shown.

> 66 When kids read and study literature, they learn about all the mechanics and artistry involved in writing. They can also learn to recognize these elements as they pertain to television and video. By watching and discussing programs with their kids, parents can help teach their kids to notice and critique the many facets of the art form— point of view, casting, subtext, directing style, script, music, and so on. Parents can help their children learn to appreciate good programs and become discerning, analytical viewers. 99
>
> *Kate Taylor*
> *Director of Children's Programming and Producer,*
> *WGBH, Boston PBS station*
> *Mother of three, ages 4, 13, and 16*

Granted, there's nothing like the pure pleasure of watching a good TV program or movie, enjoying your suspension of disbelief, traveling to other worlds, and meeting people through the electronic magic of it all—without analyzing everything you see. But it's also nice to have some inside knowledge about what makes the medium work so successfully.

Print is no longer our primary source of news and information. According to a study by Children Now, a media advocacy group in Oakland, California, on any given day 65 percent of children get their news from television, while only 44 percent read a newspaper. Television has long since taken over as our main channel of information—for parents as well as children. This brings us new obligations as parents. For instance, we parents need to assert ourselves publicly and call on the television and cable industries to provide a significant number of hours of quality children's programming. In addition, parents need to appeal to the government to make and enforce regulations ensuring that these industries meet their public interest mandate for children.

At home, we not only need to be involved in what, when, and how much our kids watch, but also help our kids learn how to "read" TV. When kids learn a few of the basics about how programs are produced, they become more critical viewers, better able to interpret media messages and benefit from a viewing experience, and less likely to be manipulated. These basics include an awareness of screen production techniques such as camerawork and editing, the ability to discriminate between fact and fiction, and an understanding that TV and video are businesses.

As a Matter of Fact...

According to the International Reading Association, the mind retains:
- 10 percent of what is read.
- 30 percent of what is heard.
- 50 percent of what is seen and heard.

The major proponents of media literacy define a media-literate person as one who has "the ability to access, analyze, evaluate, and produce communication in a variety of forms."

149

Programs are not purely mirrors of society or windows on the world but carefully constructed products, created for the most part by talented people. According to the Center for Media Literacy, there are three major parts of the media literacy movement:

1. *learning to balance or manage one's media "diet"*

2. *learning specific skills of critical viewing—that is, learning to analyze and question what's on the screen, how it's constructed, and what may have been left out. You can clue kids in to the construction of video communications by letting them know that:*

   • *a program reflects a point of view, and you don't have to agree;*

   • *if it's fictional, the program isn't "real," and that actors and everyone else involved are paid to tell a story—to make believe;*

   • *programs come in different forms or genres: information, news, and entertainment (comedy, drama, cartoons);*

   • *they have the power to:*

       —*figure out if what they're seeing is real*

       —*spot the production elements that convey the feeling*

       —*decide if they agree with the point of view*

       —*turn off the set if they don't like what's on*

       —*tape a program if the timing is inconvenient*

3. *critical or social analysis—who produced the media we experience and for what purpose? What are the political, economic, and social forces that converge to shape the cultural environment in which we live our lives?*

   • *movies and TV programs are created by professional craftspeople, talented in techniques such as sound, lighting, camerawork, editing, and special effects, and that their work is often meant to generate a mood or emotion;*

> • *programs make money by selling commercials to advertisers, who in turn make commercials to sell you their products; both the programs and commercials are made to appeal to the groups of people the advertiser wants to reach.*

Linda Ellerbee, producer of Nickelodeon's *Nick News,* said, "Media literacy education will make the difference between whether kids are tools of the mass media or whether mass media is a tool for kids to use. It's just that simple. Kids must be able to read and write, and they must be able to read TV."

Keep in mind that your kids' media literacy, like print literacy, will also depend on their ages and other developmental factors. Your 5-year-old may want to understand why some things look scary, but he probably won't worry (yet) about being in a target market. Your 12-year-old, on the other hand, will be fascinated to learn that advertisers have intentions for her disposable income.

There's a difference of opinion on whether it's appropriate to teach media literacy to kids. Some people feel TV's already too dominant in kids' lives, and we shouldn't devote any more time to it.

A report by the Carnegie Foundation for the Advancement of Teaching stated: "Next to parents, television is perhaps a child's most influential teacher." Echoing this on a show devoted to media literacy on National Public Radio's *Talk of the Nation,* Professor Henry Giroux of Penn State made the point that school is not the main educator of kids anymore; television is. He urged schools and parents to teach kids to navigate and critique what they watch. TV is part of our kids' lives whether they watch it four hours a day or four hours a month, so there's merit in helping them become media literate.

Personal Note
· · · · · · · · · · · · · · ·

Jane's son Noah, now in college, had an assignment in a high school course on pop culture that required him to log eighteen straight hours of TV ads from one selected station source. He was amazed at the quantity of junk that was on and the frequency of commercials. Sometimes a saturation diet is more telling than a starvation diet!

As a Matter of Fact...

Prior to kindergarten, the average child has seen 5,000 hours of TV.

We agree with the many interested organizations, such as the National PTA and the National Council of Churches, in recognizing the importance of media literacy programs because the media are powerful communication tools which deserve study. In addition to TV's general educational benefits is the reality that some kids learn better visually than from reading. Media literacy programs acknowledge these benefits and can help our kids' maximize their TV viewing, even as we seek to limit the viewing they do. See the Chapter 6 "Resources" section for organizations to contact to set up a media literacy program in your community or school.

Media literacy programs regularly acknowledge the "bottom line" motivation underlying TV and video programs. On broadcast and cable this means the advertiser is a key player. Kids need to be made aware that television is business, and commercials pay the freight. Media literacy programs focus on how advertisers seek to identify and reach a target audience and sell them a product. Kids become more aware of the structure of commercials, how products are presented and "positioned," and how some facts may be distorted or concealed to build credibility and invite the viewer's interest in a product.

An advantage of video is that (at least for now) children's videos don't include commercials, although they may carry ads for other tapes by the same supplier. However, videos are commercial vehicles, and it's important to make your kids aware of this. In fact, there are many elements to point out to the kids that reflect savvy business strategies on the part of video suppliers: product placement (productions often include shots of recognizable products in sets and scenes), print inserts (even coupons) with tapes, previews of other programs produced by the same studio, acknowledgments to advertisers in the credits. None of these tactics is necessarily harmful or inappropriate, but kids should recognize advertiser involvement. In fact, this more subtle advertiser presence can afford a small independent producer the extra dollars required to produce a good tape.

There are marketing strategies advertisers employ in video, just as they do in broadcast. Alert your kids to these ploys. For example, toys and products are often developed into videos, which then serve as a vehicle to license and merchandise more goodies for the kids to want and more reasons for them to tug at your purse strings. In a 1994 *TV Guide* issue on kids' shows, writer James Kaplan quoted Gary Krisel, president of Walt Disney Television Animation: "The toy companies will say, 'We'd like to have seven more characters and ten more vehicles.'" When their discussion turned to Disney's *Gargoyles* show, Krisel admitted that their consumer-products division was very active, and yet there were times when Kenner, which will be manufacturing the *Gargoyles* action toys, asked for expansions of cast and accouterments that Krisel claimed he resisted.

As a Matter of Fact...

The New York Times reported (10/8/95) that 55 percent of kids in a recent survey said they change the TV channel when a commercial comes on.

You can discuss these business aspects of the TV and video industries with your kids and remind them of the role advertisers and production companies play in determining what they produce. Together you can foster some healthy cynicism and enjoy talking back to the set during commercials. And whether or not your kids have the benefit of a media literacy program in their school, you can expand your kids' awareness of how programs are constructed to invite their interest, hold their attention, and influence their responses.

153

Extend the Viewing Experience

Make some of your viewing times also "doing times," and build in opportunities to follow up with a fun activity that relates to the program. Occasionally, a video will come with an activity-oriented print piece inserted in the sleeve, included by the producer as a value-added incentive. The suggested activities can reinforce the video's content, extending the viewing experience and inviting the viewer to come back again and again to view the tape. This is certainly true with how-to programs. For example, *Making Homemade Musical Instruments*

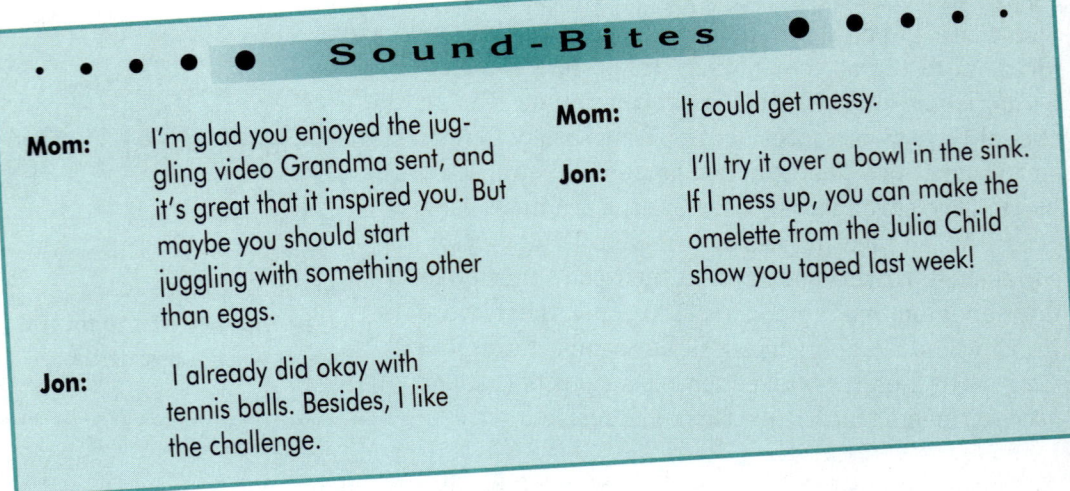

Sound-Bites

Mom: I'm glad you enjoyed the juggling video Grandma sent, and it's great that it inspired you. But maybe you should start juggling with something other than eggs.

Jon: I already did okay with tennis balls. Besides, I like the challenge.

Mom: It could get messy.

Jon: I'll try it over a bowl in the sink. If I mess up, you can make the omelette from the Julia Child show you taped last week!

offers onscreen recommendations of things from around the house, like an empty oatmeal box, that your kids can use to make a banjo. There are many choices featured in the tape and some simple steps for assembling the parts. The kids can follow the directions, and the tape remains a visual reference for repeated viewings when the kids want to start another project.

When no activity materials, lyric sheet, or story summaries are included, try to choreograph your own follow-up ideas. This isn't a make-work suggestion for parents or for projects that are more appropriate to school. Rather, it's an opportunity for more fun things to do together or to engage the kids in something entertaining when the TV is turned off.

Sound-Bites

Jenny:	Let's make the birdhouse that was in the video.	**Dad:**	Lumberyard.
Dad:	What do we need?	**Jenny:**	And some finish nails.
Jenny:	The card that came with the tape says we need some soft wood scraps, like pine or fir . . .	**Dad:**	Probably need to go to the lumberyard for those, too.
Dad:	Have to go to the lumberyard.	**Jenny:**	The tape should have been about going to the lumberyard. We'd be all set for the trip.
Jenny:	A dowel . . .		

Related Reading

Clip film and video reviews from the paper and magazines and save them for when the videos come out. Get the kids to read them after they've seen the video and see if they agree. Watch for articles in magazines and books that relate to subjects covered in favorite videos. And, of course, reading the book before the movie, or even after, is usually fun and interesting as a point of comparison. Many videos are literature-based, so reluctant readers may well be motivated to read the book after viewing the video.

Conversations and Reviews

Keep a book of family-written reviews and ratings of shows they've seen. Siskel and Ebert wannabes will enjoy the opportunity to be resident critics, and members of the family can enjoy reading each other's reviews. For further discussion, compare and contrast your home reviews with those you've clipped from magazines and newspapers.

News Story

Have your child read an article from the newspaper and tell the story to you in ninety seconds, the length of an average TV news story. What did they have to leave out? Use a big sporting event, a recent weather phenomena, or an appearance by the President as the source if you need a suggestion. You can also suggest they tell an original "news" story from an event in their experience.

As a Matter of Fact...

The average length of a television news story is ninety seconds.

Field Trips

Be creative about trips that can reinforce a particular video. For example, an aquarium visit after a film that features sea life or even after seeing an aquatic star like Shamu the whale can extend the viewing experience. Science and art museum visits can expand your kids' interest in many subjects and might be more acceptable if "triggered" by a video. Even grocery shopping can take on added meaning after seeing a cooking show.

How-to Activities

After watching cooking, gardening, or crafts shows, put together some materials from around the house that the kids can use to do their own projects.

Make Your Own Videos

If you have budding producers, directors, or writers in the house, encourage them to make their own videos. You can rent or borrow the equipment if you don't own it. And there are often local access cable production options in your community. Most cable companies' contracts with the cities they serve require they provide coverage of town meetings, local news and sporting events, and offer free community production facilities, along with training. Making videos is hands-on media literacy. It brings home the lessons of how programs are structured and how they reflect a point of view. But beyond media literacy, making videos is just plain fun. For a kid who keys in on the impact of music, suggest he or she use a tape recorder to make a soundtrack of music selections that evoke different emotions or enhance the drama or a scene. For kids who are in love with the production process, look for *Nickelodeon Director's Lab,* a CD-ROM video suite for making mini-TV productions, music videos, and cartoons. Another resource for kids is the *YO-TV Production Handbook* by the Educational Video Center. The guide takes kids through the steps of putting together a crew, writing, researching, shooting, editing, and even exhibiting a video program (see "Resources" section for details on ordering). Making flip books is a fun way for kids to follow up watching an animation special. It can be fun for kids to design their own video covers for shows they'd like to produce. If you begin to think along these lines, then the ideas are endless, and viewing can lead to doing.

TV time is most valuable when you preselect programs and when you monitor what goes on in front of the set—eating, talking, homework, chores, and other activities. By cultivating critical viewing skills in your kids, you're helping them develop into intelligent, discriminating viewers. So if you make TV watching a dedicated activity, plan ahead, and make an effort to watch together and understand the medium better, you will all appreciate the programs more fully. In addition, expanding viewing into related discussions or activities maximizes what the kids have watched. It takes an involved parent to orchestrate these valuable experiences for their kids and make TV a plus in their lives, but the rewards for you and your kids will be well worth it.

Family Activity

News at Six

Putting together a newscast involves a lot of decisions:

> Which story comes first?
>
> Which part of the story gets told?
>
> Which pictures of the story will you use?
>
> Which story gets the most time?

Try this with friends and family. Take turns being news anchor or reporter in the field.

You'll need:

a video camera

a desk, chair, and weather map

tape recorder or CD player for background music and sound effects

clock with second hand or a digital watch

news from: sports, family, neighborhood, front page

friends and or family who are game to participate

Pick an event and plan a thirty-second news report. Shoot it using props, music, and camera angles to enhance your presentation. Now give yourself a minute to present the same news story again, expanding your use of music, visuals, narrative, interviews.

Play back your pieces and talk about how time influenced your news reports and how the props, music, camera angles, and other elements affected your presentations and your audience's reactions.

Just the Ticket to Talk

How Videos Can Trigger Meaningful Discussion

To rent Shakespeare or not to rent Shakespeare, that is the question...

Video presents exciting opportunities to pass along values, exchange ideas, and open doors to the hearts and minds of our kids. Video certainly isn't the only way in, but it's an excellent way to start a dialogue.

In this chapter, we'll see how a movie or special-interest title can help you to "jump-start" nonthreatening discussions by the familiar glow of the TV screen. As a catalyst for discussing difficult topics or important values, video can make for memorable conversations. Keeping the focus on the screen and not on the viewers can make kids feel safer about discussing loaded or threatening issues. But don't expect the family to launch automatically into a fascinating discussion as soon as the credits roll. You need to set the stage and try to spark discussion with a question or comment. Anything that seems too planned or puts the kids on the spot is likely to send them running.

When you ask, "What did you do in school today?" do your youngsters answer, "Nothing"? Then you're amazed to hear them respond with the correct answers to the history or literature questions on *Jeopardy!* Or you sit down together to watch a show about an immigrant family, and the kids will say they read the story in class. Then they mention a newcomer to the class

Tune In the Topics

- Using Video Strategically
- Video and Values
- Take Advantage of Video to Tackle Sensitive Topics
- Using Tapes to Tap Special Interests
- How You Ask and How You Listen Make the Difference in What They Tell You
- Family Activity: Pitch Your Idea

161

who shared her experiences and feelings about being the butt of prejudice. If you join the kids to watch, listen carefully and you will often find ways to introduce questions or subjects so naturally they won't realize they're being "pumped."

In this chapter, we suggest ways you can take advantage of video to address topics you'd like to discuss or values you'd like to impart. We also provide some examples of titles that present attributes you may want to foster in your children, life experiences you seek to discuss with them, and activities and special interests to which you want to expose them. Even for issues that often are hard to talk about, you may find video can offer a backstage pass to what concerns or interests your kids.

Using Video Strategically

You can also use video to trigger discussions on values and ethical issues, enhance your kids' interests, and also to help them through tough times, for example in dealing with stressful life experiences like divorce or a family move.

• • • • • **S o u n d - B i t e s** • • • • •

Mom 1: Eric just called. His fish died today. He loved that fish . . . there's going to be some crying tonight.

Mom 2: Last year, when Lucy's parakeet died, I found this great video on pets that dealt with the death of a favorite pet. She must have watched that video fifty times. I'll bring it to you tomorrow.

Mom 1: In the meantime, what'll I do? I planned on making fish for dinner!

Introducing Topics and Issues

Sometimes you need to strategically select a program on a topic you want to talk about. Other times, it's a matter of having your antennae up to take advantage of what the kids are already watching . . . to pick up on elements like a character's behavior, subplots, or the writer's point of view. Or course, every time you sit down to watch something with your kids there needn't be a curriculum or hidden agenda. But many viewing experiences can open up opportunities for learning and personal growth, with video as the stimulus.

TIP

Watch a video together to introduce topics or issues.

Video is a comfortable medium for kids, making it possible to discuss sensitive topics like divorce, sexual mores, and ethical issues more objectively, leaving the door open to talk on a more personal level as well. Just avoid making the exchanges teachy or confrontational.

Imparting Information

Video resources on topics you'd like to introduce to your kids can be found in books, compendiums, and magazine articles. Columnists occasionally suggest videos to supplement their subject, so look for video resources listed in articles on topics you'd like to introduce to your kids. If you're reading an article about kids and the homework battle, for example, you may be surprised to discover there's an array of videos for kids on that very subject.

If you keep blank tapes near the VCR, you can pop one in and record a broadcast or cable program that speaks to something you think will be of interest to your kids. Coming up are lists of suggested videos to trigger discussions on: attributes you want to foster, life experiences, and worthwhile pursuits.

163

Priming Them for Upcoming Cultural Experiences

For younger kids, there are many opportunities to use videos to preview plays, music, even art and artists in museums the family is planning to visit. This will give you a chance to address some of the themes and issues raised before going to see the performance. For example, if there's a local production of *The Sound of Music*, renting the movie ahead can introduce the kids to the characters, the subject of the war, and situations like the eldest Trapp daughter having a boyfriend in the Gestapo. The kids should find the theater experience even more meaningful after this preview and exchange.

Personal Notes
• • • • • • • • • • • • • • •

Jane, husband Jerry, and their teenagers were five days into a rained-out beach vacation. After reading, bowling, board (and bored) games, and window shopping, Mom and Dad, baby boomers who met in film school, suggested what they hoped would prove a fascinating combination viewing for the family—Francis Ford Coppola's Apocalypse Now *and Eleanor Coppola's* Hearts of Darkness, *a documentary about the making of the film. Besides being an excellent behind-the-scenes view of filmmaking,* Hearts of Darkness *is quite a study of Coppola's ego and how it affected the production, the cast and crew, and his family. It raises ethical issues concerning responsibility, creative control, and more. Everyone enjoyed the short and the feature, and both videos sparked a dynamic family dialogue, lasting well into the evening.*

Complementing a Family Viewing of a Longer-Format Program or Film

Short subjects can be great ingredients to spice an evening's viewing and trigger interesting dialogues. You can try documentaries, pretaped news clips, feature stories time-shifted from informational shows, how-to videos, and shorts. Combining some shorter material with feature-format shows can complement the subject of the main program by offering another perspective on the subject or a counterpoint. Using some creativity in planning a

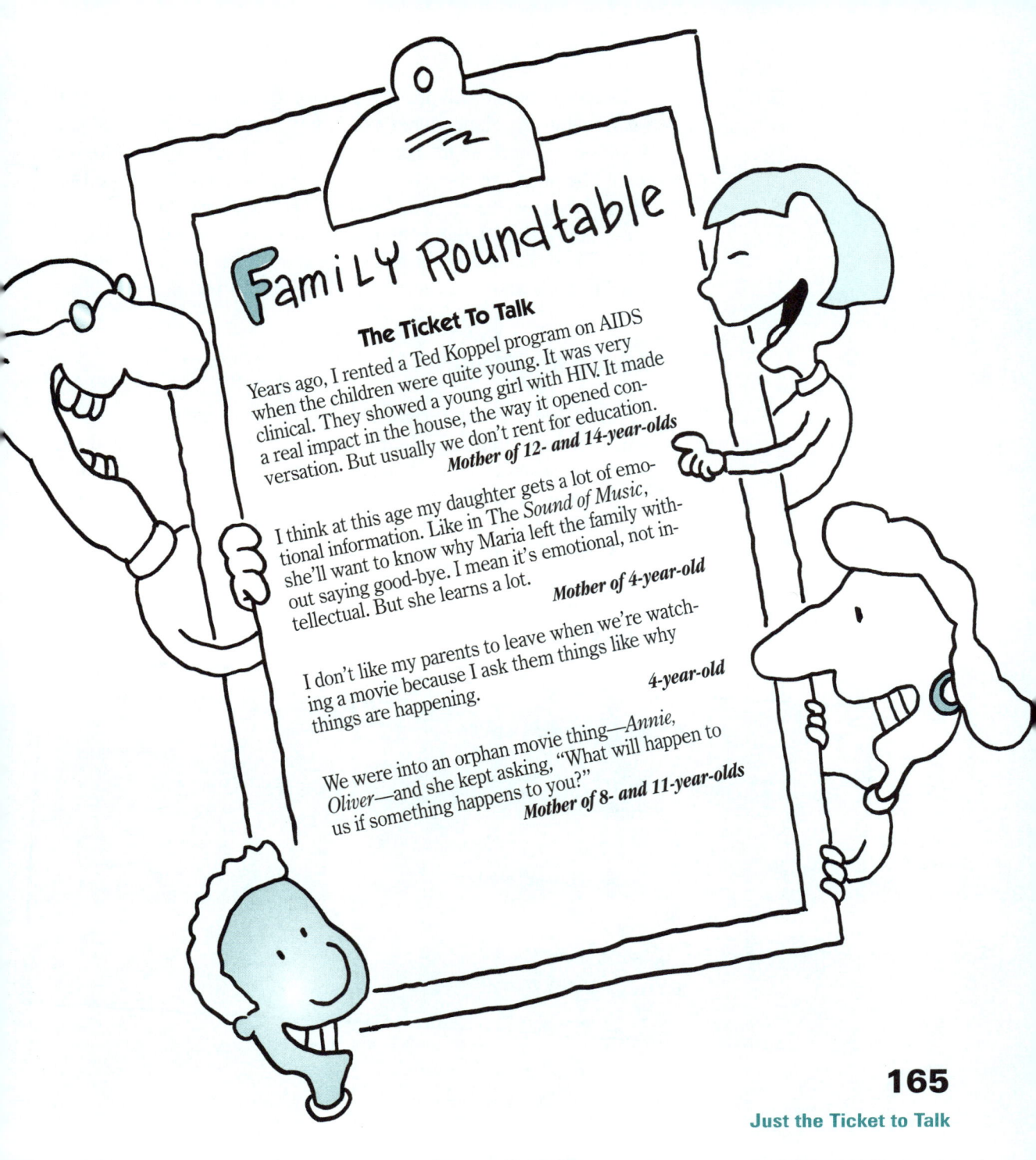

Family Roundtable

The Ticket To Talk

Years ago, I rented a Ted Koppel program on AIDS when the children were quite young. It was very clinical. They showed a young girl with HIV. It made a real impact in the house, the way it opened conversation. But usually we don't rent for education.
Mother of 12- and 14-year-olds

I think at this age my daughter gets a lot of emotional information. Like in The *Sound of Music*, she'll want to know why Maria left the family without saying good-bye. I mean it's emotional, not intellectual. But she learns a lot.
Mother of 4-year-old

I don't like my parents to leave when we're watching a movie because I ask them things like why things are happening.
4-year-old

We were into an orphan movie thing—*Annie*, *Oliver*—and she kept asking, "What will happen to us if something happens to you?"
Mother of 8- and 11-year-olds

viewing sequence will provide an opportunity for a different kind of viewing experience when the family is together. For example, a news segment about recent research on teens and smoking could be added to the evening's viewing of a 1950s classic that deals with teenagers, like *Rebel Without a Cause.* Or perhaps a news show did a behind-the-scenes piece on a recently released film. Tape it and save it for when the film is out in video . . . you'll have a short subject to go with the feature.

Video and Values

Helping kids learn right from wrong is a major task for parents. In fact, there's a library of books, from the Bible and the Greek classics to an avalanche of new publications, responding to this age-old challenge of imparting values to our children. Recent publications on values number close to a dozen, including a bestseller. But Roger Rosenblatt, writing in *The New York Times Magazine,* cautions about these new books: "Few of these works are especially learned or revealing except about the troubled public feeling they tap."

• • • • • Sound-Bites • • • • •

Mom: I rented *To Kill a Mockingbird* for you for the weekend.

Claudia: Thanks, Mom, but we saw that in school after we finished the book.

Mom: So what did you think about it? I mean, wasn't Atticus Finch a great lawyer?

Claudia: Better than O.J.'s. At least he had heart. Gotta go to Anna's to work on our extra-credit project. I'll be back by dinner. By the way, Mom, you asked me the same question when I finished the book.

Why has this long-standing interest in children and values taken on such heightened importance today? A variety of factors have combined to tug at the family. Today's kids contend with many stresses—less time with parents and more responsibilities. Front-page headlines, news soundbites on the radio, and images on TV chisel away at our kids' innocence. The media's focus on scandals and fallen heroes from sports, government, even religion can cultivate an early cynicism in our kids. To top it all off, kids learn early on that the economy no longer promises that schooling and hard work will translate to a rewarding job, a house, and the American dream of "having it all."

It's no wonder that kids are often cynical, confused, and pessimistic. Standards, once defined by clearly articulated values and monitored by parents and the community, have become elusive. In today's information society our kids have almost unlimited access to input from an unprecedented array of media that show a world of conflicting values. No longer are the family and immediate community our children's only moral influences. It's sobering to realize that today's children spend far more time listening to the voices on TV than in conversation with their own parents.

While TV can be a boon, it can also open the door to inappropriate information—words and images kids may not be ready to receive. The people who produce and sell the news, talk shows, sitcoms, and docudramas don't share a consistent worldview to pass down to the younger generation. More to the point, most of them don't acknowledge a responsibility to hold their programs up to a moral yardstick. In fact, the range of acceptable codes of conduct in society itself, which TV both reflects and influences, makes it difficult to promote common values for children.

As a Matter of Fact...

Parents spend on average less than 40 minutes per week in meaningful conversation with their children, while children spend 1,680 minutes per week watching TV.

167

The Media Aren't the Only Problem and Can Even Be a Solution

A 1995 *New York Times* poll on popular culture revealed that Americans blame television more than any other single factor for teenage sex and violence. But it's simplistic to point a finger only at TV, since our kids live in a world crowded with influences, including media, parents, policymakers and advertisers.

As acknowledged, the media have certainly perpetuated the message that all is not right with the world, often resulting in the deflation of kids' motivation to be the best they can be. Educator Peter Gibbon, in a 1993 *Newsweek* article, observed: "We have traded exemplary lives and heroes for information, irony, and reality. . . . My generation was raised on *The Adventures of Ozzie and Harriet*. My students watch *Married with Children*. We admired Rock Hudson and even thought that was his name; my students know he died of AIDS. . . . We listened to preachers like Billy Graham. They were amused by Tammy and Jimmy. I liked Elvis Presley. They like him, too, but they know he died bloated and drug-infected."

But it remains important to keep perspective on the impact of the media alone. James Halloran, director of the Centre for Mass Communication Research at the University of Leicester, reminds us how easy a target the media can be: "The attack on television does not really represent a new phenomenon. Throughout history, technological innovations in communication have been received with hostility. . . . What people are saying now about television has been said before by their forebears about films, comics, magazines, and

As a Matter of Fact...

- Television is sending kids mixed messages about the moral condition of society. According to a report by Children Now, what young people see on TV makes them think people are mostly dishonest (49 percent), care more about money than about people (54 percent), are selfish (46 percent), and talk back to their parents (51 percent). On the other hand, kids also report that what they see on TV makes them think people take responsibility for their actions (54 percent) and have generally good morals (61 percent).

- A survey of youngsters found that 82 percent said television should help teach kids right from wrong.

the press." Though the media are not solely to blame for having a negative impact on kids' perceptions and values, we still need to hold producers, distributors, and exhibitors responsible for having a conscience about what they present. There's just too much information out there for parents alone to monitor and screen.

William Damon reassures us in *The Moral Child* that ethical development is part of a child's normal growing up and that children constantly think about moral dilemmas in the course of their daily lives. He concludes that we need to engage kids in discussions that give them opportunities to reason things out. We need to expose them to lives that reflect moral commitment because they will not learn simply by being told.

As a Matter of Fact...

A 1995 study on how children are portrayed on entertainment television found that "few role models are presented to help teach children how to handle the many important social and family problems they face in real life, with surprisingly few shows offering examples of children coping with such problems." On commercial broadcast networks, a majority of the child characters are seen involved in antisocial behavior, which often yields positive results for them.

Extending Damon's work to video means that by watching selected videos together, we can expose children to good examples and discuss what we've viewed. TV and video *can* have a positive effect. Since the medium has proven so powerful, especially with young and impressionable minds, why not put it to good use? With the VCR, you can choose from a cornucopia of video products to address the values you believe in and want to pass along to your kids. As author and psychiatrist Robert Coles notes: "If a moral life has strength and coherence, the movies aren't likely (at their worst) to topple things. At their best, they can prompt . . . ethically charged reveries."

To give an idea of how videos can model certain values and trigger discussion, we offer this general list of some of our own favorites. We've coupled these viewing suggestions with the values we as parents believe can build character and contribute to rearing sensitive, caring beings. Many of our suggestions for

169

movies and TV programs converted to home video are likely to be available in your video store. For the harder-to-find programs produced exclusively for home video, we've included the names of distributors and suppliers and the target ages indicated for those titles. The chapter's "Resources" section includes supplier addresses. Always keep in mind your own kids' ages and development when selecting what's appropriate for them to view.

Attributes to Foster and Videos That Help

Respect for cultural diversity and ethnic pride

African Journey (Wonderworks)
Big Bird in China
Big Bird in Japan
Chanuka at Bubba's (Monterey Home Video)
Dances with Wolves
Glory
The House of Dier Drear 6–14 (Public Media)
Lilies of the Field
The Milagro Beanfield War
Pepito's Dream
Pow Wow Highway
Stories from the Black Tradition 5–14 (Children's Circle)

Civic responsibility and democracy in action

Advise & Consent
All the President's Men
American Dream
Brother's Keeper
The Candidate
First Monday in October
Gandhi
It's a Wonderful Life
The Last Hurrah

Mr. Smith Goes to Washington
Norma Rae

Concern for the environment

Dawn Saves the Trees (The Babysitters Club) 6–10 (A*Vision/Kidvision)
Eco, You, and Simon, Too 2–6 (3E Communications)
50 Simple Things Kids Can Do to Save the Earth (CBS Schoolbreak
   Special—David Eagle)
Free Willy
Gift of the Whales (Miramar)
Never Cry Wolf
Shamu & You (Video Treasures)
You Can't Grow Home Again (Children's Television Workshop)

Courage and perseverance

Children of a Lesser God
The Diary of Anne Frank
Gandhi
Marie
The Secret of NIMH
Silkwood
The Terry Fox Story

Fair play

The Human Race Club 6–8 (Just for Kids)
The Lean Mean Machine
Searching for Bobby Fischer

Friendship

The Berenstain Bears and the Trouble with Friends 3–6 (Random House)
Bridge to Terabithia 10–14 (Public Media)

Charlotte's Web
A Cricket in Times Square 3–6 (Family Home Entertainment fhe)
The Fair-Weather Friend—The Human Race Club (Just for Kids)
Goonies
Stand by Me
Winnie the Pooh's Making Friends 3–7 (Walt Disney Home Video)

Handling jealousy

All About Eve
The Little Mermaid
Madeline and the Dog Show 3–6 (Sony)

Honesty

A Boy's Life
King of the Hill
Pinocchio

Imagination

Beetlejuice
The Electric Grandmother 6–10 (LCA)
Gryphon 6–14 (Public Media)
Imagine That! 3–6 (Golden Book Videos)
The Little Prince (The Will Vinton Collection) 3–6 (Golden Book Video)
The Nightmare Before Christmas
Tucker, The Man and His Dream

Importance of family

On Golden Pond
The Railway Children 6–10 (Thorn EMI)
A Raisin in the Sun
Swiss Family Robinson
A Tree Grows in Brooklyn

Integrity
- Dead Poets Society
- Guess Who's Coming to Dinner
- Inherit the Wind
- The Long Walk Home
- Mr. Deeds Goes to Town

Loyalty
- Homeward Bound
- The Incredible Journey
- Stand by Me

Respect between the sexes
- Adam's Rib
- Annie Oakley
- Berenstain Bears—No Girls Allowed 3–8 (Random House)
- Free to Be . . . You and Me (fhe)
- Woman's Place 8–14 (VIEW Video)

Taking care of your body
- Baby's First Workout up to age 3 (HPG Home Video)
- Funhouse Fitness: The Funhouse Funk 6–10 (Warner Home Video)
- Workout with Daddy and Me 3–6 (fhe)

Taking initiative
- Sounder
- Stand and Deliver
- Where the Red Fern Grows

Taking risks for growth
- Breaking Away
- The Dark Horse

Europa Europa
The Little Engine That Could 3–6 (MCA)

Understanding handicaps

Best Boy
Dominick and Eugene
The Mask
The Miracle Worker
My Left Foot
Rain Man
Stanley & Iris
Walking on Air 10–13 (Public Media)

Whatever values you want to explore, there is probably a video to help you in your effort.

Take Advantage of Video to Tackle Sensitive Topics

You can use video to offer perspective and solace during stressful life experiences. Divorce, death, moving, sibling rivalry, changing schools, and making friends are issues that require real-life skills to handle well. Unfortunately, these issues are easy to avoid because they're so loaded for everyone involved and they create unusual stress. Even with the best intentions to help kids deal with issues directly, parents, teachers, or other concerned adults can go overboard by overly directing a discussion or placing too much emphasis on their own experiences. This often leaves little room for kids to process what's going on and compare it to other kids' experiences in similar circumstances. Here, an appropriate video can

174

Mom 1: This video about having a new baby in the house is supposed to be for 2–4-year-olds, but my 7-year-old has watched it over and over. You know, Alex hardly talked about his feelings about Megan for the whole first year she was here, but this tape suddenly got him talking about his anger and resentment when she first arrived and all the ups and downs and changes that came with having another person in the family. Can you believe it? He's been sitting on that stuff for a whole year, and we thought everything went so smoothly for him.

Mom 2: Hey, I never got over my brother's arrival, and he's going to be fifty in April. Do you think Alex would let me borrow the tape?

fill the bill and diffuse the directness of a "planned talk" that older kids, in particular, can find awkward.

If you do choose a program to help kids through a stressful or difficult experience, watch it with them or be around when they're done watching. Ask open-ended questions, like those suggested later in this chapter that will invite your kids to share their own thoughts and experiences.

Here are some programs we suggest you try for life transitions and times of conflict.

Life Experiences and Companion Videos

Bedtime

Baby's Bedtime Stories to Remember (Sony)
Bedtime Stories 3–6 (Random House)
Ira Sleeps Over 3–6 (fhe—Family Home Entertainment)
The Land of Pleasant Dreams 2–6 (Bridgestone)

Coming of age

Anne of Green Gables
Biloxi Blues
Empire of the Sun
Hope and Glory
A Tree Grows in Brooklyn

Death

Bridge to Terabithia 10–14 (Public Media)
The Fig Tree 6+ (Public Media)
The Little Princess
Old Yeller

Drugs/alcohol

Cartoon All-Stars to the Rescue 6–10 (Disney)
Nightmare on Drug Street 10–14
A Tree Grows in Brooklyn

*Family changes—new sibling/remarriage/family move/divorce/
aging relatives*

Cocoon
Driving Miss Daisy

Fried Green Tomatoes

Hey, What About Me? 2–7 (KIDVIDZ)

Let's Get a Move On! 4–12 (KIDVIDZ)

Mrs. Doubtfire

Necessary Parties 6 + (Public Media)

Sometimes I Wonder 3–8 (Media Ventures)

When Mom and Dad Break Up 6–10 (Paramount)

Fears/courage

The Berenstain Bears in the Dark 2–8 (Random House)

Home Alone

Talks About Dinosaurs and Monsters

The Wizard of Oz

Illness/hospital stay

The Adventures of Jimmy, Judy and AC (Baldacci Productions)

Mr. Rogers

Sesame Street Visits the Hospital

Peer pressure

The Human Race Club 6–8 (Just for Kids)

Lord of the Flies (1963 version)

The Outsiders

Pretty in Pink

Stand by Me

School issues—new school/social difficulty at school

Getting Ready for School (Random House Home Video)

Preschool Power 3–6 (Concept Videos)

Who Will Be My Friend? 3–6 (Golden)

Sex

The Miracle of Life (Crown)
What Kids Want to Know About Sex and Growing Up 8–12 (Pacific Arts)
What's Happening to Me? 10–16 (Starmaker)
Where Did I Come From? 6–10 (Starmaker)

Sibling rivalry

Jacob Have I Loved
The Parent Trap

Using Tapes to Tap Special Interests

You can use special-interest videos to interest your kids in subjects you'd like them to explore, like sailing or gardening, to introduce them to people you'd like them to encounter, like violinist Itzhak Perlman, and to tap the values exemplified by different experiences, like the satisfaction of working with one's hands.

> ● ● ● ● ● Sound-Bites ● ● ● ● ● ●
>
> **Mom:** Eddie, come see this low-cal cooking video I rented. They're making some delicious snacks.
>
> **Eddie:** What, tofu-and-yogurt cakes? Fishsicles? Seaweed snaps? Do they have lima bean salsa?
>
> **Mom:** No, but maybe you should have your own cooking show.

178

Many of us would love our kids to try hobbies and activities we ourselves have never experienced, and video is an opportunity to introduce these experiences and get a little background, too. Here are some suggestions.

TIP

Show a video to introduce topics and issues.

Worthwhile Experiences

Appreciation of animals

Animal Babies Just Want to Have Fun up to 3 (Karl/Lorimar Home Video)
Animals Are Beautiful People (Warner)
Baby Animals
Born Free
Farm Animals (Music for Little People)
National Velvet
Paws, Claws, Feathers, and Fins 4–10 (KIDVIDZ)
Ring of Bright Water

Nutrition and exercise

Fun Fit with Mary Lou Retton 6 and up (Warner)
Hip-Hop Animal Rock 6–11 (PolyGram)
Tip-Top with Suzy Prudden, Vol 1 & 2 3–6 and 7+ (Warner)

Cultural experiences

Beethoven Lives Upstairs 5–12 (The Children's Group)
Don't Eat the Pictures 2–7 (Random House)
Jazztime Tale (fhe)
The Red Shoes

Enjoying the outdoors

Bugs Don't Bug Us 18 mos.–6 (Bo Peep Productions)
Get Ready, Get Set, Grow! 6+ (Brooklyn Botanical Gardens)

Exploring one's creativity

Be a Cartoonist 8–11 (Random House)
Look What I Made 6–10 (MCA Home Video)
Richard Scarry's Rainy Day
Shari Lewis Presents 101 Things for Kids to Do 3–6 (Random House)
Squiggles, Dots, & Lines 5–12 (KIDVIDZ)

Introducing people and events

The Bridge on the River Kwai
The Buddy Holly Story
Glory
Good Morning, Vietnam

The environment

Captain Planet and the Planeteers 6–12 (Turner Home Entertainment)
Help Save Planet Earth 8–18 (MCA/Universal)

Learning about the real world

Kids Get Cooking 5–12 (KIDVIDZ)
Miniature Miracle: The Computer Chip (National Geographic)
Piggy Banks to Money Markets 5–12 (KIDVIDZ)

Doing individual sports

Cycling for Success 12 and up (Fox Hills/Media)
Karate for Kids 6–10 (Bright Ideas Productions)
New Games for the Whole Family (Dale N. LeFevre)

Doing team sports

Play Ball with Reggie Jackson 7–12 (ESPN)
Reach for the Skies with Spud Webb 8–12 (Sony Wonder/SVS)

180

Reading for pleasure

The Chronicles of Narnia 7+ (Public Media)
The 5,000 Fingers of Dr. T.
Reading Rainbow
Shelley Duvall's Bedtime Stories 3–6 (MCA)
Stories to Remember 4–11 (Lightyear Entertainment)
20,000 Leagues Under the Sea

Holidays

Animated Hagaddah (Scopus Films—London—Ltd.)
Charlie Brown Thanksgiving
Eyes on the Prize (Blackside Productions)
Miracle on 34th Street
The Nightmare Before Christmas
Snowman (CC Studios)
The Speeches of Martin Luther King, Jr. (MPI)
The Ten Commandments

Working with one's hands

Don't Wake Your Mom 3–10 (A&M)
JuggleTime 5–12 (JuggleBug)
Look What I Grew: Windowsill Gardens 6–10
Making and Playing Homemade Instruments 6–14 (Homespun)

How You Ask and How You Listen Make the Difference in What They Tell You

There are ways to talk to kids that can turn them on instead of turning them off. We can ask nonthreatening questions which open discussion instead of ending it. For example, after watching a movie character steal something, ask,

Do you think he made the right decision?
Or
It looks like she didn't think she had any other choice.

Sound-Bites

Allen: What a put-down. I mean, the kid in that show works his butt off to earn the money to buy those shoes, and then that other kid says they're nerdy.

Dad: So are you saying he should have bought the other style?

Allen: It's not like the shoes are going to make him popular or anything. I mean, he's not very cool. He should've saved his money or done something else with it. He should get the shoes he likes; he can make his own style. What's "in" all changes so fast anyway. This week one pair of shoes is the big deal, next week it's a special book bag, after that it's something else. You practically need to win the lottery to keep up.

Dad: You're pretty cool to be onto the game.

The trick is not to shut down conversation by offering opinionated and critical responses to your kids' comments about what they've watched. Be supportive of their views and open to their comments about what they're watching. This will involve them without intimidating them.

Lenny: *That kid in that scene looks dorky.*

Dad:

Response A: *Don't be silly. He seems pretty nice.*

Response B: *He obviously didn't impress you. What makes you think he's dorky?*

Response B acknowledges Lenny's viewpoint and asks him to explain how he came to it.

Monica:	*That girl Julie in the film we saw yesterday should've made the team. She's a way better athlete than Mandy what's-her-name.*
Dad:	
Response A:	*No way. Julie's a good athlete, but she skipped practice. She didn't deserve to make the team.*
Response B:	*Mandy seemed like a team player. She was pretty sensitive to the other kids at the tryouts, and the coach character said she didn't miss any practices.*

Response A negates Monica's take on the situation, but in Response B, her dad points to positive aspects of the girl who did make the team.

When you phrase questions and generate discussions with your kids, offer nonjudgmental observations and avoid making dead-end comments that shut down a conversation. Instead, share your own feelings and provide accurate information. For example:

Bill:	*"Cool motorbike!"*
Mom:	
Comment A:	*Motorbikes are so unsafe. I don't know why they have shots of kids tooling around on them. I'd be horrified to think you'd ever do anything like that.*
Comment B:	*I worry about motorbikes. I've read that thousands of kids are injured on them every year.*

Comment B doesn't make Bill feel defensive and refers to factual information that backs your fears.

183

Randy:	I want a puppy like the one in the show.
Mom:	
Response A:	They're too much work. Be happy with your fish.
Response B:	I know you do, and he's so cute. But the family in the show had a big yard, and the father works at home. They obviously could deal with the time and attention a puppy takes.

Response B acknowledges Randy's feelings but also gets him thinking about the feelings of the puppy!

The art of discussion after a video is not to put the kids on the spot by relating it to their own experiences. Give them time and space to think about your comments, to process them and feel comfortable about responding. Judy Price, vice president for Children's Programming at CBS, recognizes how TV can trigger meaningful talk: "It can be a way to get your kids to open up with things they're not comfortable discussing in the first person. . . . We have to show up to help them complete the experience. Otherwise, we're dropping the ball in a big way."

Where your child is in his or her development is also a factor in phrasing your comments and questions. Young children

> **"** It is important for parents to watch a range of television programming with their kids and even more important to discuss what they see. This gives parents a chance to offer some guidance as kids begin to shape their taste, values and critical thinking skills about the medium. **"**
>
> **Kate Taylor**
> Director of Children's Programming and Producer,
> WGBH, Boston PBS station
> Mother of three children, ages 4, 13, and 16

relate most everything to their own experiences and think concretely, so they're more apt to respond to questions and comments based on what they know. But older kids can generalize to other people's lives, so you can talk to them more abstractly. Here are two examples of comments you might offer if you took these developmental differences into account when watching *E.T.,* during the scene where the kids hide E.T. in the closet.

> Comment to your 4-year-old:
> *What would you have done with ET?*

> Comment to your 11-year-old:
> *Boy, the big brother took all the responsibility on himself by going along with the younger kids and hiding E.T. from his mom. Sometimes it's hard to know what to do.*

Try to pursue these dialogues in an open-ended, nonconfrontational ways so your kids will feel a secure and welcome context to share their feelings and opinions. Whether it's basic values or treasured life experiences you want to pass along, or major life hurdles to surmount, keep in mind what Joy Overbeck offered in a *TV Guide* article: "Television can jump-start difficult discussions, helping parents give their kids the guidance they need in their bewildering crossing from childhood to adulthood."

Family Activity

Pitch Your Idea

Do you get antsy on long car rides and every ten minutes wind up asking, "When are we gonna be there?" Try this game to help the time sail by. Become a producer and try to get the studio executives to support the show you want to make. The producer is the driving force behind a video. Her responsibilities include overseeing the budget, casting, music, and shooting and editing processes.

You'll need:

4 packs of different-colored index cards
 I color is for names of familiar
  characters from films and programs
 I color is for motivations for
  characters to take some action
 I color is for conflict, or tension that
  drives the story theme
 I color is for locations

Each person chooses one card from each color pack and combines them to present a concept for a film or program. Make your idea funny or dramatic and try to convince the group to back your show. You might find yourself working up an idea that has

Who
Casper the Friendly Ghost

Where
in New York

Theme, conflict, or tension
driving a cab (Unfortunately, no one can see him at the wheel and he has trouble getting customers.)

Motivation
to earn money for the homeless.

After everyone's presentations, vote on the show that should get produced. Just be sure no one votes for their own show.

8 Telefuture Is Here

The New Media

Even as we adjust to the impact of TV and video, we're dynamically fast-forwarding to new videolike formats and information and entertainment delivery systems, mostly by way of the computer. All of a sudden, parents have more than the TV and VCR to monitor. The menu of choice includes CD-ROM, pay-per-view cable, satellite dishes, and perhaps the most promising, online services such as America Online, Prodigy, and CompuServe, with access to the Internet and World Wide Web. The infinite variety of programming delivered through this medley of media brings up a whole new set of what, when, and how much decisions.

"It might be the new media but it's going to be old by the time I get my turn."

This chapter provides an overview of the new media options—the hardware and the programming, the benefits of investing time and money in introducing them into your home, the concerns you need to address in deciding what's appropriate, and the when and how much of it all.

How to plan the most meaningful itinerary for our kids as they travel through the electronic universe? Today's children have been born into the computer culture. The rest of us, according to Sherry Turkle, author of *Life on the Screen,* are no more than naturalized citizens. Many of us don't even know what "cyberspace" is, but some of our kids are already at home in the wired world of online communication. Kids' facility with computers has given them control, and some parents may feel

Tune In the Topics

- Surveying the New Media Landscape
- New Game, New (and Old) Rules: Concerns and How to Avoid Them
- Shopping the New Media
- The Integrated TV: You Screen, I Screen, We All Screen—But Which Screen?
- Family Activity: Plan Your Own Video Game

left behind on the high-tech highway. Even the most computer-savvy among us are stymied by the same issues that have surfaced regarding video and TV viewing. And new issues concerning privacy and etiquette have accompanied the new media.

The following pages consider the parental prerogatives of limit setting discussed earlier in relation to the new media, and in light of a new set of issues: parents' inability (due to lack of knowledge or time) to sample what's available and to accommodate these added options into the family's busy life. Sampling a CD-ROM or previewing a video may give you a handle on what your child's experience will be like. Online, however, is always new, depending where your child may choose to go, so you can never know all the available experiences without being there at every moment—even with "parental controls" in place.

If you're intimidated by new media jargon, hardware, software, and protocols, read on and chill out. You'll find that managing your kids' computer experiences, like managing their video viewing, boils down to the same old parenting story.

Surveying the New Media Landscape

Your kids are growing up in a world of computers and new technology. They've probably experienced computers and online communications in school, at a museum, at the local Boys and Girls Clubs, or at their friends' houses, so you'll want to get up to speed. There are even new media arcades and "cybercafés" (like Cybersmith in Cambridge, Massachusetts) with banks of computer terminals sporting menus of software and online options you can choose from, with charges by the minute. Initially technically forbidding, scarce, and expensive, computers are now so user-friendly and affordable that millions of households are learning to learn to talk the talk and walk the walk.

TIP

Read magazine articles, peruse the books, and visit museums, libraries, and cybercafés or computer stores to familiarize yourself with the multimedia options now available, even if your present pocketbook can't afford them.

66 *I am 150 percent behind my children being computer literate. I have no doubt that when our daughter who's still at home is an adult, the world won't function on a paper level, so she might as well learn how to get around computers now. Besides, there are terrific games and educational CD-ROMs like Oregon Trail which add a creative twist to the learning experience.* 99

Bob Vila
*TV personality/host
and correspondent on NBC's* Today *show
Father of three, ages 10, 16, and 19*

Benefits: The Feel-Good-About-It Part

The biggest incentive to get us moving from scratch pad to mouse pad is to appreciate that the computer represents a wonderful opportunity for education through technology because it can approximate most closely the way we learn—interactively. In her book *Mind & Media: The Effects of Television, Video Games, and Computers,* Patricia Marks Greenfield recognized back in 1984 that the computer is favored over TV by children because it's programmable, interactive, and dynamic.

The introduction of each new medium promises a host of unique capabilities to deliver more exciting experiences than the media that came before. Radio made the spoken word come alive in broadcast dramas and instantaneous news reporting. When television appeared, it took over as the medium for drama and entertainment, and radio specialized in what it does best—music and news. Lloyd Morrisett, president of the Markle Foundation, which funds the use of communications and information technology for social benefit, notes multimedia's capacity to integrate formats and present an array of information in one place:

> *Before multimedia, the Shakespearean play was on television and the book was in the library; the soap opera on television and the synopsis of past episodes available over the telephone; the symphony was on the stereo, the score printed, and notations were in a book. In the world of multimedia all of these and more will be available on the electronic screen to be called up when the producer or user deems it necessary.*

As the platform for multimedia, the computer integrates and displays sound, print, video, photographs, and graphics in programs that give the user the opportunity to branch off in a variety of directions, taking multiple pathways to related information and often to a variety of solutions to the same question.

One of the reasons computers and interactive programming really can deliver on their promise to entertain and educate is that in many ways they mimic the ways our brains work. Their architecture, combined with well-designed programs, can anticipate how we receive and process information, how we respond, what gives us pleasure, and how we learn. Computer software and online communication can provide:

- *rapid access to information*
- *ease of use*
- *enhanced self-esteem through creative self-directed learning*
- *accommodation to different styles of learning*
- *challenge to different cognitive skills, in addition to reading and writing*
- *preparation for a world that fully integrates the computer in our personal and professional lives*

Kids prefer to learn, rather than being "taught." In other words, they want to experience as much as they can firsthand and be in control of their own learning. Today's computers offer kids access to thousands of programs on floppy disks, CD-ROMs, or through online options. Kids can usually operate the hardware with ease and are very comfortable with the manipulative aspects of navigating from option to option by using the keyboard and mouse.

As a Matter of Fact...

- A 1991 study found that kids ages 14–18 who played Nintendo performed better in tasks involving observation, evaluation, inductive and deductive reasoning.

- Over one-third of all U.S. households have PCs.

The most successful computer programs for kids put them in the driver's seat, with rules of the road and a map to guide them, and take advantage of the ways kids learn best—with hands-on, age-appropriate challenges and content. The interactive format allows them to find and even create information rather than just consume it. Used in the right doses, even computer games can give kids mastery as they advance to higher levels, enhancing their self-esteem along the way. They offer powerful motivation with long-term appeal because the challenges are built in, and the players gain a feeling of control.

191

Good interactive software accommodates individual styles and rates of learning as well as differences in reviewing, storing, and integrating the material at hand. In a 1993 study conducted for multimedia developers, researchers reported that educational products that will succeed in the future will be designed to engage users and take advantage of how people learn:

> *Learning is a self-paced process of discovery. . . . The "felt response" to learning is enjoyment, expanded sense of well-being and appreciation. Education, as it is implemented today, is anything but that. It reflects an inherently unequal teacher-student relationship, the use of forced repetition, right answer-ism and retention of fact. The market for learning will be led by those title developers who can rekindle the flames of curiosity and possibility. Virtually every category of "self-help" and "do-it-yourself" book will become interactive and delivered on a variety of media and formats.*

When kids use educational and entertainment software, they develop new skills of inducing rules and patterns, unlike board games where rules are spelled out beforehand. Kids engaged with computer games take information from different sources at the same time and integrate it. They work at the flat two-dimensional computer screen but operate in a three-dimensional reality. Spatial skills come into play, and visual information from a variety of sources must be coordinated. For example, the popular CD-ROM game *Myst* has its players going through doors to get into new rooms, going to a library to turn the pages of a book and access what's inside, going up and down winding stairwells, into elevators and turning corners to explore new vistas.

Remember, each new medium introduces the potential to educate, entertain and enlighten, and now there are computer products and programs that do just that. So get up to speed on what's out there!

Options: A Multimedia Menu of Hardware and Programming Software

Hardware

Platforms

The hardware is the machinery, from the computer itself to peripheral devices such as disk drives and printers. There are basically two personal computer platforms (architectures) from which to choose, each type running on a distinct "operating system," which determines software compatibility:

• IBM, referring to IBM or the IBM-compatible machines produced by many other manufacturers like Compaq, Dell, and Gateway. IBM compatibles typically run on DOS or the Microsoft Windows operating systems, meaning that they will run software expressly designed for that system.

• Macintosh machines, built by Apple Computer and only recently by a few other manufacturers. Macs run on an exclusive operating system that pioneered many of the features now found in Windows.

Overall, there are many more IBM-compatible machines. But the Macintosh remains very popular with educators, kids, and first-time computer owners because of its ease of use. Leading developers of kids' software generally design their programs for both platforms, so you will often be offered the choice of ordering a title that's compatible with Windows or Mac (and sometimes both, meaning that separate disks are provided).

Peripherals for the computer include everything from the mouse and mouse pad to external hard drives and CD-ROMs, built-in or external. These devices must also be compatible with the type of computer you own.

RAM and Hard Drive

You've no doubt heard people talk about the RAM (Random Access Memory) and storage on the hard drive of their computers. Besides a computer's inherent processing speed, RAM and hard drive storage are the two key measures of a computer's capacity.

Your computer's RAM determines how much information the machine can handle at once—the more RAM you have, the more you can do. Multimedia and graphics programs, for example, require more RAM than word processing. Many people purchase additional RAM for their computers because the programs they want to use require more than what came installed in their machine.

The hard drive is where you store your programs and the documents you create. If your family wants the flexibility to operate many different programs and to create a lot of files and projects, it's best to invest in extra storage capacity.

Modem

If you want to use one of the online services (such as AOL, CompuServe, and Prodigy) and to have access to the Internet, you'll need a modem, which is literally the computer's telephone, connecting it to the outside world. Setup requires communication software that you can customize with information about your computer, frequently called numbers, and so on. The phone line attached to the modem will be tied up while you're online, so if you choose to use your home phone line, you'll be incommunicado while the modem is in use.

Software

Computer software, such as games and learning programs, are distributed on diskettes (usually 3.5-inch disks), on CD-

ROMs, via online services, or already installed ("bundled") on your hard drive or packaged with your CD-ROM drive when you purchase your computer (as a value-added incentive).

The range and special applications of software continues to grow, from office-oriented programs to home finance to fun and games. Kids' software is generally classified into such categories as creativity, reference, education, and entertainment/recreation. The division into these categories seems odd to us—when you watch a child playing a good math game, you'll see he's being entertained. Why use "entertainment" only for shooting/action games?

And don't forget the creative uses of the standard office and productivity tools, such as word processing (for composing letters, reports, term papers), databases (to keep track of books read, movies rented, coin/stamp/comic collections), and spreadsheets (for science and math, or for baseball fans to record and analyze annual stats by team and player). These tools are often combined in so-called "integrated" packages, such as Microsoft Works and Claris Works, which sometimes come bundled with the computer at purchase.

Diskettes
Most software comes on one or several diskettes that you insert into your computer to copy the program onto your hard drive. Diskettes are also a handy portable medium onto which you can copy programs or documents to bring to school or work, or to store for safekeeping.

CD-ROM
The CD-ROM is a high-capacity compact disc similar to the standard audio compact discs that play your favorite music. These CD-ROMs, however, store more than sound—they can include video, print, photography, and graphics as well as audio. This "multimedia" capacity, combined with the speed and mem-

ory of today's computer hardware, has driven the growing popularity of family-oriented CD-ROM software. There's a growing list of excellent titles, a selection of consumer magazines and catalogs that review and offer this product, as well as departments in a variety of retail outlets from computer stores to bookstores and mass merchants. An indicator of the growing market for CD-ROM is that one publishing company, Random House, is reaping larger revenues from their CD-ROM encyclopedia than from their printed and bound version, even though the print version is much more expensive.

If you haven't had firsthand experience of CD-ROM technology and can't fathom what it is, imagine using a CD-ROM encyclopedia to research the Nile River in Egypt. Your past experience would probably bring to mind paging through the "E" volume in your encyclopedia and looking up "Egypt" to find a column or maybe a full page with a picture devoted to the subject. CD-ROM multimedia introduces video and sound (perhaps an Egyptian song) as well as maps, statistics, and other traditional text and graphics you might find in a printed version. Beyond that, software format offers a menu of options from which to choose, and with a click of the mouse you can select the sources and material you want. Interactive CD-ROM presents information in engaging ways on multiple levels, often in intricate game formats with users getting the information they want at

As a Matter of Fact...

The investment banking firm Jeffries & Co. projects that nearly one in three households will own a CD-ROM drive by the year 2000, compared to the fewer than 5 percent that did in 1990. About one in two homes will own a personal computer.

their own pace. Some information appears in "hypertext" (graphically called out by underlines or highlights), indicating to the user that related material is "hyperlinked" and can be accessed by clicking on the underlined or highlighted word(s).

196

Online

In contrast to software, which is self-contained on your computer, the beauty of online computing is its "real-time" aspect, introducing a range of instantaneous experiences, including e-mail (electronic messaging to send and receive mail online), electronic bulletin boards to read and post messages on topics of interest, access to a host of consumer and specialty publications, "chat rooms" where you can meet and talk with other folks in real time on topics of special interest, direct feeds from national and worldwide news services, catalog/mall shopping, and more. Lively graphics and menus present a wide variety of options and facilitate the user's choices, and you can even download some computer programs and other documents from an online source onto your hard disk. Many kids who have access to online services already display an amazing facility in navigating their way through the maze of choices.

There are several services available at this writing. The three major services are America Online, Prodigy, and CompuServe. Microsoft Network, which comes bundled as a feature of Windows 95, promises to be a major competitor in the near future. Basically, you purchase an online on a subscription basis (much like cable TV) and access it through your computer and modem. Although each service charges differently, the general idea is that a new subscriber gets a certain amount of free time for signing up, then pays a basic monthly rate plus hourly fees. Of course, the costs add up the more time you spend logged on. You can expect to pay about $10 a month for the first few hours per month you spend online, with hourly charges once you exceed that allowance. Monitor your time because charges can mount up and some services charge extra for particular services that they provide within the general subscription. The major providers offer online help, access to the Internet and World Wide Web, and parental control options, including monitors who watch language and etiquette (called "netiquette") in the kid chat rooms.

The Net and the Web

The Internet and the World Wide Web (WWW) provide tickets to an incredible wealth of information: resources to explore, an exponential enhancement to your local school and public libraries, and your kids' gateway to e-mail with unlimited "mousepal" opportunities for correspondence.

The Internet is a vast interconnected complex of computers and computer networks located all over the world and connected by a common addressing scheme. Internet addresses, with their unusual combinations of characters, can seem bewildering, but easier methods of access are being developed. (Humorist Dave Barry commented that you create an Internet address by having a crazed squirrel run across your keyboard.)

To connect yourself, you need to sign up with a service provider or one of the online services and install software that allows you access. Most of the information on the Internet is text-based, and finding your way around can be complicated, but it's easier with one of the navigators such as Gopher which have easy-to-follow menus. You can download files from the Internet and post messages on over seven thousand topics on electronic bulletin boards called Usenet newsgroups.

The WWW is information on the Internet in a collection of graphic "home pages"—screens of information with pictures, links to other sites, information, or video/sound clips. It's easy to access the information by pointing and clicking, allowing you to travel among different sites without even having to know the locator address. The graphics are inviting, and guides and listings to sites are available online. Presently, the best Web browsing software is Netscape, available from your Internet service provider or downloaded from their website on the Internet. Keep in mind it's easy to access the Internet and WWW through one of the commercial online services. For a quick online reference, see the "Cyberglossary" at the end of this chapter.

The World Wide Web is easy for children to use and its colorful and dynamic visuals and sound are appealing. Sites for kids, hosted by volunteers and by kids themselves, are growing daily. The easiest way to start browsing is to go to any site that serves as a directory for other sites. This is very useful, since the Web has no central directory of its own.

Check out this sample cybervisit to get a sense of what a child might experience while browsing—one sample browse out of infinite possibilities.

Start at "Interesting Places for Kids," one of the many directories for kids:

http://www.crc.ricoh.com/people/steve/kids.html

(By the way, the beginning of the locator is pronounced "http,dot,dot,slash,slash www dot.")

This directory is hosted by a parent who tells a little about himself and his daughter and provides you with a choice of places to go, including art and literature, music, toys and games, Web pages for and by kids, and more. If you click on Web pages, for example, you come to another list of choices—one of which is "Courtney Elizabeth Carter's 11th Birthday." As you read along on this page, you see a scan of Courtney's picture on a baseball card and learn that her older brother posted the page for her, requesting that visitors post birthday messages. A list of things Courtney likes to do includes playing Nintendo, collecting thimbles, and playing violin. Each of these interests is hyperlinked to other sites so that if you click on violin, for example, you can visit new information with hyperlinks to yet other sites about violins.

You can go back to the first page ("home") of "Interesting Places for Kids" and click on another area, such as art and literature. The literature choices, for example, are vast. You can read poetry by Wordsworth or by kids, or you can hit the "Shakespeare at MIT" site, click further and read *Hamlet*, criticisms of *Hamlet*, and more. The "Art" index as well as the "Collections by Kids" index are both linked to "Fridge Art Gallery" hosted by IBM, which posts thirty pictures a month e-mailed by kids.

As you surf these sites (visit by clicking from one to the other) you meet real people and realize that much of the net has a folksy grass-roots feel. There's always an opportunity to interact by sending comments or posting your own messages.

Other directories that will link you to sites of interest to kids are:

Kids' Web:

http://www.primenet.com/~sburr/index.html

and the Kids on the Web:

http://www.zen.org/~brendan/kids.html

When addressing any net or Web location, remember that you must include every letter and dot correctly or you won't find the location you seek. Sometimes you won't be able to find the location your looking for, which can be frustrating, but chalk it up to the fun of exploration. Sometimes a site or the server is busy, or some little gremlin interfered!

Once you decide to bring a computer into your life, it's important to have access to good technical support, for those times you need advice, or the machine or a

As a Matter of Fact...

- Reasons cited for using the WWW: 85 percent of respondents use it for browsing, 57 percent for entertainment, 51 percent for work, 47 percent for research.

- Three-quarters of WWW users browse at least once a day, 42 percent one to four times a day, and 16 percent more than nine times a day.

program actually goes down. Support can come from the manufacturer or where you bought your computer. You may want to inquire about technical support or even try the tech support number before you make a purchase.

Nicholas Negroponte, director of the Media Lab at MIT, forecasts the ultimate pervasiveness of the Internet:

> *The mass media have more or less insulted the American citizen by assuming the couch potato to be a beer-drinking boob, too tired to do more than channel surf. . . . Kids are proving this wrong . . . all over the United States and from all economic levels.*

He anticipates a "smart TV" that learns each particular viewer's preferences and automatically provides them. Among multiple forms of entertainment, Negroponte predicts most will be delivered by the Internet.

New Game, New (and Old) Rules: Concerns and How to Avoid Them

We'd all line up for the newest, best computer and a vast selection of software if we could afford them, especially if we

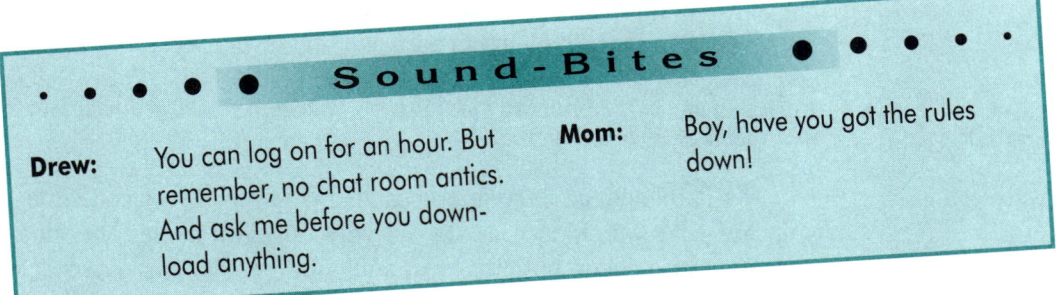

Sound-Bites

Drew: You can log on for an hour. But remember, no chat room antics. And ask me before you download anything.

Mom: Boy, have you got the rules down!

could be assured that we were getting our kids the best education that money could buy. But life's not that simple. Not all books are classics, not all comic books are bad. Not all video is mindless eye candy, and the computer is not necessarily a direct link to all things educational.

Concerns: The Minefields Out There and How to Avoid Them

Many parents are worried about some exits the kids can take on this information superhighway; these can lead to a daunting list of concerns similar to those parents face concerning TV. Setting limits with confidence around the computer screen presents the same challenges for parents and their kids as around the TV screen. Parents who are knowledgeable about the options available are better positioned to stand guard on behalf of their kids. In a column entitled *Kids Online, Parents on Edge,* columnist Nathan Cobb of *The Boston Globe* points out the computer gap between kids and parents: "Indeed, it is frequently the difference between low-tech parents and high-tech kids that causes the computer to become a family issue." It's also important to appreciate that any damaging effects the electronic media can have on children are not intrinsic to the media but grow out of the ways the media are used. So what else is new?

Consider the following questions in your effort to maximize the multipurposed computer Cobb calls "learning tool, amusement arcade, community center, and homework machine."

How can I limit my kids' use of video games whose dominant theme is violence?

The violence in computer games is especially profound because it's our kids who are actively engaged in the shooting down of objects, targets, even animated people. No longer are they passively watching violence; they're now participants in it.

Is this violence innocuous, like playing cops and robbers, or is it more insidious and closer to reality? It depends on the program and context. For example, is the game a karate match or a war simulation? As with questionable video choices, discuss this distinction with your kids, taking advantage of these circumstances as learning opportunities. Be ready to provide alternative programs, even some the kids may not know about, and limit the time they play games you consider too violent.

Should I limit screen time and let the kids decide which screen to use—TV or computer? Or should computer time be separate from TV time?

As we discussed in Chapter 3, we recommend a maximum of about two hours of recreational screen time (TV and/or computer) on weekdays and more on weekend days. (If there's schoolwork to be done on the computer, it shouldn't be counted toward screen time.) As with all viewing, time is a critical factor that needs to be allocated and monitored. Remember, with the video software, "the show" isn't ever really over. Games can be played again and again, and many include enough levels of challenge that the adept player can keep at it for hours. Online environments are even more open-ended, and can be totally intoxicating places. Alan Randall, president of East West Educational Development Foundation, whose mission is to further computer access, recognizes this attraction: "They're interactive, and as a result they suck your brains up. By that I mean they're engrossing and they're enthralling because they respond."

Even if my kids are involved in worthwhile programs, should I still be concerned about how much time they spend at the computer?

You might want to increase the time limit for computer screen time if your child is using educational programs. However, too much time on the computer, even when the kids are

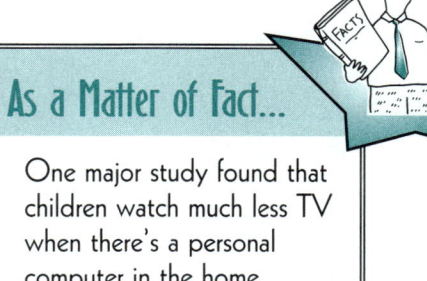

As a Matter of Fact...

One major study found that children watch much less TV when there's a personal computer in the home.

involved in worthwhile programs, is a concern because it usually represents a solitary and physically static activity. Our society is already seeing the results of both couch- and mouse-potatoism on the overweight profile of our children.

In addition to health concerns, there's also the issue of socialization. Although the onlines afford opportunities for communicating with other kids and adults through chat rooms and e-mail, those experiences will never measure up to being with other people, engaged in live conversation, sharing activities, interacting together. So again, it's a matter of balance. Whatever a given family decides is right for them, they still should include exercise, socialization, homework, and household obligations in the mix.

Time's Up! is a program parents can purchase to help the family monitor computer screen time. Parents can program in the time limit and access for each child in the family and thereby limit the online time each spends. Designed for parents inexperienced with computers, *Time's Up!* gives a two-minute reminder before the time limit is up, and then exits the child from the program, restricting access to it and all other applications according to preset time limits. However, time limit programs, like the use of other locking devices, may say to your kid, "I don't trust you." Ideally, you should aim to build internal controls in your children by setting up limits on computer time that you can explain clearly and maintain easily. Of course, it's a challenge to monitor computer use when you're not around, so you may decide a program like *Time's Up!* is necessary.

What can I do to ensure that my kids aren't exposed to inappropriate conversations and information exchanges in chat rooms and on bulletin boards? How widespread is the problem of sexual predators on the Internet, and how do I prepare my kids to recognize and report any behavior of this kind?

There are two major safety issues concerning children on the Internet that warrant your attention: monitoring your kids' access to all the information available, and protecting them from unwanted encounters. Bulletin boards offer options for publicizing one's interests, including sexual information, and chat rooms can be populated with rude, crude visitors whose conversations challenge any code of decency. Although there are all kinds of information out there on the net, and none of it is regulated, it's really not that easy to come across outright pornography. One has to go looking for it. Of course, if kids go searching, they may find it.

Ernie Allen, president of the Center for Missing and Exploited Children, comments on the issue of online predators: "It's not a huge number, but it does indicate that there are risks. Certainly there are risks in everything a child does." He goes on to say the technology can give a false sense of security. Being in cyberspace is like being out in any public space where strangers meet. Instruct your kids not to give out their name or address on the net, to stay in kid-appropriate chat rooms, and to report inappropriate chat or bulletin board notices. You can also consider *SurfWatch* Software, a program that can block up to 1,500 sites containing material SurfWatch considers inappropriate for children in defined target ages. Regular updates stay current, and parents may also indicate which sites they want blocked. You can also get the brochure, *Child Safety on the Information Highway,* from the National Center for Missing and Exploited Children, or call the Interactive Services Association and Surfnet Software for more information. Use "Resources" section for phone numbers and addresses.

How can I help my kids avoid being commercial targets?

Beyond concerns of privacy on the Internet is the problem of sites that are actually advertisements or marketing surveys masquerading as informational programs, becoming known as "blended ads." These "blended" sites will no doubt proliferate and parents should watch them carefully—informa-

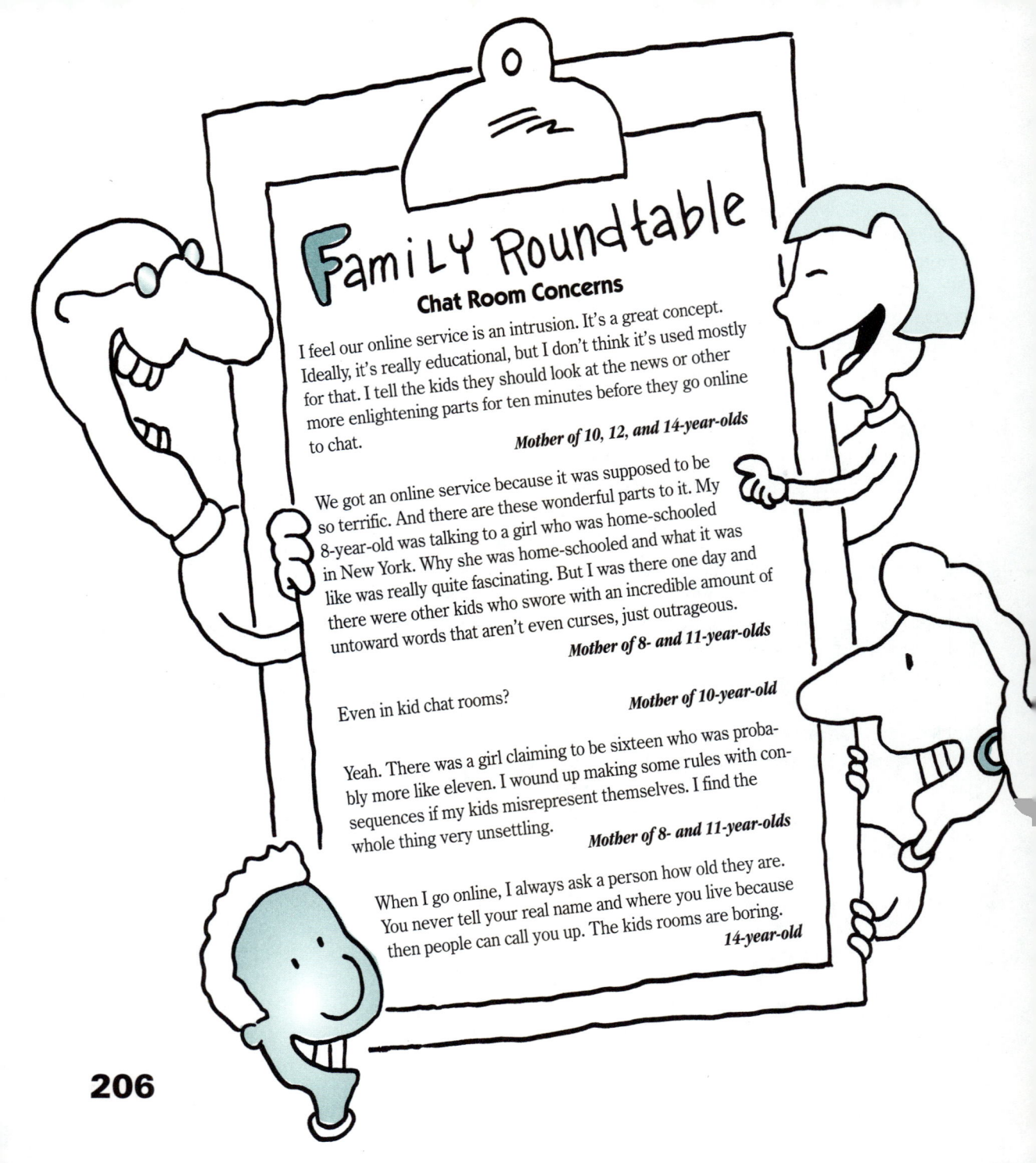

Family Roundtable

Chat Room Concerns

I feel our online service is an intrusion. It's a great concept. Ideally, it's really educational, but I don't think it's used mostly for that. I tell the kids they should look at the news or other more enlightening parts for ten minutes before they go online to chat.

Mother of 10, 12, and 14-year-olds

We got an online service because it was supposed to be so terrific. And there are these wonderful parts to it. My 8-year-old was talking to a girl who was home-schooled in New York. Why she was home-schooled and what it was like was really quite fascinating. But I was there one day and there were other kids who swore with an incredible amount of untoward words that aren't even curses, just outrageous.

Mother of 8- and 11-year-olds

Even in kid chat rooms?

Mother of 10-year-old

Yeah. There was a girl claiming to be sixteen who was proba-bly more like eleven. I wound up making some rules with con-sequences if my kids misrepresent themselves. I find the whole thing very unsettling.

Mother of 8- and 11-year-olds

When I go online, I always ask a person how old they are. You never tell your real name and where you live because then people can call you up. The kids rooms are boring.

14-year-old

206

tion and advertising are often hard for kids to separate. An example of a site that pretends to be entertainment for children but is really a marketing survey is **kids.com.com.** When a child visits here, she must register by answering a long questionnaire, including age, town, type of computer. Even one unanswered question requires her to go back until the form is complete. After registering, she can click on sites to play, but many of them are more marketing, such as one that offers prizes to sign up friends. This type of survey for entry to a site entices kids to provide information that should be protected. Use some of the information we've provided on media literacy to cue your kids to recognize blended advertising. For their protection, you should warn them never to give out any information online.

Regulating the Internet

The Telecommunications Act passed in 1996 attempts to regulate the Internet. However we feel this isn't the best route to protect children, because it might violate the rights to free speech. In fact at this writing, the law is being tested in the courts. Jerry Berman, director of the Center for Democracy and Technology, comments on the Internet regulation: "It would be a mistake to drive us, in a moment of hysteria, to a solution that is unconstitutional, would stultify technology, and wouldn't even fulfill its mission." There are protection options under discussion now that don't require government involvement, and industry and government are getting closer to agreeing on non-government-regulated controls. Navigator programs are building in protection devices, and hosts of sites are considering addresses on the World Wide Web that would have voluntary ratings in their Internet addresses. One example, presently under development, is Kid Code, which will label questionable Internet addresses with warnings.

Your regulation of online and Internet use as well as your supervision of other activities on the computer call into play your priorities as a parent: spending time with your kids, talking to them, building trust, being there. In addition, consider the following:

- *Discuss with your kids inappropriate sites they shouldn't access, and why.*

- *Develop trust as you would when they get older and go out with friends without parental supervision. Have them inform you "where they'll be."*

- *Acknowledge that the anonymity of online chat rooms sometimes inspires kids to masquerade as other people, changing their age or sex, flirting, giving misinformation, and saying things they wouldn't say face-to-face. Talk about how to handle this temptation.*

- *Browse when the kids aren't around to familiarize yourself with the options and programs they might use.*

- *Check in and ask them to show you favorite sites while they're online. Play with them, plan and solve problems together.*

- *Check out reviews of software in resource books and magazines listed in the "Resources" section at the end of this book.*

- *Limit screen time to two hours (for both TV and computer) during the week.*

The subject of online etiquette is fairly new but serious enough to have garnered attention in the press. Some online services have guides or monitors who try to maintain decorum in the sites for children. For example, America Online has on-line etiquette rules, called "Terms of Service" (TOS). If members are chatting in a room and violate TOS, a guide might notice and send a warning or even shut down the connection if it's a third offense. Violations range from using curse words to typing all in caps. There are no such guides or monitors present on

Internet sites. *Family PC Magazine* surveyed the three leading services for their own precautionary parameters and offered some online rules and responsibilities for kids and parents to follow:

Kids' Online Rules:

- *Don't give out your phone number or address without parental permission.*

- *Don't arrange to meet anyone you encounter online without first checking with your parents.*

- *If you come across inappropriate language in a forum or via e-mail, notify your parents and member services by sending a copy of the message.*

- *Remember, you are in control of your online interactions—you can always log off or exit. As long as you don't reveal your last name, phone number, or address, you are safe.*

Parents' Online Responsibilities:

- *Get to know the terms of service for your online provider so you know the kind of rules it enforces.*

- *Get to know what areas your children are going to online so that you can effectively discuss issues that come up and warn them away from potential danger.*

- *Monitor your children's online activity as you would monitor their television viewing.*

- *Remind your children of the rule about not giving out their name, address, and phone number.*

TIP

Review online rules and responsibilities with your family.

As a Matter of Fact...

When Senator Edward Kennedy's wife, Victoria, attempted to get online to find the senator while he was participating in a computer bulletin board forum sponsored by "The Congressional Quarterly," she was refused entry and told she wasn't authorized to join the discussion. Turns out, she had blocked the family computer from access to "chat rooms" in order to keep her son and daughter from listening in on adult online conversations. "I wasn't thinking in terms of town meetings where Ted might be speaking," she said and then went on to describe the blocking device as "too much parental control for my own good."

Keep in mind that balance remains the key in choosing good programs, monitoring screen time and use, and including both the TV and computer in a well-rounded life for your kids.

Shopping the New Media

When it comes to which programs to select, purchasing software is pretty much analogous to choosing video. However, the price tag is bigger; and there's limited rental availability of computer software (except for game software for Nintendo and Sega, which are widely available).

There is a growing library of computer software and multimedia product for children that includes some terrific product as well as some rather simplistic treatments of content and interactivity. Great promise is there, and more good product is becoming available, but high production costs and the still-limited penetration of CD-ROMs in the home contribute to the production of lower-quality product.

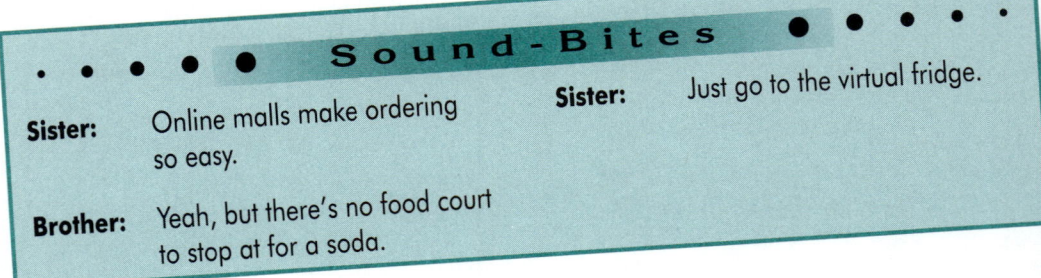

• • • • •   S o u n d - B i t e s   • • • • •

Sister: Online malls make ordering so easy.

Sister: Just go to the virtual fridge.

Brother: Yeah, but there's no food court to stop at for a soda.

The time you spend researching what's available and locating where to buy, rent, or borrow will save you from second thoughts about value, appropriateness, and the conflicts that may ensue when the wrong stuff finds its way onto the hard drive. And you always have the opportunity to return software if you don't feel it measures up to expectations.

In this section, we'll discuss criteria to consider in your purchasing decisions, a sampling of good product that's available and where to find it, options for affording access to kids who don't own computers, and opportunities for computer education.

Criteria to Consider in Making Purchasing Decisions

Read the Box

Most computer software packaging offers some information that can help you decide whether you'd like to try the program. Ask yourself:

- *Is the program compatible with your computer (Windows vs. Mac)?*

- *Do you have the necessary equipment to run the program and use it to its fullest performance (color monitor, sufficient RAM, a CD-ROM drive, and so on)?*

- *Is the price comparable to similar programs?*

- *Is there a description on the box that gives a clear indication of the content and elements in the program?*

- *Is a suggested target age indicated?*

- *Has the program won significant awards or notices from the press and media?*

- *Does the package invite curiosity and reflect quality?*

- *Is the publisher or label one that you recognize and trust? If you're satisfied with the quality of other programs produced under the same label, you can be fairly confident in their product.*

- *Is there a rating from the Recreational Software Advisory Council?*

Sample Product Before You Purchase

Beyond reading the box, if possible you should preview a program to truly know whether it measures up to your standards. There are a variety of ways you can "test drive" products before you buy them. Software Publishers or retail stores that carry their programs may offer a free demo disk. You can also check out some program demos online. KidSoft is a club that offers samples of programs they distribute. Your local and school libraries or children's museum may already own the program you're considering or offer you other options to investigate. Cybercafés also serve as retail outlets and offer a wide range of demo software. After-school computer clubs and classes and computer camps will allow your kids to sample a variety of software. Finally, families in the neighborhood may provide suggestions of what they enjoy.

If you have the opportunity to look beyond the package and actually sample programs before purchasing them, review our "Software Green Light Test." Computer software requires the same evaluation you give to your selections for appropriate video viewing.

> **TIP**
>
> *Stop in at a computer store to test out some programs.*

Software Green Light Test

- **High Production Quality**
  Does program reflect high-quality production—quality animation and graphics, clarity of sound, speed?

- **Interface Design**
  Is the software easy to "navigate"? Are there easy-to-read icons for moving through the program, exiting, and returning to the program? Are hints accessible? Is the program exploratory, with the option to switch to a practice area? Is it customizable and expandable, holding its interest level and value?

- **Age and Development Appropriateness**
  Is the content developmentally appropriate for your kids' age range, and does it satisfy interests they've expressed?

212

- **Entertainment Value**
  Does the software have high entertainment value? Even for programming with a strong educational agenda, it's important that it be entertaining, or it won't succeed in winning the attention of a young audience.

- **Stimulating Content**
  Are the content and its presentation intellectually and creatively stimulating, asking kids to learn new information or skills, question assumptions, solve problems, and think critically?

- **Ease of Use/technical Support**
  Is the program compatible with your computer and system setup, and is it easy to install? Is there a phone number provided for technical support should it be required?

- **Awards**
  Has the program won any awards, especially those specifically for children's software, like Parents' Choice?

- **Positive Values**
  Does the program reinforce positive values?

- **Fair price**
  Is the price fair (usually in the $30–$50 range)?

Ratings

The Recreational Software Advisory Council (RSAC) was established by six trade organizations, led by the Software Publishers Group. Their rating consists of three categories: nudity/sex, violence, and language, with five levels within each, 0 representing the least objectionable. For example, a game with level 2 in violence might include humans being killed or injured or a reward for injuring a threatening creature. Rewards for killing a nonthreatening creature bumps the game to level 3. A level 1 on the language scale includes mild expletives, a level 3 has strong, vulgar language or obscene gestures. Similarly, very specific and weighted descriptors for the nudity/sex scale are used to determine a rating. The bases for giving a rating are more carefully defined than those for movies and may well get adopted for other media. The rating is presented in a graphic that looks similar to a thermometer, and it appears on the software package or on an insert.

An Overview of Product Offerings

We suggest you start by reviewing the following inventory of available software, organized by conventional industry categories:

Creativity: Writing and Art Programs

Heading the list of writing programs are *The Writing Center* (ages 7–adult) by The Learning Company and *Story Book Weaver* by MECC. *The Writing Center* allows kids to choose ready-designed formats such as newsletters or reports. In both programs the word processing function is integrated with a graphics application that allows the student to select from a photo database and then resize, crop, and so on. A spelling corrector is included. *KIDPIX* by Brøderbund is an excellent example of a paint/draw program that includes wacky brushes like "splatter" and "drippy paint," rubber stamp selections, paint tools for special effects, and the all-time favorite, the firecracker eraser tool, which blows up an unwanted picture.

> **TIP**
>
> *Take some time alone to explore your child's creativity or reference software so that you can help apply the capabilities of the programs to homework assignments.*

Reference

CD-ROM encyclopedias such as *Microsoft Encarta* and *Grolier's* provide much of the basic information of book encyclopedias, and also allow kids to check out related topics and to delve deeper into the information with the click of a mouse. For more serious writing and research, the CD-ROM *Microsoft Bookshelf* includes a dictionary, quotation dictionary, almanac, thesaurus, and more.

Education

These programs cover almost any subject you can imagine, from the three R's to typing, storybooks, and problem solving. Davidson's *Math Blaster* (ages 6–12) and The Learning Company's *SuperSolvers Outnumbered* (ages 7–9) are good examples of programs that drill math facts and problem-solving experiences in fun ways through exciting action games. Reading programs for younger kids include *Talking Reader Rabbit* (ages 3–7) by The Learning Company.

Learning Adventure

This category incorporates history and science and is well represented by *Amazon Trail* (ages 10–adult), published by MECC. Traveling through time, kids journey on the Amazon, exploring rain forests, solving mysteries, and facing danger. This category also includes *Sim City Enhanced* by Maxis and Interplay, which is a simulation program that allows kids to build environments that require the interplay of power plants, transportation, jobs, and taxes, in order to make a viable city. This is fun for kids over 9, especially with a parent who will be won over by the intricacies of the evolving city. Kids learn problem solving, how a city grows, and sophisticated planning strategies. The CD-ROM version includes full-motion video clips.

TIPS

- Play along with your kid on learning adventures. Together you'll be able to pass more levels and gain enormous enjoyment out of working together.

- Reintroduce software that your kids haven't played recently. If it's a quality product, chances are your child will get reinvested You can also change the "option" or "preferences" to alter the content or challenge level.

In addition, kids can explore *Sammy's Science House* (ages 2–5, Edmark), including his Workshop, Weather Machine, Acorn Pond, and more. Kids follow their own curiosity and learn about sorting and sequencing, natural science, habitats, and so on. Logic and problem solving are integrated, as well as creative activities in which players can animate from a blueprint or even make a movie. Other fun programs are available for teaching numbers or letters but may not be so important for the youngest group. Programs for this youngest computer user group should be exploratory, varied, and offer depth and variety.

Entertainment and Video Games

A worthwhile title in this category is *Microsoft Arcade,* offering five arcade games including *Tempest,* in which enemy aliens chase the player over changing geometric screens.

Most kids are familiar with Sega and Nintendo game systems, which have been around in different forms for years. These are usually the first computer games children get and are either handheld or plugged into the TV. Each system comes with its own software on cartridges (carts) or CDs and are not compatible with any other hardware.

As a Matter of Fact...

- A Sports Illustrated for Kids study found that 25 percent of kids who play video games play between two and three hours a day, while 70 percent play for up to an hour.

- 93 percent of boys surveyed and 78 percent of girls play video games.

Online

If you're shopping online service providers and considering from among the major three, here are a few items to help with your decision:

America Online (AOL) sites for kids include the Academic Assistance Center, where kids can post a question that will be answered within twenty-four hours by a volunteer teacher. Chat rooms for kids allow kids to "talk" to each other in real time about any topic. Scheduled guests appear regularly and kids can participate in Q&A sessions with guests from the world of sports, politics, and entertainment. A parental control option is part of the package. We recommend this service.

Prodigy has sites similar to AOL's—one called Homework Helper, which gives kids the ability to research a topic through thousands of newspapers and periodicals. There are ten moderated bulletin boards especially for kids on which to post thoughts and questions. Online versions of *Sports Illustrated for Kids* and installments of the popular Babysitters Club book series are on Prodigy. Sesame Street, which attracts 55,000 log-ons a month, is one of the only sites for very young readers.

CompuServe has kid-specialized sites, such as Kids and Teens chat rooms, although this service is not as rich for kids as AOL and Prodigy.

Where to Find the Good Stuff

Luckily, your search for quality software will be easier than for quality video. You have many resources from which to learn about products, in addition to the variety of retail outlets that sell computers, including:

As a Matter of Fact...

- Commercial online services are a $795-million industry, as opposed to CD-ROM sales, which are $2.5 billion, and video game sales, which are $3.8 billion.

- The total of net users has grown by over 1000 percent in the past three years.

- 30–40 million people have net access at least to e-mail in over 160 countries.

- *catalogs (see below)*
- *information sources, such as computer and parent magazines and newsletters (see below)*
- *online catalogs*
- *computer stores, like Circuit City, Computer City, or CompUSA, which often have their own mail-order catalogs*
- *bundling options with hardware purchase*
- *clubs, museums, library, camps, school*

Catalogs are a good way of finding out what's out there. A terrific catalog is KidSoft, which calls itself "The Source for Prescreened Quality Software." Thorough explanations, thirty-day guarantees, and informative help on their 800 number make this a great resource for parents. The catalog is part of a club membership. When you join, you get a CD-ROM with samples of many programs. If you like one, you can call the Kid-Soft 800 number, arrange payment, and have it unlocked (via code) from the CD-ROM or shipped directly. The CDs and a magazine come four times a year for $29.95. One hesitation is that it's difficult to distinguish the line between editorial and advertising in the KidSoft magazine.

If you know what title you want, you can also call one of the mail-order houses, which usually have very good prices and overnight delivery. You can also get tech support from some of the warehouse 800 numbers like Mac/PC Connection, Tiger Software, and MacWarehouse.

Information Sources include *Kids' Educational Software Advisory,* a newsletter for parents of children ages 3–12, written by experts and unbiased because they do not take ads. The newsletter features reviews of new software and articles covering topics such as what to do if your child loses interest in the software you buy. *Children's Software Review* is a bimonthly newsletter for parents and teachers, featuring software and hardware news and reviews broken down by age group, from preschool to upper elementary, and rated on a number of dimensions, including ease of use and educational content. A one-year subscription is $24. CSR also provides a database of nine hundred reviews on America Online (HOMEPC) from "Newsstand" on the option menu. Magazines on the newsstands that review kids' media monthly are *New Media, CD-ROM Today, Family PC, Family Computing,* and *Parents' Choice. That's Edutainment! A Parent's Guide to Educational Software,* by Eric Brown, is the best resource we can recommend for understanding the ins and outs of hardware (which will help when you are ready to make the major purchase) and the top software titles. The book features one hundred two-page software reviews, which describe and rate titles based on eleven criteria, including educational value, entertainment value, audio quality, and technical support. It also comes with a CD-ROM with demos of titles reviewed in the book, and includes helpful age and subject indexes.

To compare hardware and software prices, read ads in newsstand magazines like *Mac World* and *PC Magazine* and see the "Resources" section.

Publishers You Can Depend On

A few select publishers of kids' software products are widely celebrated for the quality of product they produce, in particular Brøderbund, Davidson, The Learning Company, and Edmark. These are certainly not the only good publishers out there, but their products are consistently of high quality.

Options for Affording Access and Education

Perhaps the subject of new media doesn't speak to you since you've yet to purchase a computer or you have a computer without multimedia capability, CD-ROM, or modem. Or maybe you have everything, but you're thinking about your niece who doesn't have a computer. Robin Raskin, in her *Family PC* article "Bridging the Gap," cautions, "Computers have the power to change the way children learn, to give them access to worlds full of information they gather. But if only some children benefit from this power, we are headed for a world that's more factionalized than ever. Don't just stand by and let that happen." There are options for those kids who are growing up in this multimedia world but don't have immediate access to it.

Some computer societies and user groups are in a position to set up computer clubs for kids. They can facilitate organizing such groups, and they often have the membership expertise to run these groups or participate in meetings and other services. To find a group, call the Association of Personal Computer User Groups (APCUG) locator number or call Apple to find a Mac group. If there is no user group in your area, work with your child's school to start an after-school computer club or start your own.

Summertime also offers the possibility of sending kids to a computer camp or finding a camp that includes computers in its roster of activities. This can be costly, but it could prove to be significantly less than the investment in one's own hardware and software. These camps can be great for both the initiate and the computer whiz kid. Gregg Keizer, a contributing editor to *Family PC,* writes: "Activities offered by an outstanding summer program require equipment, software, and expertise most families and schools can't easily provide. Scanners, multimedia presentation software, digital cameras, camcorders, a wide variety of the latest software, and teachers who know how to put these devices through their paces are a combination that's tough to duplicate at home."

When shopping computer camps, Keizer points to the importance of finding a program with a proven record, up-to-date software and hardware, and plenty of computers and counselors. He holds up three camps as standard-bearers: Futurekids in Los Angeles, The Technology Camp at Epiphany in Seattle, and Computer-Ed High-Tech Camp in Newton, Massachusetts. Fees average about $200/week. Aside from camps and clubs, remember to check out community and school libraries and local museums.

The Integrated TV: You Screen, I Screen, We All Screen—But Which Screen?

Many people are wondering what the primary display device in our homes will be with the convergence of the telecommunication industries. Phone companies, cable companies, broadcast companies, and video companies are already partnering with manufacturers of computer hardware and software in an unprecedented variety of links and relationships that fore-

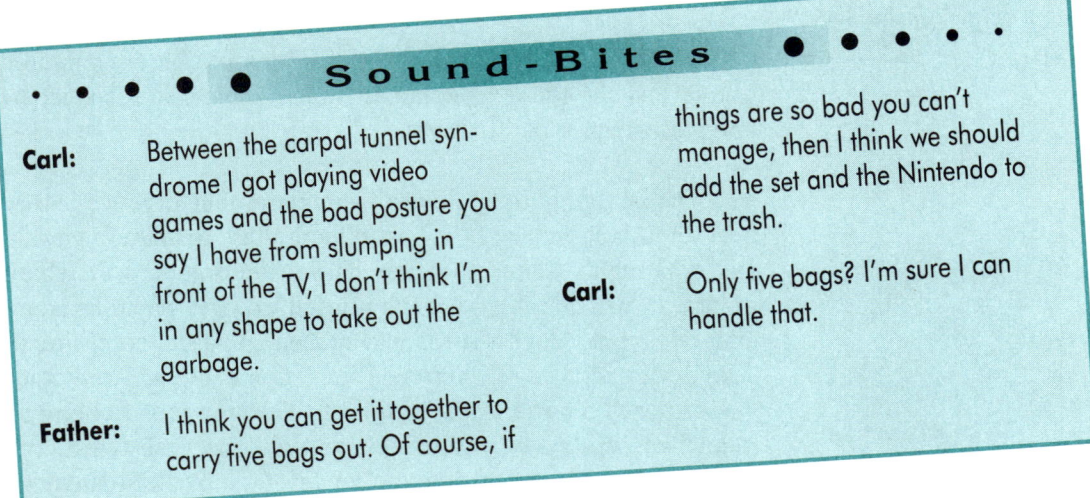

S o u n d - B i t e s

Carl: Between the carpal tunnel syndrome I got playing video games and the bad posture you say I have from slumping in front of the TV, I don't think I'm in any shape to take out the garbage.

Father: I think you can get it together to carry five bags out. Of course, if things are so bad you can't manage, then I think we should add the set and the Nintendo to the trash.

Carl: Only five bags? I'm sure I can handle that.

cast the merger of the TV screen and the computer. In the not-too-distant future a full array of learning, entertainment, cultural, compositional, and computational tools will be accessed through computers and displayed on high-definition TV screens.

Personal Note
· · · · · · · · · · · · · ·

Karen remembers her first interactive TV experience at age 4, way before the "age of interactivity." She was an avid fan of a kid show called **Winky-Dink and You.** *They mailed viewers a little piece of vinyl to put on the TV screen as a drawing surface for a weekly treasure hunt adventure. You were virtually drawing on the screen. One day she was looking everywhere but couldn't find her vinyl. When* **Winky-Dink** *came on, Karen couldn't bear the thought of missing the interactive segment, so she got her crayons and drew right on the screen.*

There are precursors to what are now truly interactive programs. *The Mickey Mouse Club* in the 1950s and *Zoom* in the 1970s invited kids' input through mail-in suggestions and contributions. *U to U* on Nickelodeon touts itself as the first interactive TV program to merit the name. While it features a series of five or so action-packed information segments, all based on ideas sent in by kids via fax, phone, home computer, or mail, it's still primitive interactively compared to e-mail, bulletin boards, and the sophistication of computer games and CD-ROM programs that offer choices in response to the performance of the player.

The benefit of this television-computer convergence is that we can ultimately have the best of both: high resolution visuals and top quality sound together with a multimedia mix which reintroduces and integrates the printed word. It was television, in fact, that devalued written and spoken language, according to Lloyd Morrisett of the Markle Foundation. "The written word had almost no place in the world of television mostly because television was a world of images, but also because the television screen was a poor medium for print. . . . Written language is an essential element of culture, an economical and rich way to convey meaning, relatively cheap to produce, and convenient to use. These age-old merits will have newfound value in the world of multimedia." Print is once again in the foreground. Today, kids are e-mailing friends and relatives; they're enjoying creative writing software programs and adding music to their own haiku and limericks and graphics to their short stories. They can highlight and take notes from online news text and from literature programs.

In the end, some fundamental things prevail. Whether the arena is defined by the TV screen or computer screen, whether selecting a video, a CD-ROM, or an online service, your role as a parent remains the same. Parents need to ensure that kids have access to the best programs and are carefully supervised in their use. They need to balance screen time with outdoor time, together time, and time for those ongoing commitments. Wherever possible, kids need to be included in decision making. They should be active participants in their own education and entertainment, learning themselves how to monitor the time they spend in front of the screen and exercising judgment about the quality of what they watch. That way, today's channel-surfing couch potatoes can join yesterday's dinosaurs and become curiosities like 45s, slide rules, and kinescopes—remember them?

Cyberglossary

Access. The means of getting into an online system.

Address. A destination for mail or files at an online site.

Browser. Software used to search for information on the World Wide Web. Netscape and Mosaic are examples of widely used browsers.

Chat. Online conversation in which two or more people type back and forth.

E-mail. Short for "electronic mail." A message passed via computer.

Forum. A theme-specific gathering place where users can download files and chat.

Internet. A system of networks allowing worldwide communication among remote computers.

Newsgroup. An area where people discuss a topic by exchanging messages.

Online. Any situation in which computers are talking to each other.

Search engine. A means of finding information on a database or on the Internet; usually accessible through a service provider.

Server. The focal point of a network, the computer through which you connect to the Internet. The server is maintained where you have your Internet account (for example, one of the online services).

Website or home page. Locations on the Internet or World Wide Web established by individuals, companies, or organizations of any kind.

World Wide Web. System allowing easy access to linked data on the Internet; a subset of the Internet with the capability of including graphics.

Family Activity

Plan Your Own Video Game

Have you ever enjoyed making up your own endings to stories or changing familiar plots so the characters do different things and different things happen? That's basically what computer games are all about. They start with a main idea and then go off in many different directions, leaving the player in the driver's seat to steer the story where you want it to go.

You'll need:
just a paper and pen

Start with Your Main Idea (Theme)
Establish the main character(s) and the story context or main setting.

First-Level Choices
Set up five choices that your main character could make early in the story.

Introduce other characters and locations.

Second-Level Choices
Set up three choices that could be made from each alternative in the first level.

Introduce more characters and more locations.

Third-Level End
Establish the "winning" or end of game arrival point.

9 We're the People

Advocate for Meaningful Kids' Media

The most profound impact you have on your kids' viewing happens at home every day when you select appropriate content and timing of programming. But beyond the living room, you can also help make a significant difference to your kids' viewing options by adding your voice to the call for quality children's media and the regulation of the airwaves and online services available to them.

A broad agenda of issues from violence on TV to monitoring cyberspace travel invite your attention. There are many opportunities to influence those in the communications industry who provide the programming, and those in government who regulate the providers. Your time and personal style will dictate whether you register your opinions individually, join an existing advocacy group, or organize your own effort.

Max Frankel, in a 1995 *New York Times Magazine* article, "Alas for Hamelin!", notes the irony in government regulation of this domain: "Children can't be treated as mature consumers. That's why government does not let children buy cars, guns, liquor, or cigarettes. The elementary idea that children need the moral direction and protection of adults, backed by the force of law, governs policy in virtually every sphere of American life— except television, the most pervasive influence of all."

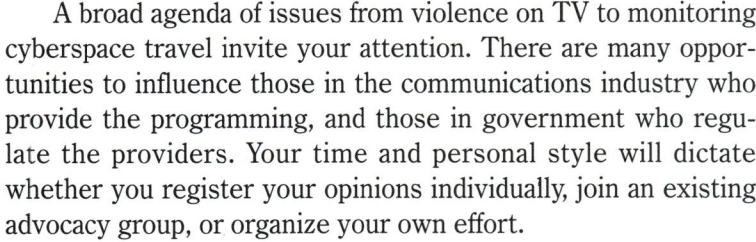

Tune In the Topics

- The Children's Television Act Is a Case Study in Advocacy: What Does It Say and How's It Been Working?
- Why and Whom to Lobby?
- How to Lobby: The Government, Communications Industry, Advertisers
- Where to Sign On: Overview of Child Advocacy Groups
- Family Activity: Advocate as a Family

This chapter addresses the many ways you can advocate for accessible quality programming for your kids. The process may involve you in writing, calling, faxing, or e-mailing your congressional representatives, government regulators, advertisers, and broadcasters. In putting together this chapter, we talked with Peggy Charren, founder of the Boston-based Action for Children's Television. Active from 1968 to 1992, ACT worked for more choice in quality children's programming and the elimination of exploitative commercials targeted at kids. Her thirty years of experience as an advocate for quality children's television have given Charren a valuable perspective and insight on these issues. Throughout this chapter we've sprinkled excerpts from our talk with Charren, whose own experience shows what can happen when an individual takes on the challenge to deliver the best media possible to kids.

The Children's Television Act Is a Case Study in Advocacy: What Does It Say and How's It Been Working?

In a 1995 *New York Times* op-ed piece, the past and present chairmen of the Federal Communications Commission, Newton N. Minow and Reed Hundt, crystallized the issue of children's television: "Broadcasters once accepted that nurturing children is part of the public interest. In 1951, when TV was still new and broadcasters wanted to convince adults that buying a TV set would enrich their children's lives, twenty-seven hours of children's programming aired each week, much of it high-quality. But over the years, commercial TV has virtually abandoned its responsibility to kids. Increasingly, children's programs—at least on commercial TV—have become less about education and enrichment and more about merchandising. Today, broadcasters too often see children simply as consumers." This downward trend in children's programming was the impetus for

Dad 1: So let me get this right. If I read all the reviews, clip them and save them, scan the catalogs for the best, pound the pavements to find who's renting and selling the award-winners, go to the library to see if they have anything good, lay down some ground rules and enforce them, watch what the kids are watching, monitor what they see at the neighbor's house, limit viewing time to an hour a day and insist it be after chores and homework, then I can let them watch, and I can enjoy a clear conscience while they do?

Dad 2: After you write your congressman to lobby for better programming, I'd say you'd have it covered.

the 1990 Children's Television Act, which serves as a case study in advocacy. It illustrates the dogged effort required not only to get a bill passed, but more importantly to ensure regulations are clearly articulated and successfully enforced—the true test of whether legislation is working.

The 1990 Act was the result of years of work by ACT and their advocates, reflecting the necessary activities for advocating on a small scale all the way up to getting a law passed, something most of us probably won't do. Although the 1990 Act was passed unanimously, it was first vetoed by Ronald Reagan. It took another major effort by ACT, in conjunction with other organizations and concerned members of Congress, to finally get it through after a new Administration took over. Charren credits Massachusetts Representative Edward Markey, who sponsored the bill and rallied support from other legislators, as a superhero for children's television. She observes it isn't enough to have concerned citizens, you need to have someone rooting for you in Congress. Charren observes: "The Children's Television Act is a wonderful focus through which to see whether or not broadcasting is serving the needs of the community. You have to do some monitoring first to find out what your stations are doing. You can do some of it in the TV listings. The 'public interest' workings of the station are a sham unless they fulfill the mandate of the Act." In summarizing the law, she points to its three components and the issues each raises for clarification and enforcement . . . the areas where she feels efforts must be focused today:

- *Every broadcaster, in return for its license, must provide some programs specifically designed to serve the educational needs of children.*

Work must be done here because a problem arises in the definition of what constitutes programs specifically designed to serve children's education. Many of the broadcasters have tried to pass off shows like *The Jetsons, America's Funniest Home Videos,* and *X-Men* as educational . . . much as the Administration in the 1980s redefined ketchup as a vegetable (thereby undercutting nutritional requirements for school lunches in their effort to reduce costs). Another problem is that the airing of these shows often occurs at times that aren't compatible with the real-life schedules of kids: during dinner hours, early weekday mornings, or late in the evening.

- *The 1990 Act puts a limit on the number of commercial minutes permitted per hour during the week and on weekends.*

The limits are set to change to 10.5 minutes per hour on weekends and 12 minutes during the week. This weekday limit allows for more commercials for children than for adults in prime time. This needs adjusting downward.

- *A small endowment for children's television, which had been expected to be funded at about $10 million, was established, to be administered through the Commerce Department.*

Actual funding didn't commence until 1992, and little has been allocated to date. Recent funding was for only about $2 million. This could represent the last monies that get allocated, since the present Congress is trying to do away with the Commerce Department altogether and is also trying to cut its preexisting commitments to public television and the endowments for the arts and humanities. Funding needs to be increased and guaranteed.

Why and Whom to Lobby?

Unfortunately, kids' TV isn't a protected wonderland of entertaining and educational goodies available whenever kids are ready to watch. And the information superhighway isn't a yellow brick road leading to a safe universe of fun and enlightenment. We can't totally insulate our kids from the real world of violence, sex, foul language, and the aggressive advertising that often pays the freight to serve it up to us. But there are steps we can take to limit our children's exposure to these influ-

Sound-Bites

Hank: I can't believe there's nothing I want to see that's on now when I can watch. Too bad the VCR's out being fixed.

Mom: Why not write a letter to the stations and tell them how you feel?

Hank: Yeah, like they're really going to care what I think.

Mom: Maybe it won't change things, but they won't know they have things to change if no one ever tells them.

Hank: What are the phone numbers? I'd rather call. That way they'll hear sooner.

231

ences. We can also help ensure that a reasonable amount of quality educational media designed specifically for kids is available for them to enjoy. One forward step was the 1990 Children's Television Act, which stipulates that stations licensed by the Federal Communications Commission (FCC) must broadcast programs "specifically designed to meet the education and information needs of children." However, most broadcasters are not living up to the mandate of this legislation, and the FCC has had to step in to refine the regulations and their enforcement.

The Issues

Issues around children and the electronic media will continue to surface with changes in communication technology. The longest-running debate centers on broadcast television and the fact that broadcasters are not adequately meeting their obligation to the public. We the people own the public airwaves, and it's important to remember that our government licenses the use of the airwaves to broadcasters. The 1934 Communications Act, in acknowledging the public's ownership of the airwaves, declared that in return for a license to broadcast over these airwaves, each station has a responsibility to serve the public. In effect, this established the broadcasters as public trustees. Unhappily, our kids' needs and rights are not being adequately served by the broadcasting industry or its advertisers, even with the existence of the 1990 Act.

Looking ahead, the new digital technologies will provide many options, including more frequencies available for programming. Existing stations are likely to receive five or so additional frequencies free for their use to offer programs and sell advertising. A 1995 *New York Times* editorial suggested that by offering this wider bandwidth gratis, Congress will be making needless additional "handouts" to the broadcasters who aren't presently meeting their mandate to provide adequate public service and children's programs in exchange for their licenses on their existing frequencies. The *Times* suggests that since the new frequencies are worth tens of billions of dollars they should be auctioned off: "With this alternative, Congress could raise money and preserve free over-the-air television. Unfortunately, the House and Senate commerce committees knuckled under to the broadcasters in September of 1995 and put digital auctions aside."

The question of digital auctions is one of many topics for parent advocacy today. Other issues relate to sections of the recently passed Telecommunications Act as well as the actual enforcement of the 1990 Children's Television Act. A coalition of more than a dozen national education, consumer, and child advocacy groups are urging the FCC to set stricter standards for compliance with the 1990 Act. Groups include: Center for Media Education, National Education Association, National Association of Child Advocates, Consumer Federation of America.

The Telecommunications Act is very complex, regulating an industry much larger than health care. Two areas for parents' concerns relate to provisions for the V-chip and for Internet regulation. These provisions may appear protective but in fact raise censorship issues. In addition, advocacy groups need to address the fact that media companies are not required by the Act to provide community access or educational programming in exchange for operating and profiting in the communities they serve.

There are other bills before Congress or other agencies as well. Goals 2000 is a bill meant to enhance elementary and secondary education. As part of this, Title III-autho-

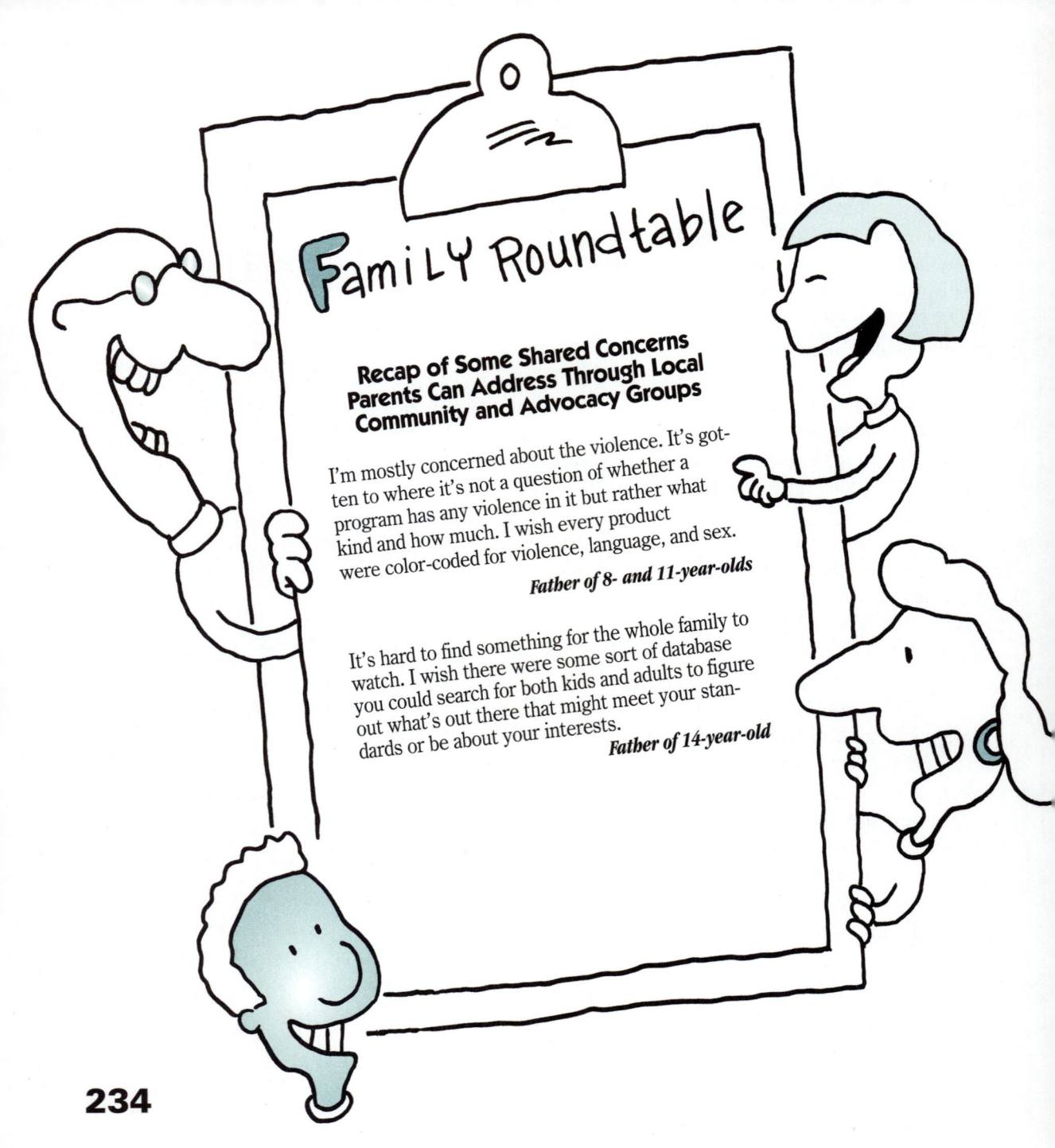

Family Roundtable

Recap of Some Shared Concerns Parents Can Address Through Local Community and Advocacy Groups

I'm mostly concerned about the violence. It's gotten to where it's not a question of whether a program has any violence in it but rather what kind and how much. I wish every product were color-coded for violence, language, and sex.

Father of 8- and 11-year-olds

It's hard to find something for the whole family to watch. I wish there were some sort of database you could search for both kids and adults to figure out what's out there that might meet your standards or be about your interests.

Father of 14-year-old

rized money is to be spent to wire some schools and libraries as models and catalysts to attract other money to be spent for similar purposes. The moneys for this program are being cut back.

Wiring schools and libraries for the information superhighway would help assure universal access. To this end the Commerce Department and the Department of Education are also supposed to put money into this endeavor. Similarly, the Telecommunications Infrastructure Assistance Program, under the National Telecommunications Information Administration, has set aside money for networking communities. Parents need to keep track of these proceedings and advocate for money to be kept at high levels. Proceedings are also done at the state level on issues of universal access, rate setting, and other issues of interest to parents.

If you elect to get involved, it will most likely be one of these concerns that will call you to action:

- *guaranteeing a minimum amount of educational programming specifically targeted to children*

- *defining what constitutes "educational programming"*

- *assigning reasonable time slots for quality children's programs—making them available when children are most likely to watch*

- *informing the public about the degree of violence and sex in programs targeted to children during times they are frequently watching*

- *auctioning off the new spectrum of frequencies to be made available through compressed digital technology*

- *ensuring children's access to the new technologies so some kids don't get a second-class technological education*

- *establishing guidelines for the online services*

As a Matter of Fact...

Only 7 percent of the computers in the nation's schools are able to support the requirements of the latest software.

- *rating computer entertainment software*

- *monitoring advertising online that masquerades as information*

- *developing guidelines and limits for acceptable advertising to children with a special focus on alcohol and tobacco products*
- *implementing media literacy programs in the schools*
- *regulating and enforcing all these safeguards*

The Targets

Principally, it's the broadcasters, advertisers, and your government representatives and regulators who have to be lobbied regarding protecting and ensuring children's rights *vis-à-vis* the various communications media.

Since local stations must apply to the government for their licenses and they select the programming they'll carry, local broadcasters should be a primary target in voicing your concerns. Broadcast television remains the one free media source available to everyone who owns a set (98 percent of the population).

Advertisers who buy commercial time on programs you find questionable, or who target inappropriate ads to your kids, need to hear your objections and suggestions for how they can have a more positive influence (or at least a nonthreatening influence) on children's media. Read on in the "How to Lobby" section for how to approach them.

The new media and just-around-the-corner expansions of broadcast, cable, and online services demand your surveillance and involvement to ensure they serve the best interests of your kids. Parents need to assure the enforcement of the 1990 Children's Television Act, to say nothing of the new issues surfacing in the dynamic evolution of the communications industry. Speak out—advocacy really can have an effect.

How to Lobby: The Government, Communications Industry, Advertisers

As a parent you represent an important constituency, and you can have an impact from your local school board to Congress. It was parent activism that helped pass the 1990 Children's Television Act and implement media literacy programs in many schools. Parents need to keep advocating. You have many other opportunities to make a difference.

Since many broadcasters are not adhering to the 1990 Children's Television Act, that's one place parents need to turn up the volume: Lobby more forcefully, and hold the leaders of the communications industry accountable for the programming they present . . . and don't present. Charren asserts: "This is not a left/right, Republican/Democrat problem. This is the society caring about its children and the citizens caring enough to speak out about what matters."

Sound-Bites

Mom 1: I've been reading about the congressional hearings on violence and television. I wish I had the time to do something because this violence thing has gotten way out of hand.

Mom 2: The garbage that oozes out of the tube these days! Let's write a letter to our rep, or better yet, let's e-mail him. Democracy in the 1990s is getting up to speed with the new technologies.

A Strategy for Lobbying

Charren generously shares her experiences of years organizing, joining forces with other groups, working with lawyers to formulate proposals to Congress, and reaching out to the press and media. A clear and simple strategy has underscored her efforts: She has fought battles for monitoring advertising to kids, mandating reasonable time allocations for children's programming, and ensuring ongoing production of quality fare for kids.

When you become aware of a problem you want to address, Charren suggests you have the option to:

- *Work alone.*

- *Join a group working on your issue or related concerns. Initiate the formation of your own advocacy group and then form a coalition with child advocacy groups whose goals are related to the issue(s) you want to address. Use the resources available in your community of concerned peers. Try to get a lawyer to be part of your group— likewise with other professionals upon whose skills you'll need to call: marketing, writing, public relations, fundraising.*

Whether you work alone, join a group or start your own initiative, try to follow these protocols:

- *Articulate your message clearly, and define a course that will be effective. Identify options for improving children's media. If there are examples of solutions that have been effective, then use those as models. Get all the facts straight, and don't say anything until you're sure you're correct. Know what to say first, and make your arguments supported with facts, not hysterics.*

- *Target who needs to be addressed. Forge relationships with legislators and regulators. Communicate with local broadcasters, (since it's the local stations who are the licensees) and with the networks. Express your views to the advertisers.*

- *Bring attention to your cause. Send copies of your letters to the local and national press. Make phone calls, stating your business briefly and positively to the appropriate department and person. Don't say anything you'd be uncomfortable seeing on the front page of your local newspaper.*

> Parents should get involved and make a lot of noise with local stations and newspapers to assure diverse educational programming for their children. Opening your mouth really can make a difference. Who would have thought that our effort begun in a suburban community could result in federal legislation and a lot of press attention to the issue?
>
> **Peggy Charren**
> *Founder of Action for Children's Television*
> *Mother of two and grandmother of*
> *children ages 9, 5, and 2*

There are many successful lobbying efforts to point to as models and inspiration. When CBS agreed to be bought by Westinghouse Electric Corporation, Westinghouse needed the FCC to grant rule waivers that would enable it to take over the licenses of some CBS stations. A coalition of groups, including the Center for Media Education and United Church of Christ, petitioned the FCC to deny Westinghouse's application on the basis that CBS did not provide enough children's educational programming to meet FCC requirements. Before the ruling, Westinghouse agreed that it would voluntarily increase programming for children from one hour a week to two in 1996 and three in 1997.

Baltimore-based Advocates for Children & Youth, Inc., launched Campaign for Kids' TV in 1992 to make sure TV stations in the state complied with the Children's Television Act of 1990. One activity is an annual report card for the fourteen local stations that looks at hours of programming, varied target ages, quality, and locally produced programs. The project makes children's television a state agenda item, and they report the stations still have much room for improvement.

The Consumer Federation of America, the Center for Media Education, and the NAACP sponsored a study that looked at where regional phone companies are planning on building advanced communications networks for wiring the information superhighway. The study showed that poorer neighborhoods were being bypassed. The consumer and civil rights groups coalition informed the media of their findings, which got media play in major outlets. This survey will help support bills in Congress for universal access.

The Center for Media Education prepared a study in 1992 on station compliance with the Children's Television Act. Their findings showed that broadcasters were not making an effort to adequately serve the educational and informational needs of children and that many stations were not providing the minimum information required by the FCC. Subsequent to the study, CME requested stricter guidelines be formulated by the FCC. At this writing, the FCC is in a process of examining new guidelines.

Lobby the Legislators and Go on Record with the Regulators

Effective lobbying requires understanding the basic process involved in writing and enforcing laws. Often it's only after a bill is passed that the important implementation details are worked out. This is done through the regulatory agencies, which have oversight over the legislation and see that it's enforced. Often the very goals of a bill are diluted or trivialized during the process of working out the nuts and bolts. In the case of the 1990 Children's Television Act, it was a long haul to get the bill passed, and the full story cannot yet be told, since the broadcasters are not adhering to its mandates.

The Children's Television Act is a good example of why advocates need to monitor the regulators. At this writing, parents and children's media advocates are lobbying the FCC to ensure the regulations are defined clearly and are carried out. In addition to monitoring enforcement of the law, advocates are addressing their concerns to their local stations and newspapers. They're "making a lot of noise," which Charren says is necessary. Advocates have been able to keep discussion of the negotiations on the front-page news as well as in the op-ed pages. These issues are attracting attention from the highest levels of government. Vice President Al Gore and his wife, Tipper, in recognizing the importance of addressing these concerns, convened a "Family Re-Union IV, Family and the Media" conference on the subject of children's media, which included President Bill Clinton, entertainment and advertising executives, over 850 educators, child advocates and politicians, and other professionals in children's issues and in children's media.

Program the Broadcasters and Sell Solutions to the Advertisers

Truth is, the broadcasters know how to do right by kids. The problem is that they're not motivated to do so, even though they could be subject to a challenge when their licenses come up for renewal. They're probably not that fearful, since the Children's Television Act doesn't presently have enough teeth in it to hold them accountable. What does motivate the broadcasters is the bottom line, which means they must look for the largest audience to deliver to their advertisers. There is no mass audience of children similar to the audience for prime-time programs because children comprise many audiences, based on their ages, interests, and abilities. Charren regrets that the broadcasters' attitude seems to be that if there isn't a mass market, there's no market: "Nobody thought that serving the public was always going to win the ratings game, or you wouldn't need to have a legal mandate. And programming for children is a special problem because three-, seven-, and twelve-year-olds are like three different species."

In the early days of TV, when the industry was trying to get families to buy sets, they had every reason to offer a menu of programs that generously included the kids. And Charren harks back to the 1970s when CBS was doing wonderful programming for children: *Captain Kangaroo,* news inserts between cartoons, the *The CBS Children's Film Festival* on Saturday afternoons, and more. She recalls, "They actually had twenty people in their news department dedicated to children's programs." Then deregulation of children's television in the early 1980s happened, which loosened government control on the broadcasters, and it all went out the door. The news shows disappeared, as did the film festival. *Captain Kangaroo* went from five days a week to a once-a-week 5 A.M. slot when the audience was still sleeping. "You don't have to tell the industry how to do good," Charren noted: "They know. It's just that unless they feel they have to, they won't."

Broadcasters need to hear from you about the programs you *do* value. Let them see where they succeed for children and for parents. Let them know the shows that exemplify quality viewing and why they win your support. Rally them to provide more programs like nature series or special-interest shows. It's clear from their programs that the cable and video industries have recognized that significant target audiences do exist for children's programming. So let the broadcasters know you're turning more and more to cable and home video as an alternative to the scarcity of good programming available on their local stations.

Charren identifies this advocacy goal as follows: "If the stations don't start really acting like they're the trustees of the public airwaves, the public should take the signals back and auction them off and use the money to fund a strong, meaningful, serviceable public telecommunications system." Now that additional spectrums will become available through digital technology, we should work to ensure there will be space dedicated to children and families.

> ## As a Matter of Fact...
>
> - Two-thirds of American homes with TV have cable.
>
> - Cable's prime-time audience has increased by more than 24 percent since October 1994, while that of the networks has declined by nearly 7 percent.
>
> - The children's cable station Nickelodeon has an average audience equal in size to that of the three networks put together, even though it's seen in one-third fewer homes.

Advertisers

Advertisers are also trying to move into home video and online services. Their influence on the airwaves should stand as a warning to us all to be watchful of how they will seek to influence these media as well. They've already made inroads in video and on cable by turning licensed characters into programs such as *Care Bears* and *X-Men;* they then market an avalanche of goodies that lure kids to the retail marketplace in search of action figures and logo lunchboxes. The online services are carrying advertising and underwriting websites. Since kids represent an over $11-billion market, it's reasonable to assume that advertisers will also extend their reach into cyberspace shopping malls and ad-supported informational material that could bias the content without users knowing the source. One such example would be a movie review option underwritten by a major studio whose own films comprise most of what's included. Parents need to be vocal when they feel the advertisers have crossed an acceptable line in targeting their kids.

Advertising Age and other trade publications indicate that in the future there will be a blending of advertisement and information so that children will not be able to tell if they're getting unbiased information or if they're being sold to or used to gather marketing information. An example of this, discussed in Chapter 8, is KIDCOM, the thinly masked advertising survey pitched as an online playground for kids. This blending is exploitive and should be stopped. The developments in advertising to kids online is mirroring the history of advertising to kids on television. Of course, TV advertising to kids is now somewhat limited due to ACT's twenty-year-plus advocacy in this area. With the onlines, however, advocates must once again get involved on behalf of kids. The advertisers are sophisticated, and the problem is now even larger than that seen in television because of the interactive nature of the new media. Advertisers can speak to kids by name and request information from them. Safe spaces on the information superhighway, akin to public television, should be guaranteed to kids so they're not always put in a commercial environment. Educational services, like public playgrounds, should be ensured, as should access to all

Personal Notes
. . . .

Karen's son Nate, when confronted with some nasty, prejudiced comments from someone in a popular online chat room, demonstrated kids can advocate, too. He summoned the online guide to make him aware of the conversation, posted a complaint to the perpetrator, and then privately "instant messaged" the other people in the chat room, asking them to also go on record.

kids. Kathryn Montgomery of the Center for Media Education calls this our "electronic legacy."

One aspect of the history of broadcast advertising has been marked by the flagrant disregard for children's health, including relentless advertising of sugared snacks to kids. Action for Children's Television won some important victories that set an example for future advocacy in this area. They succeeded in getting clearly defined breaks inserted between programs and ads so kids could distinguish between them. They also succeeded in prohibiting main characters like Captain Kangaroo from being spokespeople for advertised products. ACT also enlisted the cooperation of the American Academy of Pediatrics to put an end to advertising vitamins to children. Prior to this ban on vitamin ads to kids, one third of all commercials directed to children were for vitamins. Three principal advertisers produced commercials presenting their vitamin products like candy, even though the bottles themselves had warnings to keep the product out of the reach of children.

According to *Advertising Age,* the most lively debate at the 1995 conference of the Association of National Advertisers centered on TV violence, with several members calling it "the most pressing issue facing advertisers today." The question remains, what will they do about it? Set up a ratings system? Who will define the ratings if they do? Will industry self-regulation work? Many

As a Matter of Fact...

In the early 1970s, 16 minutes per hour of commercials were directed at children. Today, thanks to the 1990 Children's Television Act, it's between 10.5 and 12 minutes.

TIPS

- **Demand strong enforcement of the Children's Television Act from the FCC and compliance by local stations.**

- **Write and call local TV stations and key advertisers and advocate for quality children's programming.**

FIGHT T.V. VIOLENCE

245

children's advocates feel the ad industry must be monitored, especially in their participation in children's programs that include violence or other inappropriate elements.

If you're particularly disturbed with an advertiser who's supporting an inappropriate show or advertising to young people when they shouldn't be targeting this demographic (as some alcohol and tobacco companies do), you always have the option to boycott their product. We feel, however, that you can be quite influential by calling and writing them and getting your letters published in the press, letting them know your concern and also letting them know what existing kids' programs and ads *are* appropriate. Contact consumer or customer relations departments to express your views.

Where to Sign On: Overview of Child Advocacy Groups

When redressing a particular issue related to children and media, you have many options for rallying people to your cause beyond individual letters and phone calls. You might look into

Sound-Bites

Anna: Why are you in an online chat room for parents, complaining about kids' chat rooms?

Mom: I'm not complaining about kids' chat rooms in general, just some of the language that gets by the online monitors.

Dad: I wonder if there are online picket lines . . .

working with one of the established children's media advocacy groups like the Center for Media Education in Washington. Since ACT disbanded, CME has proved the most active and influential group, keeping the flame alive and advancing the cause of government and industry adherence to acceptable standards for children's programming. Under the stewardship of Kathryn Montgomery and Jeffrey Chester, the center has focused on two main areas: improving the quality of children's television, and fostering a public-interest vision for the new media and the information superhighway. The center organizes and educates other nonprofit organizations on its focus issues, serves as a clearinghouse for the news media researching issues in electronic media, and prepares FCC and FTC filings. Its policy work is more at the regulatory level rather than legislative. CME works in concert with other groups, such as the American Library Association, the National PTA, and the Black Child Development Institute. The information superhighway issues it focuses on include:

- *ensuring that children from all walks of life have access to the online infrastructure and can reap its benefits*
- *advocating policies that provide safeguards against advertising targeted to kids that masquerades as programming*
- *ensuring sufficient mechanisms for noncommercial educational services*

If there's no appropriate advocacy group near you, or if you have an issue you don't feel is being adequately addressed, you may choose to start your own group. If you do, you can organize a coalition of existing groups to work with you. To identify which groups you could partner with, Charren suggests you begin with groups that care about children's needs in a general way. See who's on their boards of advisors or directors. Read their mission statements, and see if their goals and activities are compatible with your concerns. An alliance with an established group can save you time and resources. Their memberships also represent significant numbers you can point to as supporters if you work together with them. Here are some groups whose state affiliates you should consider approaching in your quest for a coalition:

American Federation of Teachers

American Library Association

American Psychological Association

Consumers Federation of America

Consumers Union

Mainstream religious organizations, such as the National Council of Churches

National Association for the Education of Young Children

National Education Association

National PTA

State Academy of Pediatrics

State Association of Elementary School and High School Principals

If you decide to start your own group, Charren advises that you:

- *get a lawyer and incorporate as a nonprofit so you're positioned to raise and disburse funds*
- *run your organization as if you were a public company*
  - *have an outside board of directors*
  - *have a financial audit every year*
  - *remember not to say or do anything you'd be uncomfortable seeing on the front page of your local paper*

Basically, this is all about staying squeaky clean, since opponents may try to discredit you or your organization or at least distract opinion from your advocacy message.

Whatever you endeavor to do, draw upon your strongest skills and interests—letter writing, making calls, getting publicity—to bring attention to your cause. You can win the attention of other parents and concerned citizens by placing op-ed pieces or letters to the editor in local or regional papers expressing your concerns about children's programming. Don't forget to highlight the shows, broadcasters, and advertisers you feel are doing a good job. Copies of published pieces sent to the stations and advertisers will demonstrate the attention you can attract and will help them recognize the positive publicity they receive when they hit a home run in delivering quality shows to families.

There is at least one group focused on every issue we've discussed. For media literacy there is the Center for Media Literacy in Los Angeles. The CML wants Congress to assist the media literacy movement in the United States with legislation that would appropriate funds in three important areas:

- *stimulate research*
- *promote training of teachers in media literacy*
- *encourage the development of additional educational resources for a variety of ages, applications, and audiences*

Beyond lobbying government and industry, you may find that a media literacy program in your school or community could be a productive focus for your energies. Consider a collaboration between your schools and your cable company to create a media literacy program for kids. An outstanding example is *The TV Tool Kit,* produced by Continental Cablevision of Massachusetts. *The TV Tool Kit* consists of print and video components for use by teachers, parent-teacher organizations, and parents at home. This full-media literacy education program for children is the result of a partnership of the cable company, parents, and schools. See the "Resources" section for how to contact Continental to receive materials and information on this worthwhile model.

New technologies like computer games and the Internet increasingly will demand our involvement as watchdogs and advocates for our kids. Digital compression would offer each local station potential access to up to six more signals through which to air programs and sell advertising. This could provide a real opportunity to take advantage of this added electronic territory for our kids, but history cautions us about the broadcasters' bottom-line motivations. In fact, this new electronic territory was almost given away to the broadcasters in legislation that passed both houses of Congress and is still under consideration. Advocates for auctioning the digital spectrum got media attention just in time for some senators to reconsider the giveaway.

TIP

Read the newspapers or contact CME to keep current on the issues and pending legislation concerning the communications industry and its impact on children.

Advertisers are very responsive to their customers. Broadcasters are responsive to their advertisers and their viewers. Legislators are responsive to their constituents and regulators have a mandate to formulate guidelines and ensure that they be followed. But advertisers, broadcasters, and legislators often pay lip service to what's best for America's kids. Let them all put their money and their power where there mouths are. They'll be more likely to adhere to the Children's Television Act and to future regulations for quality children's programs and responsible advertising to kids if parents remain vocal in their support for their kids' welfare.

Remember, kids love TV. Most of us do. Kathryn Montgomery of the Center for Media Education calls our attention to the fact that "Since the earliest days of television, children have been among the heaviest users of electronic media." We can imagine a time when the screen, in all of its incarnations, will fulfill its potential to deliver a readily accessible treasure of learning and experience for all kids. It can happen. This book demonstrates how you can apply your own parenting skills in the arena of electronic media. In these pages, we've tried to alert you to appreciate how your child's development fits into choosing appropriate programming and software, and to provide guidelines on how to use these resources. When the important challenges you confront daily involve the screen, we've directed you to use your VCR as one versatile resource to help teach your kids about balance in their lives, compromise within the family, self-regulation, and the importance of developing a set of values to live by. Keep an eye on the news and the dynamic changes in communications that will have an influence on your kids. Think about where telecommunications will be twenty or thirty years from now, when your kids may be parents themselves. Advocate both in and beyond your home for sensitive, entertaining, and enlightening programs for your family. Then you can truly feel good about turning on the set!

Family Activity

Advocate as a Family

Advocate together for quality kids' media. No matter how small your effort and no matter what your cause, your family will be gratified by the experience of exercising their rights as citizens. Here are a few suggestions that might invite you to join with each other and "get involved."

- Review your newspaper's TV listings for a given day, and tape those children's programs on a local station with which you're not already familiar. Search through the shows and make a list of those you consider worthwhile and those you feel are worthless. Use Chapter 4's "Green Light Test" to help you with your assessments. See how the offerings line up. Write and let the station manager know your opinion.

- Form a group of station monitors. Assign someone to each local station and have them log the good and poor children's programs broadcast for the week. Again use the "Green Light Test" as a standard list of criteria. By the end of the week, every station will have been monitored every day. Gather this information together with your thumbs-up and

thumbs-down assessments. Communicate your findings to the stations, and write a letter to your local paper with your "informal study" and recommendations for more of the good stuff.

- Arrange for a legislator or kids' media expert to speak at your school. Ask them to focus their talk on how kids and families can make a difference in children's media.

- Write your congressmen/congresswomen with your views regarding any pending legislation concerning kids and the media.

- Tape Saturday morning ads. Fast-forward through them, and log how many were for unhealthy snack foods. Write the station managers with your findings and opinions.

- Petition support at a school or community fair for legislation under consideration regarding children's media. Send the signed petitions to your legislators.

- Write producers who are making worthwhile programs available, acknowledging your support and encouragement that they keep up the good work, and let your local paper know who's doing the good stuff.

Resources

Chapter 1
It's More Than Eye Candy

Plug into Your Kid's Viewing and Discover Video's Value

Books

For Further Reading About the State of Children's Television and the New Media

Chen, Milton. *The Smart Parent's Guide to Kids' TV.* San Francisco: KQED Books, 1994.

Greenfield, Patricia Marks. *Mind & Media: The Effects of Television, Video Games, and Computers.* Cambridge, MA: Harvard University Press, 1984.

Leonhardt, Mary. *Parents Who Love Reading, Kids Who Don't.* New York: Crown Publishers, Inc., 1993.

Lesser, Gerald S. *Children and Television: Lessons from Sesame Street.* New York: Vintage Books/Random House, 1974.

Minow, Newton N., and Craig L. Lamay. *Abandoned in the Wasteland: Children, Television and the First Amendment.* New York: Hill & Wang, 1995.

Negroponte, Nicholas. *Being Digital.* New York: Knopf, 1995.

Chapter 2
Who's Got the Remote?

Video and Parenting

Books

Bettelheim, Bruno. *The Uses of Enchantment.* New York: Random House, 1989.

Faber, Adele, and Elaine Mazlish. *How to Talk So Your Kids Will Listen and Listen So Your Kids Will Talk.* New York: Avon Books, 1980.

Leach, Penelope. *Your Growing Child: From Babyhood Through Adolescence.* New York: Knopf, 1995.

Spock, Dr. Benjamin. *Baby and Child Care.* New York: Pocket Books, 1976.

Chapter 3
Is TV Only for Dessert?

Video as Part of Daily Life

Books

For Alternative Activities to TV

Bennett, Steve and Ruth. *365 Outdoor Activities You Can Do with Your Child.* Holbrook, MA: Bob Adams, Inc., Publishers, 1993.

Bennett, Steve and Ruth. *365 TV-Free Activities You Can Do with Your Child.* Holbrook, MA:

Bob Adams, Inc., Publishers, 1991.

Black, Kaye. *Kid Vid: Fun-damentals of Video Instruction.* Zephyr Press, Tucson, AZ: 1989.

Brody, Lora. *The Kitchen Survival Guide.* New York: William Morrow and Company, Inc., 1992.

Cassidy, John, and B. C. Rimbeaux. *Juggling for the Complete Klutz.* Palo Alto, CA: Klutz Press, 1994.*

Jay, Dr. Timothy. *Cursing in America.* Philadelphia: J. Benjamins Publishing Company, 1992.

Katzen, Mollie, and Ann Henderson. *Pretend Soup and Other Real Recipes.* Berkeley, CA: Tricycle Press, 1994.

MacColl, Gail. *The Book of Cards for Kids.* New York: Workman Publishing, 1992.**

For Help Organizing Your Time

Schoefield, Deniece. *Confessions of a Happily Organized Family.* Cincinnati, OH: Writer's Digest Books, 1984.

Organizations

American Academy of Pediatrics (708-981-6771) Request pamphlets on children and television.

*Klutz has many other activity books.
**Workman has many other activity books.

Chapter 4
No Guns, No Sex, No Swearing, and They Want to Watch It Again?

How to Select What to Watch

Video Awards

ALSC Notable (Assoc. for Library Service to Children) (800-545-2433)

Coalition for Quality Children's Media (505-989-8076)

Film Advisory Board Award of Excellence (213-874-3644)

International Film & Television Festival of New York (914-238-4481)

National Parenting Publications Award (818-846-0400)

Oppenheim Toy Portfolio (212-598-0502)

Parents' Choice Awards (800-722-2939)

Special-Interest Video Association (203-8331-2891)

Chapter 5
Homework for Parents
Research Can Lead to Buried Treasure

Annotated Video Compendiums

Atkinson, D., and F. Zippan. *Videos for Kids: The Essential, Indispensable Parent's Guide to Children's Movies on Video.* Rocklin, CA: Prima Publishing, 1995.

Catchpole, Catherine and Terry. *The Family Video Guide.* Charlotte, VT: Williamson Publishing, 1992.

Cella, Catherine. *Great Videos for Kids: A Parent's Guide to Choosing the Best.* New York: Carol Publishing Group, 1992.

Green, Diana Huss, ed., et al. *Parents' Choice Magazine Guide to Videocassettes for Children.* Mt. Vernon, NY: Consumers Union, 1989.

MacAlpine, Loretta. *Inside KidVid: The Essential Parent's Guide to Video.* New York: Viking Penguin, 1995.

Martin, Mick, and Marsha Porter. *Video Movie*

Guide 1996 (updated annually). New York: Ballantine Books, 1995.

Spenser, James R. *The Complete Guide to Special-Interest Videos*. Scottsdale, AZ: James–Robert Publishing, 1995–1996.

Publications with Video Reviews and Articles on Industry Trends

On Newsstands

Billboard
Child
Entertainment Weekly
Family Fun
L.A. Parent
New York Family
Parenting
Philadelphia Inquirer
Premiere
San Francisco Parent
TV Guide (especially Children's Television Issue)

By Subscription

Children's Video Report
370 Court Street
Suite 76
Brooklyn, NY 11231
718-935-0640

Children's Video Review Newsletter
916-273-7471

Kids First! Directory
Coalition for Quality Children's Media
535 Cordova Road
Suite 456
Santa Fe, NM 87501
505-989-8076

KIDSNET Media Guide
Computerized clearinghouse for children's TV and radio.
202-291-1400

Parents' Choice
Box 185
Waban, MA 02168
617-965-5913

Organizations

American Library Association
800-545-2433
Ask for information on quality videos.

Distributors

Baker & Taylor
7000 N. Austin Avenue
Niles, IL 60714
800-325-6094

Ingram Entertainment
1125 Heil Quaker Road
LaVergne, TN 37086
800-759-5000

Rounder Kids
800-346-4445

Silo
802-244-5178

Catalogs

Columbia House (800-457-0500)
Critics' Choice Video (800-367-7765)

Critics' Choice Video Search Line (900-370-6500)
Facets Multimedia (800-331-6197)
Listening Library (800-243-4504)
Movies Unlimited (800-523-0823)
Oppenheim Toy Portfolio (212-598-0502)
Troll Communications (800-631-3576)

Specialty Retailers with a Good Selection of Children's Videos

Imaginarium (800-765-8697)
Learningsmith (800-404-2190)
Zany Brainy (610-896-5457)

Online Shopping for Kids Video

America Online (800-827-6364)
"Kids' Only" and "The Global Plaza" areas include kids' videos.
CompuServe Electronic Mall (800-848-8199)
Critics' Choice Video catalog, Entertainment Works.
Prodigy (800-PRODIGY)

Software

Cinemania (CD-ROM, Microsoft)

Chapter 6
Rewind and Play Again

A Fresh Look at What Kids Do While the TV's On and How What's On Influences Them

Books

Dewing, Martha. *Beyond TV: Activities for Using Video with Children.* Santa Barbara, CA: ABC-

CLIO, 1992. 718-935-0600
YO-TV Production Handbook. New York: Educational Video Center, 1994.

Media Literacy Organizations and Programs

Center for Media Education
Campaign for Kids' TV
1511 K Street, NW, Suite 518
Washington, DC 20005
202-628-2620

Center for Media Literacy
1962 S. Shenandoah Street
Los Angeles, CA 90034
800-226-9494

Continental Cablevision
The Pilot House/Lewis Wharf
Boston, MA 02110
800-227-7709

Ask for:
• Tool Kit and Video for Kids, Their Parents & Teachers
• A Classroom Guide to Master Control: Television Literacy for Kids
• Leading a Workshop on TV Literacy

Strategies for Media Literacy
1095 Market Street #410
San Francisco, CA 94103
415-621-2911
Offers strategies newsletter, resource lists, workshops, and educational resources.

Software

Nickelodeon Director's Lab (CD ROM)

Chapter 7
Just the Ticket to Talk

How Videos Can Trigger Meaningful Discussion

Books

Coles, Robert. *The Moral Life of Children.* Boston: Atlantic Monthly Press, 1986.

Damon, William. *The Moral Child: Nurturing Children's Natural Moral Growth.* New York: the Free Press, 1988.

Faber, Adele, and Elaine Mazlish. *How to Talk So Kids Can Learn.* New York: Simon & Schuster, 1995.

Greer, Colin, and Herbert Kohl, eds., *A Call to Character.* New York: Harper Collins, 1995.

Lickona, Dr. Thomas. *Raising Good Children.* New York: Bantam Books, 1983.

Schulman, Michael, and Eva Mekler. *Bringing Up a Moral Child: A New Approach for Teaching Your Child to Be Kind, Just & Responsible.* Reading, MA: Addison-Wesley, 1985.

Chapter 8
Telefuture Is Here

The New Media

Online Services

America Online (800-827-6364)
CompuServe (800-848-8990)
Prodigy (800-PRODIGY)

Retail Outlets That Carry a Good Selection of Hardware and Software

Babbage's (214-401-9000)
Egghead (800-598-0010)
Circuit City (800-274-8958)
Computer City (800-The City)
CompUSA (800-266-7872)

Mail Order Outlets That Carry a Good Selection of Hardware and Software

KidSoft (800-354-6150)
Mac/PC Connection (800-800-0002)
MacWarehouse (800-255-6227) Mac
MicroWarehouse (800-367-7080) PC
Tiger Software (800-888-3437)

Books

Brown, Eric. *That's Edutainment! A Parent's Guide to Educational Software.* Berkeley, CA: Osborne McGraw-Hill, 1995.

Glossbrenner, Alfred. *The Little Online Book.* Berkeley, CA: Peachpit Press, 1995.

Miranker, Cathy, and Alison Elliot. *The Computer Museum Guide to the Best Software for Kids.* New York: Harper Perennial, 1995.

Perkins, Michael, and Celia Nùñez. *Kidware: The Parent's Guide to Software for Children.* New York: Prima Publishing, 1994.

Turkle, Sherry. *Life on the Screen: Identity in the Age of the Internet.* New York: Simon & Schuster, 1995.

Magazines on Software Available at Newsstands or by Subscription

CD-ROM Today
Family Computing

Family PC
Mac World
New Media
PC Magazine
Wired

Newsletters Available by Subscription Only

Children's Software Press (713-467-8686)
Children's Software Review (313-480-0040)
Kids' Educational Software Advisory
(800-879-2441)
KidSoft Magazine (800-354-6150)
Parents' Choice (617-965-5913)

Organizations

Association of Personal Computer User
Groups (APCUG) (914-876-6678)
National Center for Missing and Exploited
Children (800-843-5678)
http://www.missingkids.org Ask for *Child
Safety on the Information Highway* booklet.

Software Publishers

Here is a selected list of dependable suppliers
whose product lines are consistently of high
quality.

Brøderbund Software, Inc.
Davidson & Associates, Inc.
Edmark Corporation
The Learning Company
MECC
Mindscape

Awards

Association for Library Service to Children
New Media Magazine's Invision Awards
(800-685-8463)

Parents' Choice Foundation (617-965-5913)
Software Publishing Association
(202-452-1600)
Also note that most of the software magazines
select top picks annually and these lists are as
useful as awards.

After-School and Summer Computer Programs

Computer-Ed High-Tech Camp, Newton, MA
(617-938-6970)
Futurekids, Los Angeles (800-765-8000)
The Technology Camp at Epiphany, Seattle
(206-329-0217)
Ask these organizations for programs in
your area.

Safety Programs for Kids Online

Surfnet Software
SurfWatch
Time's Up!

Chapter 9
We're the People
Advocate for Meaningful Kids' Media

Government

You can start to reach out to your representatives or government agencies on topics relating to media and children by calling or writing to the following:

Federal Communications Commission
Mass Media Bureau
2025 M Street, NW

Room 8210
Washington, D.C. 20554
202-418-2600

U.S. Capitol
202-224-3121
To find out the name of your senators, give your state. To find out the name of your representative, give your ZIP code.

U.S. Department of Commerce
The Herbert C. Hoover Building
14th and Constitution Avenue, NW
Washington, DC 20230
202-482-2000
For Telecommunications Act information:
202-482-1551

Advocacy Groups

Contact these groups to get involved in media and programming policy and advocacy:

Center for Democracy and Technology
202-637-9800
http://www.cdt.org

Center for Media Education
1511 K Street, NW
Suite 518
Washington, DC 20005
202-628-2620
http://www.access.d:gex.net/~cme/kidstv.html

The Center for Media Education focuses on public policy and the media. The center functions in four ways:

1. *Organizes and provides information to consumer groups and nonprofit organizations.*
2. *Researches issues related to their focus.*
3. *Prepares filings to the FTC and FCC.*

4. *Serves as a clearinghouse for news outlets.*

Center for Study of Commercialism
1875 Connecticut Avenue, NW
Suite 300
Washington, DC 20009-5728
202-332-9110

A subdivision of the Center for Science in the Public Interest, the Center for the Study of Commercialism's focus is to research and oppose commercialism and advocate for commercial-free zones in public and private spaces.

Children Now
1212 Broadway
Suite 530
Oakland, CA 94612

Children Now acts as a voice for children in the mass media and in areas of public policy. Children Now works toward three ends:

1. *Educating the public and decision makers about the needs of children.*
2. *Developing and promoting effective strategies to improve children's lives.*
3. *Reaching out to parents and children to inform them of opportunities to help themselves.*

Media Literacy Organizations and Programs

Center for Media Literacy
1962 S. Shenandoah Street
Los Angeles, CA 90034
800-226-9494

Video Supplier Index

A&M Video
1416 North La Brea Avenue
Hollywood, CA 90028
213-468-2411

A*Vision/Kid*Vision
75 Rockefeller Plaza
New York, NY 10019
212-275-2900

Baldacci Productions
23-00 Route 208 South
Fair Lawn, NJ 07410
201-703-1750

Blackside Productions
486 Shawmut Avenue
Boston, MA 02118
617-536-6900

Bridgestone Group
1979 Palomar Oaks Way
Carlsbad, CA 92009
800-523-0988

Bright Ideas Productions
31220 La Baya Drive, Suite 110
Westlake Village, CA 91362
818-707-7127

Brooklyn Botanical Gardens
1000 Washington Avenue
Brooklyn, NY 11225
718-622-4433

CC Studios
389 Newtown Turnpike
Weston, CT 06883-1199
203-222-0002/800-543-7843

The Children's Group
561 Bloor Street West #300
Toronto, Ontario
Canada M5S 1Y6
800-668-0242

Children's Television Workshop
Video Services
50 Leyland Drive
Leonia, NJ 17605
800-822-1105

Concept Associates
7910 Woodmont Avenue #1214
Bethesda, MD 20814
800-333-8252

Crown Video
201 East 50th Street
New York, NY 10022
212-572-2627/800-752-3396

ESPN Home Video
ESPN Plaza
Bristol, CT 06010-7454
203-585-2000

Family Home Entertainment (fhe)
15400 Sherman Way
Van Nuys, CA 91410
818-908-0303/800-423-7455

Golden Book Video
c/o Western Publishing
1220 Mound Avenue
Racine, WI 53404
414-633-2431

Goodtimes/Kids Classics
401 Fifth Avenue
New York, NY 10016
212-889-0044

Homespun Video
P.O. Box 694
Woodstock, NY 12498
800-338-2737

HPG Home Video
400 South Houston, Suite 230
Dallas, TX 75202
214-741-5544/800-888-1188

Jugglebug
7426 Olympic View Drive
Edmonds, WA 98026
206-774-2127/800-523-1776

Just for Kids Home Video
c/o Celebrity Home Video
P.O. Box 4112
Woodland Hills, CA 91367
818-715-1980

KIDVIDZ
618 Centre Street
Newton, MA 02158
617-965-3345/800-840-8004

Landyvision
11 Hill 99
Woodstock, NY 12498
800-777-9755

Lightyear Productions
Empire State Building, Suite 5101
350 Fifth Avenue
New York, NY 10118
212-930-4800

MCA/Universal Home Video
70 Universal City Plaza, Suite 435
Universal City, CA 91608
818-777-4315

Mirimar Productions
200 Second Avenue West
Seattle, WA 98119-4204
206-284-4700

Monterey Home Video
28038 Dorothy Drive, Suite 1
Agoura Hills, CA 91301
818-597-0047/800-424-2593

MPI Home Video
15825 Rob Roy Drive
Oak Forest, IL 60452
312-687-7881/800-323-0442

Music for Little People
Box 1460
Redway, CA 95560
800-346-4445

Pacific Arts Video
11858 La Grange Avenue
Los Angeles, CA 90025
213-820-0991/800-282-8765

Paramount Home Video
5555 Melrose Avenue
Bluhdorn #337
Los Angeles, CA 90038
213-956-5000

PolyGram Video
825 Eighth Avenue
New York, NY 10019
212-333-8000/800-223-7781

Public Media Video
5547 North Ravenswood Avenue
Chicago, IL 60640
312-878-2600/800-323-4222

Random House Home Video
225 Park Avenue South, 8th Floor
New York, NY 10003
212-254-1600

Smarty Pants Video
15104 Detroit Avenue, Suite 2
Lakewood, OH 44107-3916
216-221-5300

Sony Kids Video
P.O. Box 4450
New York, NY 10101
212-445-4321

Sony Wonder
2100 Colorado Avenue
Santa Monica, CA 90404
310-449-2100

Strand Home Video
3350 Ocean Park Boulevard, Suite 205
Santa Monica, CA 90405
310-396-7011

Turner Home Entertainment
One CNN Center
Atlanta, GA 30303
404-928-3066

Video Treasures
500 Kirts Boulevard
Troy, MI 48084
313-280-0237

V.I.E.W. Video
34 East Twenty-third Street
New York, NY 10010
212-674-5550/800-843-9843

Walt Disney Home Video/Buena Vista
 Home Video
500 South Buena Vista Street
Fairmount Building, 633F
Burbank, CA 91521
818-562-3883/800-362-4533

Warner Home Video/Scholastic Home Video
4000 Warner Boulevard
Burbank, CA 91522
818-954-6000

Warner Reprise Video
3300 Warner Boulevard
Burbank, CA 91505
818-846-9090

Worldvision Home Video
1700 Broadway
New York, NY 10019
212-261-2700

Bibliography

Books

Ames, Louise Bates, M.D., and Frances L. Ilg, M.D., and Sidney M. Baker. *Your Ten-to-Fourteen-Year-Old.* New York: Dell Publishing, 1988.

Atkinson, D., and F. Zippan. *Videos for Kids: The Essential, Indispensable Parent's Guide to Children's Movies on Video.* Rocklin, CA: Prima Publishing, 1995.

Bar-Levav, Reuven. *Every Family Needs a C.E.O.: What Mothers and Fathers Can Do About Our Deteriorating Families and Values.* New York: Fathering, Inc., Press, 1995.

Bennett, S., and R. Bennett. *Kick the TV Habit.* New York: Penguin Books, 1994.

Bettelheim, Bruno. *The Uses of Enchantment.* New York: Random House, 1989.

Black, Kaye. *Kid Vid: Fun-damentals of Video Instruction.* Tucson, AZ: Zephyr Press, 1989.

Brown, Eric. *That's Edutainment: A Parent's Guide to Educational Software.* Berkeley, CA: Osborne McGraw-Hill, 1995.

Brown, Jay A., and editors of Consumer Guide Publications, International, Ltd. *Rating the Movies for Home Video, TV, Cable.* Skokie, IL: Consumer Guide Publications, 1982.

Brown, Scott, and Roger Fisher. *Getting Together: Building a Relationship That Gets to Yes: Harvard Negotiation Project.* Boston: Houghton Mifflin Co., 1988.

Burger, Jeff. *Multimedia for Decision Makers: A Business Primer.* Reading, MA: Addison-Wesley, 1995.

Catchpole, Catherine and Terry. *The Family Video Guide.* Charlotte, VT: Williamson Publishing, 1992.

Cella, Catherine. *Great Videos for Kids: A Parent's Guide to Choosing the Best.* New York: Carol Publishing Group, 1992.

Chen, Milton. *The Smart Parent's Guide to Kids' TV.* San Francisco: KQED Books, 1994.

Coles, Robert. *The Moral Life of Children.* Boston: Atlantic Monthly Press, 1986.

Damon, William. *The Moral Child: Nurturing Children's Natural Moral Growth.* New York: The Free Press, 1988.

Dewing, Martha. *Beyond TV: Activities for Using Video with Children.* Santa Barbara, CA: ABC-CLIO, Inc., 1992.

Dosick, Wayne. *Golden Rules: The Ten Ethical Values Parents Need to Teach Their Children.* San Francisco: Harper, 1995.

Faber, Adele, and Elaine Mazlish. *How to Talk So Kids Will Listen and Listen So Kids Will Talk.* New York: Avon Books, 1980.

Field, Tiffany. *The Developing Child: Infancy.* Cambridge, MA: Harvard University Press, 1990.

Fisher, R., and W. Ury. *Getting to Yes: Negotiating Agreement Without Giving In: The Harvard University Project.* New York: Penguin Books, 1983.

Gilder, George. *Life After Television: The Coming Transformation of Media and American Life.* Knoxville, TN: Whittle Direct Books, 1990.

Ginott, Dr. Haim G. *Between Parent and Child.* Scarborough, Ontario: Avon Books, 1956.

Gordon, Dr. Thomas. *PET—Parent Effectiveness Training.* New York: New American Library, 1985.

Green, Diana Huss, ed., et al. *Parents' Choice Magazine Guide to Videocassettes for Children.* Mt. Vernon, NY: Consumers Union, 1989.

Greenfield, Patricia Marks. *Mind & Media: The Effects of Television, Video Games, and*

263

Computers. Cambridge, MA: Harvard University Press, 1984.

Heymann, Tom. *On an Average Day . . .* New York: Fawcett Columbine, 1989.

Hoffman, Paul. *The Internet.* Foster City, CA: Compaq Press & IDG Books, 1994.

Jay, Dr. Timothy. *Cursing in America.* Philadelphia: J. Benjamins Publishing Company, 1992.

Knowles, Katharine Heintz. *The Reflection on the Screen: Television's Image of Children.* Seattle: University of Washington Press, 1995.

Landsdown, Richard, and Marjorie Walker. *Your Child's Development: From Birth Through Adolescence.* New York: Knopf, 1991.

Leach, Penelope. *Your Baby and Child: From Birth to Age Five.* New York: Knopf, 1978.

Leach, Penelope. *Your Growing Child: From Babyhood Through Adolescence.* New York: Knopf, 1995.

Leonhardt, Mary. *Parents Who Love Reading, Kids Who Don't.* New York: Crown Publishers, Inc., 1993.

LeShan, Eda. *When Your Child Drives You Crazy.* New York: St. Martin's Press, 1985.

Lesser, Gerald S. *Children and Television: Lessons from Sesame Street.* New York: Vintage Books/Random House, 1974.

Levine, Milton I. M.D., and Jean H. Seligmann. *The Parents' Encyclopedia of Infancy, Childhood, and Adolescence.* New York: Thomas Y. Crowell Company, 1973.

Lickona, Dr. Thomas. *Raising Good Children.* New York: Bantam Books, 1993.

MacAlpine, Loretta. *Inside KidVid: The Essential Parent's Guide to Video.* New York: Viking Penguin, 1995.

Maltin, Leonard. *Leonard Maltin's 1996 Movie and Video Guide* (updated annually). New York: Penguin Books, 1995.

Martin, Mick, and Marsha Porter. *Video Movie Guide 1996* (updated annually). New York: Ballantine Books, 1995.

Minow, Newton N., and Craig L. Lamay. *Abandoned in the Wasteland: Children, Television and the First Amendment.* New York: Hill & Wang, 1995.

Montgomery, Kathryn. *Target: Primetime— Advocacy Groups and the Stuggle Over Entertainment Television.* New York: Oxford University Press, 1989.

Oppenheim, Joanne. *Best Choice Books & Videos for Kids* (updated annually). New York: Harper Collins Publishing, 1995.

Research & Forecasts, Inc. *Where Does the Time Go? The United Media Enterprises Report on Leisure in America.* New York: Newspaper Enterprise Association, 1983.

Schor, Juliet B. *The Overworked American: The Unexpected Decline of Leisure.* New York: BasicBooks, 1991.

Schrag, Robert L. *Taming the Wild Tube: A Family's Guide to Television and Video.* Chapel Hill, NC: The University of North Carolina Press, 1990.

Schulman, Michael, and Eva Meckler. *Bringing Up a Moral Child: A New Approach for Teaching Your Child to Be Kind, Just and Responsible.* Reading, MA: Addison-Wesley, 1985.

Simon, Dr. Sidney B., and Sally Wendkos Olds. *Helping Your Child Learn Right from Wrong: A Guide to Values Clarification.* New York: Simon & Schuster: 1976.

Singer, D. G., J. L. Singer, and D. M. Zuckerman. *Use TV to Your Child's Advantage.* Reston, VA: Acropolis Books, Ltd., 1990.

Spenser, James R. *The Complete Guide to Special-Interest Videos.* Scottsdale, AZ: James-Robert Publishing, 1995–1996.

Spock, Dr. Benjamin. *Baby and Child Care.* New York: Simon & Schuster, 1976.

Tarshis, Barry, ed. *The "Average American" Book.* New York: Atheneum/SMI, 1979.

Turck, Mary C. *A Parent's Guide to the Best*

Children's Videos & Where to Find Them. Boston: Houghton Mifflin Company, 1994.

Turkle, Sherry. *Life on the Screen: Identity in the Age of the Internet.* New York: Simon & Schuster, 1995.

Wilson, James Q. *The Moral Sense.* New York: The Free Press, 1993.

Yankelovich, Daniel. *The New Morality: A Profile of American Youth in the '70s.* New York: McGraw-Hill, 1974.

Articles

"Age Is the Big Video Use Factor," *Research Alert,* January 20, 1995.

Bates, Stephen. "A Textbook of Virtues," *The New York Times,* January 8, 1995.

Biddle, Frederick M., ed. "TV and Radio," *The Boston Globe,* March 2, 1995.

Chronis, George T. "Study of Families Says Children Spend Much Less Time Watching TV When Computers Are Available," SVP and Grunwald Associates study.

Cobb, Nathan. "Kids Online, Parents on Edge," *The Boston Globe,* February 22, 1995.

"Computers and the Family," *Newsweek,* Summer 1995.

Dennis, E., ed., et al. American Academy of Pediatrics. Committee on Communications. "Children, Adolescents, and Television." June 1990.

Dietz, William H., M.D., Ph.D. American Academy of Pediatrics Committee on Communications. "Children, Adolescents, and Television." 85 (6), June 1990.

Dietz, William H., M.D., Ph.D. "Doctors Urge Colleagues to Fight TV Violence," *The Boston Globe,* March 2, 1995.

Disney, Anthea, ed., et al. "Parent's Guide to Children's Entertainment," *TV Guide,* Summer 1993.

"Don't Let the Broadcasters off Free," *The New York Times,* Editorial, October 25, 1995.

Doten, Patti. "Tuning In & Tuning Out," *The Boston Globe,* April 6, 1995.

Frankel, Max. "Alas for Hamelin!" *The New York Times Magazine,* October 8, 1995.

The Freedom Forum Media Studies Center. "Children & the Media," *Media Studies Journal,* Fall 1994.

Friddle, Jamie, ed. Nielsen Media Research, *American Way,* April 15, 1995.

Gabriel, Trip. "A Generation's Heritage: After the Boom, A Boomlet," *The New York Times,* February 12, 1995.

Gibbon, Peter. "In Search of Heroes," *Newsweek,* January 18, 1993.

Goodman, Walter. "How TV Really Gets Away with Murder," *The New York Times,* July 16, 1995.

Graham, Ellen. "Language of Childhood: No Expletives Deleted," *The Wall Street Journal,* July 17, 1995.

Gregor, Anne. "Who's News," *The Wall Street Journal,* September 15, 1995.

Hundt, Reed E., and Newton N. Minow. "A Cure for Kids' TV," *The New York Times,* October 19, 1995.

Innerfield, Amy, ed. "Fact Sheet," *Video Business,* April 14, 1995.

Innerfield, Amy, ed. "Fact Sheet," *Video Business,* October 13, 1995.

Kanner, Bernice. "American Dialogue: LifeScapes," *Advertising Age,* April 10, 1995.

Kaplan, James. "Why Kids Need Heroes," *TV Guide,* March 4, 1995.

Keizer, Gregg. "Summertime Computing," *Family PC,* May 1995.

Kellogg, Mary Alice. "How America Really Watches TV," *TV Guide,* July 29, 1995.

Lohr, Steve. "Practicing Safety on the Internet," *The New York Times,* September 21, 1995.

Mifflin, Lawrie. "Cable TV Continues Its Steady

Drain of Network Viewers," *The New York Times,* October 25, 1995.

Miller, Eric. "The Context of Trends: The Reshaping of America," *Research Alert,* 1994.

Moon, Michael, ed. Multimedia Developer Challenges & Strategies for Success: Essential Considerations for Market Entry, 1993.

Morrisett, Lloyd N. "The Twilight of Television," The John and Mary R. Markle Foundation. *Annual Report* 1993 with supplement, 1994.

Moyers, Bill. "The Wondrous Power of Television, Video, and the Public Library," *Public Libraries,* Fall 1988.

Nolan, Elizabeth Weld. "The Human V-Chip," *The Boston Globe,* September 1995.

Pitman, Randy. "Changing Perceptions: Video and Books," *NVR Reports,* June 1993.

Raskin, Robin. "Bridging the Gap," *Family PC,* April 1995.

"Retrospective on 50 Years of Advertising," *Advertising Age,* Spring 1995.

Rideout, Vicky, ed. "Children, Values & the Entertainment Media," *Children Now Special Report,* 1995.

Rosenblatt, Roger. "Teaching Johnny to Be Good," *The New York Times Magazine,* April 30, 1995.

"Survey of Advertising on Children's TV," Center for Science in the Public Interest study, February 1992.

"Tool Kit for TV," *The TAB,* May 10, 1994.

Video Business Survey, April 14, 1995.

"Video Games," *Boston Parents Paper,* November 1994.

Whalen, Jeanne. "Myers Seeking Panel to Rate TV Violence," *Advertising Age,* October 16, 1995.

Williamson, Debra. "Building a New Industry," *Advertising Age,* March 13, 1995.

Zuckerman, Jill. "Washington Notebook," *The Boston Globe,* August 12, 1995.

Other Sources

"1994 Home Media Consumer Study: Personal Computers," LINK Resources Corporation. Framingham, MA, 1994.

American Psychological Association. Violence on Television. Parent Handout.

Peggy Charren Interview, 1995.

National Frozen Food Association, Inc. Harrisburg, PA.

Talk of the Nation. National Public Radio. July 20, 1995.

U.S. Census, 1990.